C. K. Robertson

Conflict in Corinth

Redefining the System

PETER LANG

New York • Washington, D.C./Baltimore • Bern

Frankfurt am Main • Berlin • Brussels • Vienna • Oxford

Library of Congress Cataloging-in-Publication Data

Robertson, C. K.
Conflict in Corinth: redefining the system / C. K. Robertson.
p. cm. — (Studies in biblical literature; vol. 42)
Includes bibliographical references (p.) and index.
1. Conflict management in the Bible. 2. Bible. N.T. Corinthians,
1st—Criticism, interpretation, etc. I. Title. II. Series.
BS2675.6 .C573 R63   227′.2067—dc21   2001041299
ISBN 0-8204-5569-5
ISSN 1089-0645

Die Deutsche Bibliothek-CIP-Einheitsaufnahme

Robertson, C. K.:
Conflict in Corinth: redefining the system / C. K. Robertson.
–New York; Washington, D.C./Baltimore; Bern;
Frankfurt am Main; Berlin; Brussels; Vienna; Oxford: Lang.
(Studies in biblical literature; Vol. 42)
ISBN 0-8204-5569-5

The paper in this book meets the guidelines for permanence and durability
of the Committee on Production Guidelines for Book Longevity
of the Council of Library Resources.

Printed in the United States of America

Conflict in Corinth: Redefining the System

Conflict in Corinth

Studies in Biblical Literature

Hemchand Gossai
General Editor

Vol. 42

PETER LANG
New York • Washington, D.C./Baltimore • Bern
Frankfurt am Main • Berlin • Brussels • Vienna • Oxford

For Virginia M. Robertson
1922-1999

✧ TABLE OF CONTENTS

✧ FIGURES AND ILLUSTRATIONS

✧ Editor's Preface

More than ever the horizons in biblical literature are being expanded beyond that which is immediately imagined; important new methodological, theological, and hermeneutical directions are being explored, often resulting in significant contributions to the world of biblical scholarship. It is an exciting time for the academy as engagement in biblical studies continues to be heightened.

This series seeks to make available to scholars and institutions scholarship of a high order, and which will make a significant contribution to the ongoing biblical discourse. This series includes established and innovative directions, covering general and particular areas in biblical study. For every volume considered for this series, we ask the question as to whether it will push the horizons of biblical scholarship. The answer must be *yes* for inclusion.

In this volume, C. K. Robertson has explored comprehensively the issue of intra-church conflict in Corinth. Robertson focuses his study on 1 Corinthians 1–6, detailing the concerns, and attending to them critically and judiciously. Using a systems analysis approach and following on the work of L. A. Coser, who argues that conflict is not inherently negative, Robertson argues for a multi-dimensional understanding of the intra-church conflict. While many studies have been done over time on 1 Corinthians 1-6 and the conflict issues therein, Robertson brings important new directions to the scholarly discourse on Paul. This volume will have to be reckoned with in future studies. The horizon has been expanded.

Hemchand Gossai
Series Editor

✧ ACKNOWLEDGMENTS

This book is a revised form of my 1999 Ph.D. thesis for the University of Durham, written under the supervision of Prof. James D. G. Dunn. I am profoundly grateful for his wise insights and genuine concern. Thanks also go to the Episcopal Church Foundation for awarding me the Muntz Fellowship, thereby enabling me to complete the research and writing of this book. I also thank the Virginia Theological Seminary for awarding me with the Bell-Woolfall Fellowship.

One of the great joys for my family and myself during my research was the wonderful way in which we were embraced by the churches and people of Durham, England. To all of our dear friends there, and especially to the Rt. Rev. Michael Turnbull, Bishop of Durham, we are so very grateful. We also received much support and care from home, with particular thanks going to the the Rt. Rev. Dorsey Henderson, the Very Rev. Dr. Paul Zahl, the Rt. Rev. John Howe, the Rev. Canon Ernest Bennett, and the Rev. H. David Wilson. Thanks also go to Dr. Hemchand Gossai, Dr. Heidi Burns, and Sophie Appel for their editorial assistance.

A few people who deserve special recognition for being there when we needed it most are: the Rev. Michael and Gill Rusk, Stephen and Amy Yawn, Gen. Floyd and Berry Trogden, Merritt Preston (and his dear departed Grace), Dr. Charles and Karen Stewart, Dr. Hank and Sherry Nelson, Gary and Laurie Reichard, Kevin Jamison, John and Janet Jarvis, Michael Maichak, Hasty and Julie Miller, Glenna Speechley, Bill and Gayle Besosa, Will Heisler and Ray Smith, Roy and Dagmar Mason, Dr. Ken Dobson, and our St. Stephen's parish family.

Our families had to endure the hardship of being an ocean away from their grandchildren for three years. I am more thankful to them than I can say. As for my wonderful wife and partner, Debbie, and our children David, Jonathan, and Abigail, they not only experienced this adventure together with me, but have inspired me throughout it all!

✧ ABBREVIATIONS

ABD	*Anchor Bible Dictionary*
APS	American Philosophical Society
BA	*Biblical Archaeologist*
CBQ	*Catholic Biblical Quarterly,* Washington, DC
ContCh	*Continuity and Change*
EDNT	Exegetical Dictionary of the New Testament, ed. H. Balz and G. Schneider, Grand Rapids: Eerdmans, 1990
Hesp	*Hesperia*
HTS	Harvard Theological Studies
HTS	*Hervormde Teologlese Studies,* Pretoria, South Africa
JBL	*Journal of Biblical Literature,* Atlanta
JPT	*Journal of Psychology and Theology,* La Mirada, CA
JRASup	Journal of Roman Archaeology Supplementary Series
JRS	*Journal of Roman Studies,* London
JSNT	*Journal for the Study of the New Testament,* Sheffield
JSNTSup	Journal for Study of New Testament Supplement Series
JSOT	*Journal for the Study of the Old Testament,* Sheffield
JSOTSup	Journal for Study of Old Testament Supplement Series
NJB	New Jerusalem Bible
NRSV	New Revised Standard Version
NovT	*Novum Testamentum,* Leiden
NTS	*New Testament Studies,* Cambridge, MA
RSV	Revised Standard Version
SNTSMS	Society for New Testament Studies Monograph Series
TDNT	*Theological Dictionary of the New Testament,* 10 vols., ed. G. Kittel and G. Friedrich. Grand Rapids: Eerdmans, 1976
TynB	*Tyndale Bulletin*
TZ	*Theologische Zeitschrift*
WBC	Word Biblical Commentary

✧ INTRODUCTION

Tension within the early Corinthian church is not a new topic. Yet despite a recent surge of scholarly interest in 1 Corinthians, there has been anything but unanimity on several important questions. These include the precise nature of the Corinthian difficulties, the degree of seriousness of the problem(s), the impact (if any) of outside influences, the apostle Paul's own part in the whole affair, and the nature of his epistolary response. Such queries, as well as the many corollary issues that emerge from them, will be addressed in the pages that follow. As for the manner in which I have chosen to approach these questions, the title of this thesis offers some preliminary hints.

First, what is meant here by "conflict"? The word itself derives from the Latin *conflictus,* referring to "a striking together, a clash, a collision," and suggesting a "dispute or prolonged struggle."[1] The term can be used in quite divergent settings, describing a military battle, an interpersonal disagreement, an individual's personal battle within her/his own self, or dissension of some kind within a group. In Paul's time, the Greek equivalent, στάσις, referred to "recent or still existing disputes" between persons or groups,[2] and presupposed a rift in harmony that needed to be mended.[3] It was a term especially prominent in the ὁμόνοια speeches of orators like Dio Chrysostom, who linked this 'discord' with ὠμότης, ὕβρις, and ἀνομία.[4] While στάσις is found in both the Gospels and Acts,[5] the word was not used in the New Testament "for conflicts *within* the Christian community."[6] Perhaps for this reason, it is not found in 1 Corinthians, since from the beginning of the letter Paul made it clear that his focus instead concerned *intra*-church conflict. While 1 Clement later made significant use of στάσις in relation to the Corinth church, often listing it with other related terms for discord and disunity[7]—ζῆλος καὶ φθόνος, ἔρις καὶ στάσις, διωγμὸς καὶ ἀκαταστασία, πόλεμος καὶ αἰχμαλωσία, 3.2—Paul instead spoke of ἔριδες, or "quarrels," among the

Corinthian Christians (1.11) and appealed to them to have no σχίσματα among themselves (1.10).[8] Though the situation warranted his immediate attention in the letter,[9] Paul's language suggests that there was still hope for the community.[10] While some have insisted that the problem in Corinth was factionalism,[11] it will be argued in this study that there was an *underlying issue* of confusion concerning the unique identity and claims of the church in a larger system of overlapping relational networks. This confusion then resulted in conflict where it should not have existed (litigation between members) and a lack of tension where it should have existed (the incestuous member)...a "double dilemma," as will be demonstrated.[12] "Conflict" here refers to a dynamic process.

It is not simply conflict, however, but "conflict management," which is discussed in this study. The question may be raised why the more familiar term (to many), "conflict resolution," is not used here instead. However, as mentioned briefly above, the problem in Corinth was not simply the *presence* of conflict between church members, but sometimes its *absence,* as well. As will be seen, "conflict management," while it may appear to be a more modern phrase, actually has the flexibility to describe more adequately the multi-varied approach Paul took to the complex relational situation in the Corinthian church.

The phrase "systems approach" is used. By its very nature, a systemic methodology is multi-faceted, focusing on various connected patterns and utilizing various complementary tools. I wish to enjoy the fruits of recent social scientific study, from M. Douglas' research on "holiness" and boundaries and Coser's work on conflict to Chow's adaptation of networks and Friedman's study of social systems. By adding my voice to theirs, my hope is that the overall conversation may be enhanced and taken in some new directions, especially in terms of the apostle's often ignored use of familial imagery. Finally, it should be noted that my focus is on the first six chapters of 1 Corinthians, partly because of space limitations and, more substantially, because these chapters focus on issues of judgment, discipline, and intra-church conflict.

Following, then, a survey in chapter 1 of relevant literature previously written on the subject, chapter 2 offers a brief exploration into my systems methodology. Chapter 3 explores the overlapping of multiple relational networks in the one Christian community, thereby introducing into the church the standards and dichotomies inherent in those other networks. Chapter 4 then considers the ἔριδες in 1 Cor. 1-4 in terms of confusion over corporate identity and relational priorities, while chapter 5 involves analysis of two situations which exemplify the "double dilemma" facing Paul: the incestuous man and litigation between fellow members. The conclusion, drawing on all that has been said in the various chapters, poses the question: is it possible to speak of a specifically Pauline strategy for managing intra-church conflict?

NOTES

[1] See *The Oxford Dictionary of the English Language* and *The Oxford Latin Dictionary*.

[2] Jones 1978, 83. Interestingly, *homonoia*, the opposite of discord, "often lacked its negative connotation and [could] mean merely 'understanding' or 'goodwill.'"

[3] Cf. Dio Chrys. *Or.* 38, 39; Aristid. *Or.* 23.

[4] *Or.* 1.82.3; cf. also 2.22.3; 3.47.2; 11.79.4; 11.130.4; 12.74.2; 25.7.9; 26.4.8; 29.18.6; 30.11.4; 31.105.9; 32.70.4; 36.31.7; and especially 34 (14.3, 18.5, 22.2, 22.4, 34.4). Note that in 34.22, στάσις is contrasted with κοινῇ, a term found in Paul (esp. Phil. 1) with its origins in the *collegia*, as will be shown. See also Ael. Arist. *Or.* 24.4.

[5] In Acts, the term is used to describe clashes or dissensions of various kinds. In 15.2, the στάσις is between Paul & Barnabas and certain Judaising preachers; in 19.40, it is between Paul and Demetrius & his fellow craftsmen (members of Demetrius' *collegium?*); in 23.7, it concerns Sadducees and Pharisees in response to Paul's preaching of the resurrection; in 24.5, the reference is both more ambiguous and more grandiose, as Paul is described as "an agitator among all the Jews throughout the world" (RSV).

[6] Noting that this language is not taken from the New Testament, Delling adds: 'The vocabulary is obviously taken from the political sphere as in the call for ὁμόνοια' (*TDNT* VII, 571). Welborn and Mitchell add that Paul took his "conflict language" from the political sphere, although στάσις is not used explicitly. Cf. Martin 1995, 58.

[7] The first pair especially, ζῆλος καὶ φθόνος, figures prominently in 1 Clement (cf. 14.2; 51.1; 54.2). The opposite of στάσις for Clement, as seen in the epistolary conclusion, was peace and harmony (εἰρήνη καὶ ὁμόνοια, 65.1).

[8] The use of this verse as a thematic statement will be discussed later in this thesis. For more, cf. Mitchell 1992, Witherington 1995.

[9] Orr-Walther 1976, 149.

[10] In this sense, Paul was quite possibly "echoing" Proverbs 17.15, where readers were called to "quit before στάσις breaks out." This is the only use of στάσις, in the sense of strife or discord, in the Septuagint. Indeed, several verses in Prov. 17.1-19 appear to be 'echoed' in 1 Corinthians. For example, in Paul's illustration of the trying of human works as in a furnace in 1 Cor. 3.12-15, it is possible to hear clear echoes of Prov.

17.3. Other possible echoes include verse 1 in 1 Cor. 11.18ff.; verse 3 in 1 Cor. 3.12–15; verse 7 in 1 Cor. 1.17ff.; verse 9 in 1 Cor. 13. Pauline "echoes" of LXX texts will be discussed in chs. 4–5.

[11] See the discussion below on M. Mitchell's work, in particular.

[12] Again, if we consider Prov. 17, immediately following the admonition in verse 14, there is a warning against the one "who justifies the wicked and condemns the righteous."

✧ CHAPTER ONE
Paving the Way

A concern for internal group dynamics in Corinth began to emerge late in this century, due in large part to contributions from the social sciences, particularly sociology. Interestingly, until recent years the nature of conflict within a group had been an area relatively untouched by those in the traditional social sciences. As one of the most common of human conditions, interpersonal conflict may appear to be an obvious choice for countless sociological studies. However, a reader thirty years ago expecting a deluge of articles and books on the subject would have been frustrated to discover only a trickle. Though the topic of conflict was considered a priority subject at the 1907 meeting of the American Sociological Association, it has been in the intervening years "very much neglected indeed as a field of investigation."[1] The most noteworthy exception to this silence has been the work of Lewis Coser, whose ground-breaking *Functions of Social Conflict* has been praised by many scholars since its publication in 1956, although in the last twenty years, it has been from corporate management that most conflict studies have emerged, almost always with a pragmatic managerial eye towards the cessation of internal dissension.[2] Iimplications for New Testament research, on the other hand, having remained largely overlooked.

Beginning, then, with a consideration of Coser's principles and their relevance for this study, there follows below a brief review of significant works which have wrestled with the issues of conflict in the Corinthian community and Paul's response. Concluding with a summary of findings on conflict in the Corinthian church, it will be argued that another approach is needed to wrestle with the complex dynamics of the Corinthian interrelationships, particularly in light of Coser's assertions.

Coser on Conflict

While early figures in American sociology such as H. W. Odum, J. Bernard, and G. Simmel may be found on the short list of those who have called for a sociology of conflict,[3] it is really to L. A. Coser that a reader turns for greater understanding. Coser's assertion that "a certain degree of conflict is an essential element in group formation and the persistence of group life"[4] stands in stark contrast with widely held negative assumptions of conflict. Perhaps it is due to the persistence of such assumptions that Coser's work has rarely been utilized in examining the early Christian community.

Coser asserts that one of the primary social functions of conflict is "the establishment and reaffirmation of the identity of the group and [the maintenance of] boundaries against the surrounding social world."[5] Thus, conflict "always presupposes a relationship," for by separating from the "other," we more clearly associate with and understand the "us."[6] Of course, whether the "us" being discussed is a long established "us" or a very new "us" (in terms of a developmental timeline) can be significant when considering how that group might respond to its own internal conflict, for clearly a more established group will have developed certain internal mechanisms for controlling, or at least confronting, any conflicts which arise. Perhaps one of Coser's most important contributions to a study of social conflict is the line he draws between *realistic conflict*, which permits 'a socially sanctioned framework for carrying out conflict without leading to consequences that disrupt relationships within a group,' and *nonrealistic conflict*, which merely promotes the 'letting off of steam' and strengthening of the status quo.[7] The former 'serves to establish and maintain the identity and boundary lines of societies and groups,' while the latter points to greater rigidity in the group's structure, in which there is little room for internal disagreement over any matters, minor or major (see *figure 1.a*). In short, 'the more cohesive the group, the more authoritarian its structure; and the more threatened it feels, the stronger will be the demand for conforming behaviour and the greater the rejection of deviant members.'[8]

Realistic conflict	Nonrealistic conflict
A means toward a specific result	*Tension release only*
Allowance made for disagreement over real issues	*Primary issues of disagreement are suppressed*
Fear of group disintegration is minimal	*Fear of group disintegration is great*
Greater toleration of internal conflict	*Greater rigidity of group structure*

Figure 1.a—Conflict Release Continuum

Coser also considers conflict's greater intensity in closer relationships, arguing for a strong correlation between the structure of a group, its participants' active involvement within the group, and both the occurrence and intensity of conflict therein. Here again, Coser parts with conventional wisdom by noting distinctions between "conflicts which concern the very basis of a relationship and those which concern less central issues."[9] The narrowly focused psychological notion of "competing loyalties" is countered by a more positive view of multiple group affiliations or networks.[10] Thus, a crucial issue that Coser helps illuminate is the potential "function" of conflict to build up or tear down: "the institutionalisation and tolerance of conflict" in a group, rather than its suppression, can be a safeguard against group disruption or ultimate disintegration. Again and again Coser argues that conflict's presence and not its absence may point to a more stable relationship.

Coser's arguments are weighty, not least because of their inner consistency and focus of thought. They are not, however, invulnerable. In a subsequent collection of essays on conflict, several of Coser's political applications of earlier theoretical propositions raise the question of an overly amoralistic view of conflict's social function.[11] A more substantial methodological criticism arises as Coser's picture of "us" and "them" is expanded to be more multi-faceted and complex. Although he speaks of interdependence, Coser uses the term in fairly two-dimensional ways, mentioning multiple group affiliations while failing to delve into the possible ramifications of such social interfacing.[12] Yet, the impact of such interfacing on group conflict is potentially great, making this an issue which demands more attention than it is afforded. Coser leaves unanswered a more basic question, as well: the pragmatic issue of the management of conflict, alluding only briefly (in the second chapter of his

1967 *Continuities*) to some practical steps. Nevertheless, Coser remains a landmark figure in the study of conflict, not least because of his advocacy for the positive role of conflict in group development.

Of course, the essential issue here is the relevance of Coser's ideas for our study of conflict in the Corinthian congregation. Developmentally speaking, the Corinthian community at the time of Paul's writing lay far closer to "brand new" than to "firmly established" (see *figure 1.b*), a fact not always acknowledged in comparison studies between the ἐκκλησία and other more established groups such as the synagogue or philosophical school. After all, Paul himself had founded this congregation (ἐγὼ ἐφύτευσα, 1 Cor. 3.6) only a few years before 1 Corinthians.[13]

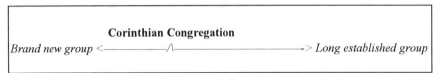

Figure 1.b—Group Development Timeline

While it might (or might not) be accurate to speak in later years of "the successful unification of strongly separate social interests in a common life,"[14] in the period of 1 Corinthians both Paul and the ἐκκλησία in Corinth were still very much wrestling with those "strongly separate social interests." In this period of growing pains, to use the phrase, the Corinthians "were in the process of defining their group identity and boundaries, a process which Paul hope[d] to influence with his letter."[15] Much of what he attempted to do in his letter might be referred to as creative (as in building a relatively new community) more than strictly preservative (as in maintaining an established community). Interestingly, beyond any infighting independent of the apostle, conflicts between Paul himself and many in the community were inevitably part of this creative process, since "Paul as apostle and community-founder [was] attempting to build a social world different in some respects from that (or those) envisaged by the members of the community themselves."[16]

Unlike a longer established group in which "more nuanced laws or specific norms coupled with definite sanctions" could be used in disciplinary and conflictual situations, the Corinthian community still exhibited only the "undeveloped beginnings of church discipline" (as seen in 1 Cor. 5),[17] and disputes that did arise were relegated to the arena of the larger surrounding society. If that meant that a lower status member of the ἐκκλησία had to suffer the results of litigation (1 Cor. 6), then at least only one piece of the whole was affected, the pressure was relieved, and the group's stability was preserved. Here, Coser's distinctions between realistic and unrealistic conflict may prove particularly relevant. Whether the choice the Corinthians made in the case of litigating members or similar dilemmas was a conscious or unconscious one is irrelevant in terms of the eventual result. But certainly Paul's very intentional response to this and other issues will also have affected the resultant development of the church community, as did the Corinthians' counter-response to Paul, and so on.

Much of what was happening in this creative period of the congregation's life demands greater attention, and several questions may arise in light of Coser's principles: What were Paul's thoughts on the distinctions between primary and "less central issues" in the Corinthian conflicts? Were there "conflict management" strategies in the Septuagint to which Paul might have been able to turn for ideas in his own situation at Corinth? Was "scapegoating" occurring in Corinth and, if so, who was the sacrificial lamb in any given issue? Such queries call for our attention.

Having touched on the complex issues involved in a study of conflict in any social group, it is now appropriate to move to works specifically aimed at understanding conflict in the Corinthian community. As will be seen, in the past century there has been a move from viewing the Corinthian tensions in purely theological terms to seeing other contributing factors at work, resulting in a greater utilisation of interdisciplinary resources. Although Coser's own work has not featured prominently in Pauline studies, insights gained through the union of various academic disciplines has resulted in the emergence of new understandings of conflict in the first-century Corinthian congregation. Indeed, Taylor argues that "both historical and social sciences need to be applied competently if satisfactory and reliable results are to be attained in social studies of extinct societies."[18] This increased momentum in socio-historical research has created a dynamic context for asking new questions about the role and management of conflict in Corinth.

Pioneering Steps

Earlier Works

Early in the nineteenth century, F. C. Baur led the discussion on conflict in the Corinthian community by focusing on what now can be termed *inter*-church conflict between Paul and the Jerusalem church.[19] Baur contended that a clear division existed in early Christianity, with a Petrine party (representing the Jerusalem Church) and a Pauline party standing "opposed to one another, holding divergent views on the subject of the redemption wrought by Christ."[20] The Jerusalem-Paul dichotomy of Baur and the Tübingen School has continued to carry influence through the years,[21] so that R. H. Fuller can rightly assert that "the ghost of Baur is far from dead".[22] At the same time, this opposing group or *inter*-church hypothesis has also faced sharp criticism.[23] For instance, J. Munck, in his extensive refutation of Baur's position, argues that the "immense simplification that Baur's theory brings with it" in the end replaces a "richly faceted historical reality" with a "colourless homogeneity."[24] Despite such protests, other scholars have continued to reach the same general conclusion as Baur, that conflicts in Pauline churches can be attributed to a single opposing group, while simply altering the identity of the opposing party.[25] G. D. Fee goes as far as saying that the Corinthian situation was "one of conflict between the church and its founder."[26] However, more recently W. Baird has revealed several flaws in the one-front hypothesis, suggesting instead that "the conflicts reflected in 1 Corinthians have arisen out of a variety of situations," some of which are primarily theological in nature but others appearing to be more socio-economic or religious in their origins.[27] Baird's conclusion is echoed here: "the analysis of conflict in 1 Corinthians should not be restricted to a single method."[28] Having said this, it is appropriate to turn now to socio-historical contributions to the issue.

A Methodological Map

In the exploration of new lands, it is the pioneers who pave the way, while homesteaders follow when the path is more familiar. Joel Barker speaks in similar terms of "paradigm pioneers," who ask the questions others dare not ask and approach the field of study with new tools or new uses of well-known tools.[29] It is the pioneers' initial work that allows those who follow in their steps to build more stable theories—critiquing, refining, expanding the initial studies. In terms of Pauline research, two pioneers in particular have contributed to new understandings of Christian community and the conflicts therein. Gerd Theissen's compilation of groundbreaking articles on Pauline Christianity and W. A. Meeks' study of Paul's social world together present a socio-historical foundation on which further studies have since been constructed. Despite valid warnings by some that "sociological interpretations of religious phenomena are inevitably reductionist,"[30] Theissen has combined sociological concepts with a historical-critical concern for prosopographic and contextual evidence in order to present "a historically plausible picture of the social constituency and social structure of the church in Corinth."[31] J. H. Schütz rightly describes the author's interests as those of a "social historian" rather than a sociologist.[32] In his movement away from the subject of inter-church conflict to "describing and analysing the interpersonal behaviour of members of primitive Christian groups,"[33] Theissen in essence steps out of the more familiar territory of his predecessors and peers and onto a different path. But how has he accomplished this?

Like other trailblazers, Theissen himself has set forth a plan, a methodological map.[34] Texts must be analysed first through a *constructive* method: one examines material sociologically not to know the individual's biography, but to question what may be learned about social status. This involves necessarily facing problems of reliability, validity, and representativeness. Second, there are *analytic* methods, which make inferences from events, from norms, and from symbols. In other words, one considers historical statements about the unusual in order to arrive at assertions about the usual, the paradigmatic pattern. Lastly, there are *comparative* procedures which consider texts coming from outside Christianity but which may shed light on the texts in question. Theissen's own consistent usage of this methodology shows that, despite justifiable criticisms directed against certain conclusions at which he arrives (see further below), Theissen represents a next step in understanding socially a Pauline community.

Theissen's inquiry into the *socio-political, socio-economic, socio-ecological,* and *socio-cultural* factors surrounding the first Christians has enabled him to account for the contrasting images that emerged in those earliest generations,[35] not in terms of a theological "law versus grace" argument, but rather in socio-historical terms of two emerging types of itinerant preachers and the respective Christian movements they represented. At the heart of the contrast, claims Theissen, is the different approach each type took toward financial subsistence. While Palestinian Christianity consisted of an intra-Jewish renewal group operating within a politically unstable and economically depressed rural setting, the Hellenistic mission was a trail-blazing enterprise in a stable, prosperous, urbanized society. For Pauline Christians, the picture of the Palestinian wandering beggar, characterized by *lack* of home, family, possessions and protection, became superseded by that of the financially independent organizer of integrated communities of faith. Thus, Theissen is able to point away from a romanticized notion of a golden age of Christian unanimity to a more grounded understanding of tension between two very different forms of Christian mission that "was overlaid with class-specific differences and tendencies already present."[36]

Such "differences and tendencies" *within* the Corinthian community, contributing to intra-church conflict, are also examined by Theissen, who uses prosopographic as well as indirect evidence. Theissen's combination of statements about the community as a whole, about individual members, and about divided groups in the community, lead to a greater appreciation of the congregation as a voluntary organisation unlike most others of its time, one in which a socially heterogeneous membership was its unique strength as well as the source of constant internal conflict.[37] With references to community *offices, houses* and private circumstances, *services rendered* to the mission, and the ability for *travel*, Theissen is able to assert that "the great majority of the Corinthians known to us by name probably enjoyed high social status."[38] Theissen notes that alone each referent does not define conclusively any statement of social status, but as the various referents are found in combinations of two or three in the New Testament, some accurate designations can be made. He also admits that this in no way negates the fact that Christians of lower status (mostly unnamed) were in the Corinthian ἐκκλησία in far greater numbers.

The crucial point, as with Meeks, is that Theissen's socio-historical approach to the Pauline texts (especially in regards to the Corinthian community) allows for new insights, however tentative they must be. For while it is true that "there is little available information to enable us to ascertain with any degree of exactitude or representativeness the social positions of the Corinthian Christians,"[39] it is equally true that "it is a step above zero to know which social strata are represented at all in early Christian groups."[40] Recalling an earlier analogy, those who follow the pioneers are in a far better position to smooth out any imperfections.

Two particular elements in Theissen's research have been the source of subsequent criticism and refinement. The first is his term "love-patriarchalism" (from a concept borrowed from E. Troeltsch), an apparent "moderate social conservatism" which Theissen observes in Paul, citing 1 Corinthians 7.21ff; 11.3–16. "This love-patriarchalism takes social differences for granted but ameliorates them through an obligation of respect and love, an obligation imposed upon those who are socially stronger."[41] Theissen further explores this concept through examinations of specific Corinthian disputes: the question of eating meat offered to idols and the problems at the Lord's Supper. In both situations, he considers the conflicts as socially, and not purely theologically, driven. Pointing to two distinct social groups within the Corinthian ἐκκλησία, the Strong (the so-called "wise" or the "haves") and the Weak (or the "have-nots"), Theissen uses an extended (and potentially controversial) comparison between the position of the Corinthian strong ones, the "wise," and later Gnosticism. Here, he lists four specific sociological criteria which suggest why the Strong were more open than the Weak to eating idol meat: (1) *an intellectual standard* based on the ability of those in a higher class to have and use written documents, (2) *faith focused on inner knowledge for salvation,* (3) *an elitism* held firmly by those of higher status, and (4) *a broader acceptance* of the surrounding culture. In short, the "haves" in Corinth were less stringent on the issue of idol meat *precisely because they could afford to be.* Paul, in Theissen's mind, stood in theory and belief on the meat issue with the Strong and wrote to them directly, yet appealed nevertheless to a respectful concern for the Weak, those who did not have the luxury of giving up their scruples in this area. Paul allowed a stratified system to continue, but under the banner of love-patriarchalism.

Likewise, Theissen asserts "that the conflict over the Lord's Supper is a conflict between poor and rich Christians."[42] This class-specific assumption is supported by assertions that the ability to provide one's own food and have a house in which to eat leads one to infer a higher economic status. But on a deeper level, his essay on "Social Integration" is less concerned with description of the conflict and more with Paul's "desire to influence interpersonal relationships in a certain direction."[43] Theissen, therefore, focuses attention on the apostle's *compromise solution,* which allowed the class distinctions to remain while the centrality of the sacramental meal subtly effected integration. The result for Theissen is, once again, love-patriarchalism.

Theissen's focus on social distinctions between the two groups in Corinth is even evident in his suggestion that there was a clear-cut division of communication between church members and Paul: a written report articulating clearly the position of the Strong, and a separate oral report that seems to have originated from below. "Might these divergent paths by which information travels have a class-specific character?"[44] Whatever the answer, Theissen argues consistently that Paul revealed in his epistolary response a level of theoretical agreement with the Stroog in the various disputes while continuing to promote concern for the Weak.

Although Theissen himself views this ethos as "insufficient" for modern society, his claim that love-patriarchalism was an important social and theological component of Paul's message to the Corinthian Christians has resulted in very different reactions. Recent scholars, especially feminist theologians, have questioned not as much Theissen's conclusion that Paul espoused a position of love-patriarchalism in his communities as Theissen's assertion that such a model had any positive value. Rather, E. Fiorenza argues that Theissen portrays a *repressive* patriarchalism, in which the apostle introduced "the vertical line of patriarchal subordination not only into the social relationships of the ἐκκλησία, but into its symbolic universe as well by arrogating the authority of God, the 'father,' for himself."[45] Such scholars agree with Theissen that love-patriarchalism has "made a lasting impact on Christianity,"[46] but conclude that this impact has been mostly a negative one. On the other side of the spectrum stand those who have not only accepted but approved of Theissen's conclusion, agreeing that "Paul's ethic does not challenge the inequities between people, but sees in those very differences the building blocks of a new type of human community."[47]

Perhaps the most interesting responses have been those which have ventured farther in suggesting that perhaps Theissen's basic conclusion is inaccurate, that he has *oversimplified* the more subtle and complex rhetorical arguments in Paul's responses to the "strong."[48] While Theissen concedes that the love-patriarchalism of which he speaks is much more prevalent in the deutero-Paulines and the Pastorals, still he insists that "it is already evident in Paul."[49] Against this view, N. Elliott argues that despite Theissen's broad statements, "no evidence is produced from 1 Corinthians that Paul requires the subordination of 'weaker members' of the Corinthian congregation."[50] As for a "natural development" of Pauline thought from the undisputed letters to the Pastorals, Elliott contends that it would be just as appropriate to speak of a very different development to other ancient writings such as *The Acts of Paul and Thecla.*. Reading backwards into difficult texts such as 1 Cor. 7.21 through the lenses of the Pastorals is, for Elliott, a "contamination [of] the way we interpret even the genuine letters."[51]

Using instead a touch of irony, D. Martin modifies Theissen's famous term to "benevolent-patriarchalism," stating that such patriarchalism may be called benevolent "only in the minds of the deluded."[52] He goes on to argue that Paul actually undermined the existing patriarchal system through a subtle epistolary strategy of "status reversal." Horrell is more careful first to set up a sociological framework in which he is then able to examine Theissen's claim for love-patriarchalism. In the end, he (not unlike Elliott and Martin) notes that "Paul's criticism of the socially strong, coupled with the absence of any explicit demand for the subordination of weaker social groups, should surely lead us to question the appropriateness of the term love-patriarchalism as a summary of the social ethos of Paul's teaching in 1 Corinthians."[53]

The second area in Theissen's research which may be criticized is his over-dependence on more *functionalist* theory and *static* terminology to describe dynamic social distinctions and interactions. However, as this criticism also touches on the conclusions of W. A. Meeks, it seems appropriate to delay such discussion for the moment and turn to the contributions of this second socio-historical pioneer.

"An Impressionistic Sketch"

Meeks' work *The First Urban Christians*, which has received high marks from many scholars and students both for its readability and for its thorough study of the subject, seems to take up the torch from Theissen in speaking of the ordinary Christian in Paul's day and in the Pauline Christian communities. Meeks asserts that as "the texts were written in some sense *for* them, and were used in some ways by them—if we do not ever see their world, we cannot claim to understand early Christianity."[54] Using "suggestive" rather than "generative" social theory, a "piecemeal" rather than altogether "consistent" application of that theory, and a more "pragmatic" rather than "pure" approach, Meeks presents an "impressionistic sketch" of Pauline groups and their members, involving "mixed strata and ambiguous status."[55] It soon becomes clear how this leads to issues of intra-church conflict.

"Paul was a city person."[56] Such a seemingly insignificant statement is for Meeks a key to understanding the uniqueness of Pauline Christianity. For Meeks, the growth of Pauline Christianity in the Roman East was linked with the mobility and connectedness of city dwellers. Yet for many persons, there also existed in this urban environment a certain social *ambivalence*. This included women who enjoyed a period of greater independence and status, only to have their positions seen by many as a threat. Jews lived in strong subcommunities and kept their faith alive, yet at the same time found themselves becoming more and more Hellenized. Indeed, most city dwellers experienced some social ambivalence in their situation, leading Meeks to ask whether there existed "some specific characteristics of early Christianity that would be attractive to status-inconsistents," or whether the Jews and women Paul mentions "would tend to stand out in any group they joined."[57]

Moving, then, to a search for greater *specificity about persons in specific churches*, Meeks states that "to be a freedman in the early years in Roman Corinth, a colony whose first settlers were mostly freedmen, would surely have been less of a social disability than it would have been in Rome or in Antioch."[58] Like other groups and associations open to them, the Christian ἐκκλησία offered Corinthian residents the possibility of fellowship, stability, and a place in the system. Meeks considers some of the possible models for the Pauline ἐκκλησία, and illustrates the limitations of a correlative connection between "model" and church (see *figure 1.c* below). In this way, through comparative research, Meeks reveals that it is both the similarities and dissimilarities with other models of its time that marked the Pauline Christian community as utterly unique.

	Possible influences on ἐκκλησία	How ἐκκλησία differs from model
Household	*Group stability and intimacy*	*Sense of unity within larger entity*
Voluntary Association	*Free choice in gathering and a sense of common purpose*	*More exclusive: resocialisation More inclusive: social stratification*
Synagogue	*Worship/ritual; belonging to the larger "people of God"*	*Different membership requirements and different leadership roles*
Philosophic/ Rhetorical school	*Focus on teaching and social functions*	*Such functions were in no way primary to the church's existence*

Figure 1.c—Models for the Church

Based on this chart, how did members of the Pauline Christian community interact with others in society? Meeks' response is found in the phrase "boundaries with gates," a description of a Pauline community as read from the letters themselves. The boundaries included *language*, which both gave a sense of belonging within the group and a sense of separation from the rest of the world, and *purity rituals,* such as in issues of idolatry and rules for marriage/sex. Beliefs may be seen as boundary markers, as Meeks argues for the "social context and *functions* of doctrine."[59] Boundaries are also seen in the strong sense of apostolic authority which Paul claimed and used as he deemed necessary. Using 1 Corinthians as an example, Meeks maintains that Paul utilized irony, sarcasm, metaphor, diatribe, corrective second-order speech, parodies, refutations, tales of personal experience, and the Corinthians' own terminology[60] in order to assert his authority and deal effectively with the conflict there.[61] At the same time, however, Meeks asserts that the boundaries in the Pauline community incorporated gates, allowing Pauline Christians to remain a part of society (albeit not always easily), unlike some contemporary groups such as the Essenes of Qumran. It is not surprising, therefore, that these "boundaries with gates" often led to a tension "between measures needed to promote a strong internal cohesionand the intention to continue normal and generally acceptable interactions with outsiders."[62]

Despite the strengths of Meeks' comprehensive study, like Theissen he leaves himself open to criticism on several counts. The first concerns his tendency to generalize about other Pauline communities from the Corinthian situation, about which we have the most textual evidence (which is arguably not all that much). Unlike Theissen, Meeks does not attempt to develop more fully his own methodology, leaving queries about the implications of several of his conclusions unanswered.[63] For example, Meeks portrays in paradoxical language ordinary Christians who might have embraced the intimacy of Pauline "small groups" out of loneliness and a need to belong, yet who clearly displayed "some daring, some self-confidence, some willingness to break out of the ordinary social structures."[64] Meeks does not answer adequately *how* this paradox could be. Like Theissen, Meeks asserts that although the Pauline Christians were in a cohesive exclusive/inclusive group, they still experienced internal conflict. While Theissen puts forth his "love-patriarchalism" argument as an answer to why Paul says at times confusing and seemingly contradictory statements in response to Corinthian conflicts, Meeks offers only "guesses" and observations, allowing much to be left unsaid. Part of this criticism must be correlated to Meeks' concern with the big picture, for in applying broad brush strokes in his representation of Paul's social world, he often leaves fine areas of detail untouched.

Finally, returning to a criticism made of Theissen earlier, Meeks employs *static* terminology and a narrow *functionalist* theory to describe the Corinthian social context. While improving on earlier more romanticized notions of the early Christian movement as "a movement of the poor, the oppressed and the unpropertied,"[65] both Theissen and Meeks fail to realize the dynamic potential inherent in their theories of social stratification. While Meeks rightly points out that status in Paul's time involved "a combination of several different, and often inconsistent, factors," he fails to account for the potentially conflicting ways these various factors may affect a person's social interactions within a group. And like Theissen, Meeks exhibits a strong reliance on a functionalist methodological approach, asserting that "the primary questions to be asked about the early Christian church are questions about *how* it worked."[66] Unfortunately, such questions may predetermine their own answers, as "certain concepts from functionalist sociology focus our attention on the relatively smooth, stable, and continuous growth and development of groups across time," while neglecting almost wholly the presence and effects of conflict within a group.[67] This failure to account for intra-church conflict beyond simplistic distinctions between "Strong" and "Weak" or "haves" and "have nots" has led G. Harris to lament that "since the rise of the interdisciplinary approach to the study of Christian origins in the 1970s, little attention has been given to the problem of social control within the early church."[68] "Little attention," however, does not mean "no attention," and a few scholars recently have risen to the challenge.

By employing sociological resources, Theissen and Meeks have opened doors to new questions of social differences, influences and friction. By making mention of Paul's argumentative skills in 1 Corinthians, Meeks has also paved the way for more detailed study of the socio-rhetorical aspects of that epistle especially. This does not mean that a focus on social problems alone is the answer to understanding the conflicts at Corinth, since this would simply represent "another [sociological] methodological oversimplification, parallel to the earlier theological oversimplification."[69] However, the broadening of methodological horizons and increase of interdisciplinary research has led to new questions and the examination of the text from "new angles of vision."[70] Indeed, many subsequent areas of study exist only because of the groundbreaking work of Meeks, Theissen, and other pioneers. Whatever their limitations or weaknesses, these scholars have set the stage well for much work yet to be done.

The Power of Language

"Rhetoric played a powerful and persuasive role in first century Græco-Roman society. It was a commodity of which the vast majority of the population were either producers or, much more likely, consumers."[71] In the years since Theissen's and Meeks' pioneering studies, much has been unlocked by use of rhetorical criticism. Although several scholars have turned to the so-called "New Rhetoric" as an exegetical tool,[72] more substantial gains seem to have come from a socio-rhetorical approach grounded in the historical-critical method. Following H. D. Betz, M. Mitchell outlines five mandates for proper rhetorical criticism: (1) It is a subsidiary of the more general historical-critical method (2) which utilizes primary sources in the form of ancient speeches, letters and rhetorical handbooks, in order to (3) argue for the rhetorical species (epideictic, deliberative, forensic) of a text and (4) demonstrate how that species is appropriate to the subject matter of the text, while (5) examining the text as a compositional unit. Following this methodology in her own study, *Paul and the Rhetoric of Reconciliation,* Mitchell utilizes comparative research with ancient Graeco-Roman speeches and handbooks in order to present her case that "1 Corinthians is a single letter of unitary composition which contains a deliberative argument persuading the Christian community at Corinth to become reunified."[73] This statement marks a radical shift in perspective from the previously common notion among modern scholars that chapters 1–4 *only* were Paul's deliberative rhetoric in response to Corinthian internal divisions, while the remainder of the letter was concerned with separate issues brought to Paul's attention by the congregation. Mitchell, following in the steps of several patristic authors (1 Clement 47.1–3, as well as Ignatius, Origen, John Chrysostom), instead asserts that *the entire letter* is a unified argument in response to factionalism, falling under the category of deliberative rhetoric.

Mitchell characterizes "deliberative rhetoric" in terms of a *future time frame*; a *set of appeals* to listeners/readers, especially an appeal to advantage (τό συμφέρος); *proof by example* (including the example of oneself); and *appropriate subjects* for deliberative discussion.[74] (Witherington amends the list to include an appeal for what is *honourable* and not only expedient.[75]) Within this general category of deliberative rhetoric, ὁμόνοια (concord) speeches "became practically a genre unto themselves, with predictable patterns, set clichés and examples, and an identifiable ideology."[76] Ὁμόνοια, here, "in its commonest sense, especially when used by writers of the imperial period, is the opposite of στάσις ('faction' or 'discord') and implies the resolution of recent or still existing disputes."[77] Mitchell asserts that within 1 Corinthians are to be found the political language and *topoi* frequently used in the ὁμόνοια

speeches and letters of Dio Chrysostom and other near-contemporaries of
Paul, including images of "oneness," metaphors of Christ's *body* and
God's *building*, and calls to "stand firm." Even the ordering of Paul's
material is far from being simply arbitrary or reactive.[78] The call for
intra-church concord in 1.10 continues to be heard throughout the entire
letter.

This focus on the deliberative nature of Paul's rhetoric, while
supplying a consistency in argument, proves to be one of Mitchell's weak
points, as her study does not seem to make allowances for the other
rhetorical genres to be present within or in conjunction with the
deliberative. As a result, her case may seem at times somewhat overstated
or forced, especially her inclusion of 1 Corinthians 15 as the last of four
sections of deliberative proof. Along similar lines, Mitchell may "protest
too much" concerning the common interpretation of Paul's use of the περί
δέ formula. Though she observes greater intentionality on Paul's part in
his writing, her dismissal of contrary opinions on this formula's use may
be premature. Also, Mitchell's claim for the letter's compositional unity
does not in itself adequately answer the difficulties of particular problem
sections, including (but not limited to) chapters 8–10 and the specific
issues of idol meat and freedom. This convoluted sub-argument demands
more attention given to it than Mitchell seems to give. Finally, her
designation of the "political" nature of Paul's rhetoric, while not overly
problematic, has been criticized by some scholars as somewhat pressed.[79]

A deeper concern is raised by B. Witherington. While affirming the
importance and fruitfulness of rhetorical study of Pauline texts,
Witherington still admits that such study is "a discipline still being
reborn," with results that are both "tentative and subject to further
correction."[80] Citing a modern "failure to interact with the wealth of
resources in the studies on the ancient Græco-Roman world produced by
classics scholars,"[81] it is not surprising that Witherington continually calls
to mind the social or historical context of several problem areas in the
epistles, including sections on marriage, litigation, slavery. In the end, the
central conviction of rhetorical studies, as voiced by Mitchell, is that Paul
"is in control of the subject matter and does not fit his advice into either
the Corinthians' framework or the order of events."[82] This directs readers
to focus not so much on hypothesised opponents *as on Paul's actual*

responses. This redirection of focus is, as will be seen, a crucial step in better understanding "the competent way in which [Paul] applies the rules of [rhetoric] in the given circumstances."[83] What, then, is the next step to be taken?

Body Language

As if in response to the question, D. B. Martin enters "an imaginative but responsible engagement with primary evidence from the ancient world"[84] in order to explore the philosophical dimensions of *body imagery*, a major motif in 1 Corinthians. Contending that the divisions in Corinth are ultimately to be understood in light of "a more fundamental, though never explicitly acknowledged, conflict regarding the construction of the body,"[85] Martin explores Paul's "rhetorical finesse" in utilising σῶμα imagery in order to confront the status quo thinking of those Corinthians who were in privileged positions, ultimately calling into question "any use of normal, upper-class status designations for the assignment of honour within the church."[86] With some finesse on his own part, Martin argues against dated views of the Corinthian conflicts in terms of proto-Gnosticism, spiritual "enthusiasm" or the influence of Judaizers, and instead asserts that the church was "for the most part split along one major 'fault line' with wealthier, higher-status Christians on one side and lower-status Christians on the other."[87] In this assertion, Martin acknowledges that his arguments "are not original" and places himself in line with those already mentioned in this chapter, beginning with Theissen. However, Martin's unique strength lies in both the subtlety and comprehensiveness of his treatment, as he proceeds to show how Paul, far from espousing a position of "benevolent-patriarchalism," actually pursued a "strategy of status reversal, siding with the Weak, directing his criticisms primarily toward the Strong, and overturning the normal expectations of upper-class ideology."[88]

Martin divides his study into two main parts, one focusing on the hierarchy suggested by the body and the other on pollution in the body, with concerns about the former "giving way" to concerns about the latter.[89] Echoing anthropological arguments for the importance of the body in wrestling with issues of purity,[90] Martin interweaves background information about the body in both the Græco-Roman world and ancient *homonoia* speeches with careful exegetical study on Paul's own unique "twists" on the traditional rhetoric. Paul is shown to have countered high-status assumptions "by dividing the cosmos into two realms, that of 'this world' and an alternative reality defined by apocalypticism."[91] By "differentiating" himself from the Strong, Paul essentially welcomed his readers into another world—another worldview—in which the dominant opinions and presuppositions which they themselves carried were turned inside out.[92] Martin shows the strategy of an apostle who is very much in control of his argument, even if he did not always win.

If there are weaknesses to Martin's thesis, they are primarily two-fold. First, Martin's portrayal of the "fault line" between "haves" and "have-nots" terms remains somewhat two-dimensional and static. As will be shown in chapter three of this thesis, there were likely more factors at work in Corinth than simply economic ones, and by seeing so much in terms of a two-group conflict, Martin leaves untouched many of the dynamics found in multiple networking relationships. Second, despite the prevalence of σῶμα imagery in 1 Corinthians, Martin's focus on it appears at times to be overstated. By seeing Paul's thinking always through the lens of the body, Martin sometimes finds himself in a difficult position, especially when discussing the apostle's understanding of the roles and rights of women in the church. While only briefly acknowledging the apparent discrepencies with other Pauline texts on women's positions, Martin's defense is that Paul, whose strategy of status reversal has been so cogently argued, now reversed his reversals when it came to women.[93] As with his view of the conflicts in a Strong/Weak dichotomy, Martin's thesis that the problems in Corinth came down to differences in views of the body seems to say more than Paul himself states, especially as the apostle used more than one image to discuss the church, albeit not usually with as much detail as his σῶμα imagery. And, as will be shown in chapter four, there is another set of terminology Paul used in regards to the interrelationships of the ἐκκλησία—familial imagery—which is even more prevalent, though more subtle, than his body language. Nevertheless, Martin's cogent and detailed work has set a new standard for exegesis which takes seriously both the text and the contextual background.

The Missing Element

Greater Complexity

A criticism of earlier functionalist studies, exemplified in Pauline studies by Theissen and Meeks, has been their "essentially static view of society."[94] A crucial and often missing element that has recently been addressed in some studies of the Corinthian community has been the relation of multiple social roles played by each member of the Pauline ἐκκλησία in relation to one another, to Paul, and to the surrounding society. Borrowing from anthropological insights into gift exchange and its effect on friendship in the ancient world, P. Marshall suggests that "patronal friendship provides us with the best social context in which to view these relations and from which to assess the different way that Paul construes them."[95] By altering the interpretive focus from party divisions or even differences between "haves" and "have nots," Marshall opens the door to greater complexity in social interactions. However, several questions remain unanswered, especially in terms of clearly defining "patronal friendship." Chow takes notice of this "ambiguity" in Marshall's study, and while admitting that "we may be asking too much of Marshall" in seeking clearer delineation between patronage and friendship, Chow still argues that it seems better, if possible, to take into account the power differences among the "friends" of Paul, when analysing their relationships with him.[96] Rising to his own challenge, Chow undertakes such a study into patronage, using *networks* as his tool.

Defining Networks

A network may be defined as "a specific set of linkages among a defined set of persons, with the additional property that the characteristics of these linkages as a whole may be used to interpret the social behaviour of the persons involved."[97] While "there is nothing revolutionary about the idea of social networks," they can "provide a slight enlargement of the conceptual repertoire"[98] in examining the multiple roles and interrelationships present in the Corinthian ἐκκλησία. Chow lists several working principles of social networks that may prove helpful to our study:[99]

(1) Ties often are asymmetrically reciprocal, differing in content and intensity. The contents which flow through personal ties can be information, material goods, or power.

(2) Ties link network members indirectly as well as directly; hence ties must be analyzed within the context of larger network structures.

(3) The structuring of social ties creates nonrandom networks; hence network clusters, boundaries, and cross-linkages arise. Individuals are connected to multiple social networks.

(4) Cross-linkages connect clusters as well as individuals. Linkages of clusters of individuals with outside resources may have important consequences for the structure of ties within clusters.

(5) Assymetric ties and complex networks distribute scarce resources differentially.

(6) Networks structure collaborative and competitive activities to secure scarce resources.

Careful to note that usage of these principles in Pauline studies is limited, Chow makes no pretence to a "scientific account of the actual situation in Corinth back in the first century," admitting that New Testament scholars lack an anthropologist's or sociologist's ability to "collect first-hand information through participation, observation or sending out questionnaires."[100] Even so, although Chow offers a powerful methodological tool in the use of network theory, disappointingly, he himself fails to use it to the fullest.

Focusing on only "one particular type of network, patron-client ties," Chow considers how a person's Christian ties to a fellow member (as sister or brother in Christ) often could clash with the social claims inherent in their other relationship, that of client and patron. Chow is able to reach plausible conclusions concerning otherwise difficult passages, such as the case of the litigating members, noting that the offending member might have been a patron to the other "silent" Christians.[101] However, by narrowing the focus of his study, Chow fails to wrestle with the larger possibilities inherent in the multiple social networks and cross-linkages to which he alludes in his working principles. The fact that "an individual would likely be involved *in a number of different relationships*, or a 'network' of relationships,"[102] means that the same individual would hold multiple roles in relation to others in the community, with some roles firmly imbedded in the "worldly" or societal sphere (or network) and others in the "spiritual" or ecclesial sphere, thus contributing to dynamic interfaces and complex situations of conflict.

Determining Social Roles

N. R. Petersen's study of social structures in Philemon concurs that the expectations of one's social role in one sphere (or network, perhaps) might "pose a threat" to the stability of the other spheres to which that person belongs.[103] While Petersen's vocabulary centres on "structures" and "roles," he quickly adds that his concept of Pauline roles and structures does not "presuppose the extent of institutionalisation of rolesbut rather seeks to show where possible where the roles are located in the *process* of institutionalisation."[104] A fascinating but, regrettably, unexplored area in Petersen's work is the role of conflict itself in the ongoing process of institutionalisation. Still, it is possible here to see several points of contact with "network" theory, though Petersen's work remains necessarily limited in terms of exploring the effects of multiple roles on congregational conflict due to its specific focus on Philemon. We can envision a jumping-off point from analysis of multiple roles and networks to further exploration into the dynamic complexities of interpersonal and intra-group conflicts.

Back to Coser and Beyond

Several concluding thoughts emerge from this overview of the literature on the conflicts reflected in 1 Corinthians. One of the chief problems of previous studies on the Corinthian situation has been their limited, linear approach. From Baur's early arguments for a Peter/Paul dichotomy to more recent theories concerning the Enlightened versus the Weak, attention has rarely turned to the more dynamic relational complexities inherent in intra-group relationships, complexities that move beyond "us/them" terminology, whatever form that terminology assumes. Insights gained from cultural anthropology[105] and socio-rhetorical analysis[106] (to name but two interdisciplinary fields) have indeed yielded great benefits. But more is needed. Chow speaks of the complex interweaving of social networks and relationships and Petersen makes complementary statements concerning the interweaving of social roles. But as has been argued here, Chow has not yet exploited the full scope of his assertions about networks and Petersen's work, commendable as it is, is focused on Philemon and not 1 Corinthians. However, these scholars point to the possibility of a methodological approach which can move beyond simplistic categories of "us" and "them" to address more comprehensively the dynamic realities of a group.

To those who are quick to impose modern methodological models on the scriptural texts, Horrell offers a general warning that while at first glance "modern sociological models may 'fit' the New Testament evidence, we must be aware of the particular way in which they *shape* this evidence."[107] After all, the Corinthian community was not the first-century equivalent of either the medieval Roman Church or a twentieth-century Western congregation. Indeed, there is something suspicious about research that begins with unspoken presuppositions which the "evidence" is then adapted to prove. Any methodological approach, therefore, must be used self-critically, with an eye towards its own capacity for contamination as well as potential discoveries.[108] In short, we return to Theissen's earlier concern for text-focused and comparative analysis, or what Clarke calls "descriptive-historical work," instead of becoming further entangled in arguments about "the theoretical advantages of one sociological theory over another."[109] By exercising a constant concern for the unique temporal and cultural environment of the Corinthian situation and Paul's own letter, we may avoid the danger of underestimating both the complexity of the first-century situation and our own distance from it.

Coser's theory of conflict raised questions that have yet to be answered (or even asked by some) concerning the role or function of conflict in the development of a group. In considering the complex situation at Corinth, Coser's continual assertion that conflict is as necessary as it is potentially destructive appears particularly relevant. For example, it is not the oft-noted *presence* of conflict within the Christian community that is remarkable as much as the relative *absence* of conflict between that community and its larger social environment.[110] From all indications, the Corinthian Christians at the time of Paul's writing were not being persecuted for their faith, were not facing public reproach or ridicule on account of their profession of Christ. On the contrary, according to Paul they were actually held in honour (ὑμεῖς ἔνδοξοι, 4.10), apparently boasting in their human σοφία.[111] Paul sharply contrasts the respected position of the Corinthian Christians with his own and other apostles' standing as the "refuse of the world" (4.13, NIV). Allowing for some rhetorical embellishment on the part of the apostle, it still remains clear that the Corinthians' situation as those who were "filled, rich, ruling, wise, powerful, honoured"[112] was quite different from that experienced by Paul himself, and other Pauline congregations such as the one in Thessalonica.

Since one of the primary social functions of conflict is the establishment of social boundaries, the *lack* of conflict in Corinth between the ἐκκλησία and its surrounding culture (including, of course, other social groups to which the Corinthian Christians belonged) may be understood, at least in part, in terms of a deficiency of the church's identity markers and boundaries.[113] From Paul's perspective, the Corinthians' boundaries were overly permeable or, using Meeks' terminology, the "gates" were open far too wide, as is evident in the confusion over purity rituals surrounding sex, marriage, and common meals, areas which were then addressed by Paul. His own reworking of their terminology—such as with "wisdom" and "foolishness" in the opening chapters of the letter—reveals Paul's perception that even the Corinthian Christians' language was somehow corrupted.

What is of particular significance here is that Paul faced a double dilemma, a dilemma that has often passed unnoticed or understated by the various scholars: the need to lessen the amount of tension and conflict *within* the Corinthian church (and integrate newcomers into the church) while at the same time *heightening a sense of conflict on the part of those within the church towards the outside world,* thus fortifying and clarifying the church's boundaries.[114] For divisions within the ἐκκλησία to abate and boundaries to be drawn tighter and made clearer, a *larger shared division* from the rest of the world had to be perceived, not only by Paul but by the Corinthians themselves.[115] This is an area of potentially fruitful study which remains to be explored in greater depth. It is because of the "double dilemma" that I have chosen to describe Paul's apostolic response as conflict *management* rather than conflict *resolution.* As will be argued here at points, while the latter phrase is less problematic in terms of potential anachronism, it is too narrow in its scope to explain Paul's creative attempts to heighten conflict in order to reduce it.[116]

Finally, Coser's work, while invaluable for raising provocative questions on conflict, remains only a step towards grasping the nature of the Corinthian conflicts and Paul's response. Building on Chow's suggestion that Paul was facing not static groups, but rather networks of relationships involving members of the Corinthian ἐκκλησία, it is helpful to draw upon methodological tools which are appropriate both to the text itself and to the dynamics of the situation. Inasmuch as *systems thinking* provides the terminology and the concepts to describe the purpose and ramifications of conflict within a series of networking relationships, it is suggested that systems principles may provide further insight into the Corinthian situation. In bringing a new voice to the ongoing conversation, we hope to build on what has been said already while extending the discussion in new and potentially valuable directions.

Having considered the socio-historical background of the discussion, it is appropriate at this time to state that *the purpose of this study is to explore intra-group conflict in the Corinthian community, as well as Paul's "conflict management" response in 1 Corinthians, in light of systems thinking and the impact of overlapping relational networks.* The thesis is divided into six chapters. Following this chapter's survey of previous studies, chapter 2 presents the methodological approach of this study in the form of an overview and analysis of systems thinking. Chapter 3 considers the nature of the problem in the Corinthian church, not in terms of reasoned theological debate or even socio-economic differences between two groups (i.e. the "haves" and the "have-nots"), but rather in terms of overlapping relational networks.[117] The chapters that follow concern Paul's response to the conflictual "double dilemma" in Corinth. Chapter 4 focuses on the problem of the ἔριδες in 1 Cor. 1–4, with particular attention given to an underlying identity crisis, in terms of the church's identity and boundaries as well as Paul's unique position in that system. The apostle's use of familial imagery is examined in some detail, especially as this has often escaped the notice of many scholars. Chapter 5 moves into the specific intra-church disputes and tensions which Paul addresses in 1 Cor. 5–10, considering Paul's conflict management strategy in light of the ancient household *consilium*. The concluding chapter of the thesis asks the question of whether or not it is possible to speak of a distinctive Pauline approach to intra-church conflict, based on all that has been said thus far.

Throughout this thesis, it is argued that the intra-church conflicts in Corinth represent a return to the familiar and the comfortable, as patterns originating within pre-existing relational networks to which many of the Corinthians belonged claimed precedence over the principles espoused by Paul. Where some commentators have chosen to focus on individual disputes wholly apart from the rest, the intentional strategy here is to maintain a systemic, and thus holistic, perspective throughout the following discussion. For now, we can start to unpack some of the terminology and concepts which will be used throughout the study, introducing some new tools but always seeking to avoid the error of forming conclusions with "a lack of concern for proper historical judgement."[118]

NOTES

[1] Coser 1956, 16.

[2] There is a link here with ancient rhetors/consultants like Dio Chrysostom, whose speeches on concord were offered with an eye towards practical results. Cf. Jones 1978, esp. 83–94.

[3] Cf. Odum 1931, 1–17; Bernard 1950, 11–16; Simmel 1955.

[4] Coser 1956, 31.

[5] Coser 1956, 38; cf. Morgan, et al. 1981, 137; also Beavers 1977.

[6] *Ibid.*, 59.

[7] *Ibid.*, 38 (emphasis mine). J. Rex has argued that opportunities for anger and conflict must be allowed in a group "to allow for adaptation and learning" (1981, 73).

[8] Himmelweit 1964, 197.

[9] Coser 1956, 73.

[10] Cf. Chow 1992 (about which more will be said later in this chapter); Clarke 1993.

[11] Coser 1967, 101–105, 223–244. Examples include Coser's interpretation of the Watts riots, in his predictions for the future of socialism, and in the apparent justification of a limitless arms build-up in the name of ascertaining "relative strength." Cf. Coser 1955, 136f.

[12] *Ibid.*, 75–80.

[13] A highly reasonable date for the church's founding is between 50 and 51 C.E., with the first epistle being written sometime between 53 and 55. Cf. Jewett 1979, 104, as well as Barrett's (Harper) and Conzelmann's (Hermeneia) commentaries.

[14] Holmberg 1990, 41.

[15] Pogoloff 1992, 250.

[16] Barton 1986, 229.

[17] Harris 1991, 20.

[18] Taylor 1992, 31, where the author rightly points to the "interdependent and complementary" nature of the two disciplines.

[19] For a summary of Baur's contributions, see Schweitzer 1912, 12–21 and, more recently, Taylor 1992, 15–25. Though Baur's "Die Christuspartei in der korinthischen Gemeinde" is still unavailable in English translation, N. Elliott (1995, 281, n. 77) notes that "some of its assumptions are represented by C. K. Barrett" in his 1968 (1987) Harper commentary.

[20] As cited in Schweitzer 1912, 13.

[21] On the continuation of the Tübingen view, see Barrett, Dibelius, Lietzmann, to name but a few. For a more recent updating of the Baur thesis, cf. Goulder 1994.

[22] Fuller 1962, 66, where he continues, "It is still widely assumed that there was a basic disagreement if not between Peter and Paul, then certainly between Paul and James."

[23] Early on, A. Ritschl criticised Baur's hypothesis (*Die Entstehung der altkatholischen Kirche, eine kirchen- und dogmengeschichtliche Monographie*, 1850, 622 pp.), while other criticisms came from G. V. Lechler (1852) and R. A. Lipsius (1853).

[24] Munck 1959, 70.

[25] Consider, for example, Schmithals' proposal of Jewish-Christian gnostics at Corinth, a refinement of Lütgert's "libertinische Pneumatiker." Cf. also Bornkamm 1969.

[26] Fee 1987, 6. Cf. Hurd 1983 (1965) for agreement about the "unified front" against Paul.

[27] Baird 1990, 130–131. It must be asserted here from the start that these different levels or dimensions of conflict—theological, religious, socio-economic—are interwoven in each conflict. The crucial point is the complexity of the problem facing Paul.

[28] *Ibid.*

[29] Taken from "Paradigm Pioneers," the second of two management consultation videos on paradigms and leadership by Joel Barker (1988).

[30] Meeks 1983, 2, in which the author paraphrases his objectors.

[31] Holmberg 1990, 56.

[32] Theissen 1982, 15.

[33] *Ibid.*, 177.

[34] Cited as the final article in Schütz' English translation in Theissen 1982, the German original of "The Sociological interpretation of Religious Traditions: Its Methodological Problems as Exemplified in Early Christianity" first appeared in *Kairos* 17 (1975), 284–299.

[35] These categories also have a prominent place in his 1978 work on Palestinian Christianity.

[36] Theissen 1982, 58.

[37] See 1982, 106. In this, Theissen stands in line with E. A. Judge (1960; 1980), as well as A. Malherbe 1983, who speaks of an "emerging consensus" in the issue of social makeup.

[38] Theissen 1982, 95; cf. pp. 73–96 for detailed examination of individuals in the community.

[39] Horrell 1996, 94. He goes on to "stress the need for caution and for conclusions congruent with the nature and extent of the evidence."

[40] Holmberg 1990, 69. Horrell also concurs "that their work remains valuable" (1996, 94).

[41] Theissen 1982, 107.

[42] Theissen 1982, 151.

[43] *Ibid.*, 163.

[44] *Ibid.*, 137. M. Mitchell (1991) and Witherington (1995) argue otherwise.

[45] Fiorenza 1987, 397.

[46] Theissen 1982, 108.

[47] Kidd 1990, 177. The author also sees this love patriarchalism as a Pauline concept that helps bridge the gap between Paul and the Pastoral epistles.

[48] See Engberg-Pedersen 1993, esp. 111.

[49] See above note 56.

[50] Elliott 1995, 65. "We never learn," Elliott continues, "what Theissen makes of the exegetical difficulties in 1 Cor. 7.21."

[51] Elliott 1995, 31–32.

[52] D. Martin 1995, 259, n. 12; cf. also 135–6, as Martin admits difficulty in pigeonholing Paul.

[53] Horrell 1996, 196.

[54] Meeks 1983, 2.

[55] Meeks 1983, 72.

[56] *Ibid.*, 9.

[57] *Ibid.*, 73.

[58] *Ibid.*, 55.

[59] Meeks 1983, 164 (emphasis mine).

[60] Talbert adds, "Just as Tertullian cited selections from Marcion before answering him, so Paul referred to Corinthian assertions before responding" (1987, xiv).

[61] Cf. Meeks 1983, 117–125, esp. 122–123. Paul's use of rhetoric will be explored more in the next section; also, cf. Betz, Litfin, M. Mitchell, Witherington.

[62] Meeks 1983, 107.

[63] Cf. Malina 1985, 347, for further criticism on this; also Horrell 1996, 35–36.

[64] Meeks 983, 191.

[65] For more on the "proletarian" views of Deissmann, Engels and Kautsky, see Chow 1992.

[66] Meeks 1985, 7.

[67] Elliott 1995, 65.

[68] Harris 1991, 1. There have been some noteworthy exceptions, as seen below.

[69] Baird 1990, 131. Here, Barton (1997) has also offered fair warning about over-reliance on any one sociological methodology.

[70] Crafton 1991, 13. Cf. also Meeks 1986; D. Martin 1995, 294, n. 4.

[71] Litfin 1994, 202.

[72] An example is J. A. Crafton's use of Burkian analysis in examining Pauline texts (1991, esp. 27–30). While there are many problems with the "New Rhetoric," several of Crafton's arguments on metaphors are convincing and should not be jettisoned too quickly.

[73] M. Mitchell 1992, 1.

[74] Cf. also Fiorenza 1987, 393; Jones 1978, 94; Mitchell 1989, 256.

[75] Witherington 1995, 75. He concurs, however, that "benefit" does play a part in persuasion.

[76] D. Martin 1995, 38.

[77] Jones 1978, 83.

[78] Cf. Mitchell 1992, 187–188.

[79] Cf. Pogoloff 1992, 90; Witherington 1995, 75, n. 10.

[80] Witherington 1995, 39.

[81] *Ibid.*, 55.

[82] Mitchell 1992, 284.

[83] Smit 1991, 215–216, in which Smit notes Paul's "effective and creative use of the suggestions for persuasion mapped out in the classical schoolbooks."

[84] From W. A. Meeks' comments on the back jacket of Martin's book.

[85] D. Martin 1995, xvii.

[86] *Ibid.*, 63.

[87] *Ibid.*, 69.

[88] *Ibid.*, 76.

[89] *Ibid.*, 136.

[90] As seen in Douglas 1966; cf. also Barton 1986, 231.

[91] *Ibid.*, 67.

[92] It is possible to hear resonances of Crafton's arguments for bringing others into a new worldview, although Martin neither suggests nor cites any specific connection.

[93] D. Martin 1995, 199.

[94] Horrell 1996, 37. Cf. also Broderick 1993, 14–15.

[95] Marshall 1987, 145.

[96] Chow 1992, 19.

[97] *Ibid.*, 30, where the author cites network analyst J. Mitchell (1969, 2).

[98] Bott 1971, 330.

[99] Chow 1992, 31–32. The predilection toward change suggested in (6) connotes a potentiality for conflict, a concept that will be explored next chapter.

[100] *Ibid.*, 33.

[101] *Ibid.*, 139–157. Cf. Clarke 1993, 68–73; also Saller 1982 for more on patronage.

[102] Dunn 1995, 52.

[103] Petersen 1985, 90–175, esp. 91–97. Petersen's reliance on Berger and Luckman's *The Social Construction of Reality* is quite evident throughout his work (see esp. 171, n. 2).

[104] *Ibid.*, 171, n. 3.

[105] As mentioned briefly, M. Douglas' work on social boundaries, applied to the Corinthian situation by Barton 1986, has important implications for this study, as seen later.

[106] Besides Mitchell's more comprehensive work, other more narrowly focused studies include Castelli 1991; Fiorenza 1987; and Wire 1990.

[107] Horrell 1996, 16–18. Interestingly, because in his own work he focuses so much time and space on both a critique of past sociological approaches to Paul and an explication of A. Gidden's structuration theory, Horrell leaves himself very limited space in which to apply Gidden's principles to both canonical Corinthian letters as well as *1 Clement.*

[108] This is also seen in Baird's concern about "methodological oversimplification" (1990).

[109] Clarke 1993, 6.

[110] Barclay 1992, 57, who remarks that this lack of "hostility" between Christians and others in Corinth, though noteworthy, is "one of the least noticed features of Corinthian church life."

[111] For a summary of the various positions on this much-discussed topic, see Pogoloff 1992; also cf. Davis 1984 for details on Jewish sapiential traditions in the Roman period.

[112] Fee 1987, 181. Cf. Orr and Walther 1976, 182, who concur that "the social position of the members [of the Corinthian church] was one of comparative calm and safety."

[113] Coser 1956, 38; cf. Morgan, et al. 1981, 137; also Beavers 1977.

[114] Witherington 1995, 75, alludes to this double dilemma but does not tease out the implications of what it means to "create community." Again, cf. Coser 1956, 38ff.

[115] Coser 1956, 34; he adds that such conflict also creates a balance between the distinct groups, a claim that will be examined in more detail later in chapter 5.

[116] The dangers of anachronism are discussed further in the next chapter on the methodological approach utilised here.

[117] Cf. Mitchell 1991, 96, who notes that "the image of inner-group contenders as disputing children is another commonplace in literature urging concord on divided groups."

[118] Witherington 1995, 58, where he alludes to the use of the so-called "New Rhetoric."

✧ CHAPTER TWO
Defining Systems

Thus far in our survey of the socio-historical literature on 1 Corinthians, we have seen that despite valuable insights from various studies, a gap remains in our understanding of the role and management of conflict in the Corinthian church. Chow's research into social networks has appeared particularly promising in this regard, illustrating how thinking in terms of ties and networks can transport us from the static imagery of "us versus them" and into a world of dynamic interfacing and complex boundaries. Yet Chow himself has not made full use of this new imagery, instead limiting his focus to only one type of interaction within the Corinthian networks, i.e. the patron/client relationship. As a result, the larger image of a network of relationships in the Corinthian congregation has been left unexplored. The gap remains.

Coser's principles may yet assist in focusing attention onto conflict's functions and management in the Corinthian community's development, *provided these principles are accompanied by a more dynamic way of engaging and describing the social networks to which many of the Corinthian Christians belonged.* Several social analysts, in both theoretical study of the dynamic realities of networks as well as practical applications of this study for counseling and negotiations, have provided some helpful methodological keys in the form of systems thinking and conflict management (or conflict resolution, depending on one's terminology). As these approaches focus almost exclusively on issues of complex group dynamics, they may provide some assistance in unlocking several of the difficulties raised by conflicting roles and interwoven relationships in Corinth.

This chapter focuses on systems thinking, giving particular attention to its history, key principles, and relevance for study of the Corinthian situation. In remaining true to not only the concepts but also the methods of systems thinking, discussion of key terms and concepts will be accompanied throughout by various diagrams and tables. The importance of "family" in systems thought will be explored, as will the suggestion that a Pauline congregation may be understood sociologically as a family-like social system. The goal of this chapter is to present a methodological approach which can be utilized with clarity and confidence in addressing the dynamic nature of the Corinthian church's conflict(s).

A Social System

Although systems terminology is not new to functionalist scholars,[1] a new level of expertise has emerged through the coming together of several seemingly separate and distinct fields including cybernetics, empiricism, family therapy and, interestingly, functionalism itself. In other words, systems thinking is not some radically new, wholly unfamiliar methodological model, but rather another step in a long line of socio-historical approaches to complex social groups or systems. Indeed, it has been argued that systems thinking is not new at all. It is as old as the dictum, "The whole is greater than the sum of its parts," and found in ancient rhetoricians' use of the "body" metaphor to promote unity within groups.[2] What is new in systems thinking is its explicit and conscious application by analysts in approaching complex networking relationships. A perfect example is seen in computers, which have made use of such systematic focus to perform not several, but several million, operations per second. Like computer systems, social systems have also benefited in recent years from concepts and tools emerging from systems thinking. Indeed, because systems thinking "deals with data in a new way, focusing less on the cause-and-effect connections that link bits of information and more on the principles of organizations that give data meaning,"[3] it becomes possible to move beyond arguments about this part or that part in a system, examining instead the system and its interrelationships as a whole. Thus, systems principles can help clarify the dynamic networking relationships mentioned by Chow.

What is being discussed here? What exactly is meant by the term *system*? Webster's Dictionary defines a *system* as "a regularly interacting or interdependent group of items forming a unified whole." Even in this basic description, certain points may be seen. First, the words "interacting or interdependent" point both to a dynamism and to a connectedness that are present in the group. There is nothing static about a system, although systems can be, and often are, resistant to change. The word "regularly" denotes that despite the dynamism within the group, there are patterns of relationships which may be studied and which prevent the group from deteriorating into chaos. Similarly, the words "a unified whole" suggest a group held together by some sort of boundaries, ranging from almost *no* boundaries, where the group within and the outside environment become virtually indistinguishable, to very *fixed* boundaries. Lastly, within the description "group of items" can be found not only simple inanimate units of study, but also highly complex "items," such as people in the Corinthian congregation who were connected to one another and to others outside the ἐκκλησία through their various social interactions. Appropriately enough, even as systems thinking has developed from the interactions of ideas from several diverse fields,[4] it has also engendered several distinct approaches in recent years (including communications theory, conflict theory and family process theory). Most of these approaches, however, share four foundational systems assumptions.

(1) All parts of the system are interconnected. "Although the assumption of interconnectedness in a system seems obvious, it is far from trivial."[5] Once it is acknowledged that the various parts of a system are interconnected, it is no longer possible to view each part as a purely independent entity. Rather, as seen in *figure 2.b,* each part of the system is connected to, and can potentially influence, the other parts. (Of course, not every part can boast the same degree of influence as other parts.[6]) Starting from a standpoint of interconnectedness may appear quite odd to many in the twentieth-century Western world, where concepts of individualism and independence are so highly prized. Interestingly, as pointed out by Malina and Neyrey, people in the ancient Mediterranean world grasped the concept of interconnectedness and saw relationships in interdependent terms.[7]

A → B → C → D
   Here, leader 'A' causes or coerces 'B' which then causes 'C' and so on.

Figure 2.a—Linear Thinking

          Here, as opposed to simple causal relationships, or even multiple
          causation (as when A + B + C = D), each of the elements can
          have an effect on one another, so that interdependence is seen
          in the overall system. It is no longer appropriate to speak only
          in linear terms when describing the interactions of such a system.

Figure 2.b—Interrelational Thinking

Of course, this begs the question of what exactly holds the parts of a system together. One answer is the principle of *equilibrium*. This affirms that every system maintains its own stability by use of self-regulating mechanisms. An example of this from inanimate systems is the auto-pilot mechanism of an airplane. Note that the auto-pilot can, and indeed does, make minor course corrections along the flight path, but always within a range and always with the express purpose of maintaining a certain fixed direction. The minor changes are allowed to prevent major, stability-challenging, changes from occurring. On a more complex social level, groups such as families or clubs develop their own mechanisms, albeit often unconsciously, which allow the group to continue a largely stable existence. However, just as self-regulating mechanisms can provide healthy and even salvific ways for a system to persevere through terrible tragedies, they can also work to prevent healing or much-needed change from entering a system.

Scapegoating or blaming—marking out one group member as the troublemaker or, in seemingly more benign terms, the sick patient—is one homeostatic mechanism that may perpetuate the continued existence of the group, but at the cost of any real growth. A family may seek counseling for the adolescent son who is failing several school subjects, but reject any notion that the boy's actions are a symptom of a deeper problem within the family as a whole. However, as shown in *figure 2.b*, when it is acknowledged that the various group members are networked into one another, it is then impossible to view problems in the system in such simplistic terms as, "This is all his fault," or "She is the problem here, not I." Eliminating such linear cause-and-effect thinking "has important consequences for diagnosis (and blaming), for prediction, and for evaluating change."[8] All are connected. All are involved, if not always equally or obviously, in the internal workings of that group, in conflicts that arise and in possible resolutions. Therefore, when problems do arise in a system, the question to ask is not, "Who is to blame?" but rather, "What is happening in the system as a whole to allow a problem or change to occur now?"

Thus, *timing* is a crucial factor. For as nothing occurs in a temporal vacuum, whenever there are signs of challenge or change in a social system, it is important to ask: "Why now?" For good or for bad, something has now broken into the formerly stable environment of the social system. Perhaps the system's "immune system" is particularly weak at the moment and an outside force has been able to invade. Perhaps a radical new discovery has rendered prior knowledge in the system archaic. In any case, a corner has been turned at that moment, and it is helpful to understand the timing of the change in order to better understand what is going on among the system parts.

(2) Understanding is only possible by viewing the whole. Related to the first systems assumption, this says that as much as the parts of a system are interconnected, they *"do not function according to their 'nature' but according to the position in the network."*[9] With data bombarding us on virtually every possible subject, it is simply not feasible to focus on this part and then that part of a given system, and assume in the end that we understand the system as a whole. It is in comprehending the mutual interactions and potential effects of the various parts that greater understanding of the system as a whole is possible. However, for the system to grow with any vitality at all, there must exist some internal boundaries between its interdependent members. *Differentiation* is necessary. Where does one person end and another begin? Without adequate differentiation within the group, the parts can become so enmeshed in one another that they are indistinguishable. This is not interdependence, but over-dependence.

Emotional *triangles* occur, as conflicted members bring in a third party to be rescuer, fellow victim, or supreme judge. Such triangles can result in the third party bearing the stress and responsibility of the others, and the entire system can become stuck.[10] To the extent that a group allows its constituent members to be differentiated from one another, yet all interdependent, that group can grow and develop.

The concept of *interactional process over informational data* offers a crucial edge to grasping what is happening in a group or system. Referring once more to *figure 2.b,* it is helpful to see the lines between the individual, connected parts as lines of communication. This communication involves not simply *messages* but also *metamessages,* not only *what* is communicated (i.e. the content of the conversation), but also *how* the communication is taking place (i.e. the tone, body language, rhetorical form of the conversation, the positioning of each conversant). In this way, it is possible to avoid becoming stuck in a morass of data and instead concentrate on the way communication is taking place within the system.

(3) A system and its environment have an effect on one another. This effect is generated by feedback enabling persons and entire groups to "make decisions and change behavior based on information about the environment."[11] Just as a system needs internal boundaries by which constituent members can be differentiated one from another, that same system needs to be differentiated from its environment while remaining open to helpful interaction with the outside world. Two complementary sets of processes by which this maintenance of selectively permeable boundaries occurs are *protective territoriality,* which keeps unwanted elements out of the system while allowing for the entrance of needed or desired elements, and *possessive restrictiveness,* which maintains member loyalties and preserves valued assets while allowing for either the elimination of wastes or the regular expeditions of members into the outside world.[12] Through these processes, the system is differentiated from its environment while maintaining contact with it.

(4) Systems are not reality, but a way of approaching the reality being studied. Thus, "defining an object as a system composed of subsystems, inputs, and outputs is just one among many possible ways we might study the object."[13] Awareness of this assumption can help us

avoid any reductionist or anachronistic errors in analysis, therefore promoting a less competitive, more complementary methodological study of the Corinthian congregation. Some opponents have argued that systems theorists have been "prone to slip into the danger of reification, or the fallacy of misplaced concreteness."[14] This is indeed a danger for all social-scientific approaches, and therefore "clarity regarding theories, models, and methods is a characteristic concern."[15] However, the constructivist position of systems thinking says from the start "systems models are not models of 'reality' so much as heuristics for different purposes."[16] Systems principles are used here in the hopes of complementing other exegetical and historical approaches to conflict in Corinth.

A more substantial critique leveled against systems thinking has been the argument that, like continuums or flow-charts (with which it is at times linked), this approach is "too abstract and global to be of much use with ideas so general as to be almost meaningless."[17] However, as hopefully will be seen here, this criticism melts away as the generalities spoken of (i.e. boundaries, triangles, change) are applied *intentionally within the larger historical critical approach.* In utilizing systems principles in a study of the Corinthian congregation, there is no suggestion that this first century social entity is a system synonymous with any modern group, or that the Mediterranean world of that period is identical with twentieth century Western society.[18] Even within its own temporal and cultural environment, the Corinthian congregation is understood as unique among other social groups. Thus, while the *terminology* involved in systems thinking is by necessity time-based, the *substance* of the theory and its elements may be discerned in social systems of other times, dressed in their own cultural and temporal garb. Insofar as the first century ἐκκλησία exhibited group characteristics such as rules, goals, communication, negotiation or boundaries, it is appropriate to examine that congregation as a social system, *while always within its own unique temporal and cultural context.* For a summary of the key systems concepts mentioned above, see *figure 2.c* below.

Systems Concept	Meaning and Significance to Group
Interactional Process over Informational Content	Focus on the "how" of interchanges between group members, not solely on the "what" of the issue in question. This involves study of metamessages.
Equilibrium, or Homeostasis	Focus on choices within the group, conscious or otherwise, *to maintain overall stability at all costs*; "Don't rock the boat" is the aim, for good or bad.
Scapegoating	When equilibrium is challenged, blame may result, *often focused on the leader challenging the group*; leverage is given to the followers, not the leader.
Triangles	Conflicted members seek to involve a third party as rescuer, fellow victim, or supreme judge, *thus thwarting any real change in initial relationship*. Paradoxically, greatest power may rest precisely in the triangled, or "most vulnerable," position.

Figure 2.c— Key Systems Concepts and their Significance

Family as the Prototypical System

A Model of Social Interactions

It has been in modern family research as well as work with churches and synagogues that the greatest fruitfulness of systems principles has been realized. Why is "family" so important to systems thinking? Clearly, the family in any age is a set of interconnected relationships, as well as a group with both boundaries and "gates" (once again using Meeks' terminology) between itself and its environment. More than any other social system, the family is, in most cultures, the primary relational group. Whatever the specific form or appearance of the family, the relationships therein are in some way differentiated both in quality and importance from all other social relationships. Saller speaks of the ancient family as the "organizing unit to satisfy basic needs and to reproduce the next generation."[19] Parson's classic model of social interactions explains the unique character of the family using "pattern variables," dyads of opposing relational roles, which allow any system to be located in its own space in the model.[20]

Parson asks whether the internal relationships are…
Universalistic: insiders are treated the same as those outside the system, OR
Particularistic: members relate to each other differently than to outsiders?

Diffuse: system members interrelate on a wide spectrum of issues, OR
Specific: system members interrelate on a few specific projects or issues?

Ascribed: system members receive membership through no achievement, OR
Achieved: insiders earn membership through some form of achievement?

Neutral: members interact with each other in emotionally neutral ways, OR
Affective: members interact with each other in emotionally affective ways?

Using these variables, then, it can be claimed effectively that "literally, only one type of social relationship can be defined as diffuse, *and* particularistic, *and* affective, *and* ascribed: the family relationship."[21] The family is, perhaps, the best social example of a regularly interacting or group of constituent members comprising a unified whole.

"Family-like systems"

In the same way, the pairing of modern religious institutions with family is not accidental, for as some systems theorists have argued, "the one work system that functions most like a family is the church or synagogue."[22] The unique character of family interrelationships has just been illustrated. However, it may be argued further that the local congregation is one of "many varieties of *family-like systems* that mimic" families without "replicating" them (see *figure 2.d*).[23] Indeed, despite some conservatism in too broad an application of systems principles, "much of what family process theorists and researchers have discovered about how family systems operate may apply to family-like systems."[24]

MODERN WESTERN FAMILY			MODERN CONGREGATION		
Internal relationships are			*Internal relationships are*		
Specific	| ✓	Diffuse	Specific	| ✓	Diffuse
Neutral	| ✓	Affective	Neutral	| ✓	Affective
Achieved	| ✓	Ascribed	Achieved ✓	|	Ascribed
Universal	| ✓	Particularistic	Universal	| ✓	Particularistic

Fig. 2.d–Modern Systems Comparison Chart

A Brief Disclaimer

It would be naive to assume that because twentieth-century churches may be described as family-like systems and, therefore, be examined using key systems principles, the same is necessarily true of first-century churches (or even first-century families). After all, in speaking of the Corinthian "congregation," as well as "family" and "household" in Paul's time, we are using terms whose meanings might very well have been different then (perhaps slightly, or perhaps radically, different) from their meanings now! This distinction is not always recognized or expressed by those who comment on Paul's "family talk." Yet if any accurate understanding is to be reached concerning Paul's familial terminology in 1 Corinthians, there is a need for greater comprehension of Roman family life, "many aspects of which will be quite alien to readers" and may "seem to militate against anything resembling modern urban family life."[25] Entering the world of Paul and his Christian "sisters and brothers" means tuning in to a different frequency than that which would be used for a church community or family household today.

The Church as a System

Of what advantage is it to use systems principles in examining the conflicts and interrelationships of the Corinthian congregation? This query may be answered by briefly considering the Pauline church in light of the four systems assumptions outlined above: (1) The Corinthian congregation was clearly a group in which there were many interconnections (see next chapter). As seen in *figure 2.e* below, the Corinthian community may be viewed in terms more dynamic than simply "Strong" and "Weak" members in contention. Because several overlapping relationships and group processes were present, a constant dynamism was inherent in the church.

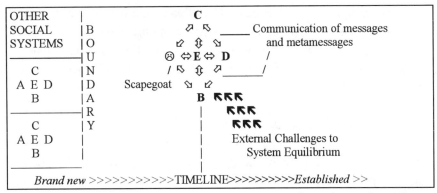

Figure 2.e—The ἐκκλησία as a Social System

Paul's use of "body" language in 1 Corinthians and of συμ- language, "If one member suffers, all suffer together" (συμπάσχει, 12.26), reveal the apostle's own acknowledgement of the emotional and spiritual interdependency in the Corinthian congregational system. Even his admonitions to his "beloved children" (4.14) suggest a systemic network of interrelationships of which he is a part. Furthermore, Paul himself understood the congregation as a whole unit, a "body," "temple," "field." His letters to the Corinthians, like those to other congregations, were addressed to the church *as a whole*. And particularly with the Corinthians, his letters were addressed to a group he himself saw in familial terms. Whereas "the Corinthians saw themselves as a *collegium*," Paul's understanding of the church was tied up with organic and familial imagery. It is easy, then, to imagine "how behaviour Paul criticize[d] could to them have seemed completely normal."[26] We must here be concerned with questions of varying perceptions of the shared relationship. Systems thinking, with its concern for the group as a whole, can assist us in viewing the contrasting images that the Corinthians and Paul held.

Concerning the system and its environment, Paul described the collective Christians in Corinth as ἐκκλησία, denoting "a very strong sense of internal cohesion and of distinction both from outsiders and from the world."[27] Yet the apostle also designated this congregation as a subset of at least two larger groups: the city (and society) of Corinth (τῇ οὔσῃ ἐν Κορίνθῳ) and the larger community of Christians in every place (ἐν παντὶ τόπῳ). Thus, the same Corinthian community which was distinct from other groups in society was, in another sense, interwoven with them through inter-relationships, so that a Christian was actually part of a large matrix of systems, all of which influence[d] one another."[28]

The Church as a Family-like System

The usage of systems principles with which to view the Corinthian ἐκκλησία is possible only because systems thinking has always been grounded in a concern for "real life" and empirical evidence. It is essential and altogether expected that as much attention as possible will be placed on the historical context and primary sources, with issues of reliability, validity and representativeness highlighted throughout the process. Above all, there is strength in systems thinking's concern with the degree of emotional interdependency in an interconnecting system.

Systems thinking works best with families and family-like social systems. This has been stated quite clearly. The Corinthian church, it may be argued, displayed many familial qualities, with internal relationships that were diffuse and not situation-specific, particularistic and not universalistic, affective and not emotionally neutral.[29] Unlike a (modern) family, however, these relationships were usually *achieved*, through baptism and entrance into the faith community, and not *ascribed* (though even this point may be debated[30]). Indeed, the ἐκκλησία was in some ways born out of the household system, and not too surprisingly "adapted the structure of [contemporary] families and applied it to the Christian family and also to a lesser degree to the Christian congregation as family."[31] Continuities between the family and a family-like system, which Paul himself promotes through his language and imagery, do allow for some continuities in analysis...with emphasis on the qualifier "some." Principles such as the focus on contextual process over internal content of information, or the resistance to change outside a small range (homeostasis), or the need for a non-anxious presence in conflict—all these can be used, though with awareness to their limits, when approaching the situation in Corinth.

Thinking of the Church in Systemic Terms

How, then, are we to apply systems principles to the study of intra-church conflict in Corinth and Paul's response to the situation? First, following Barton's realization that there is "surprisingly little New Testament scholarship" concerning "Paul's attempts to mark out boundaries between church and household,"[32] it would seem that there is room for a methodological approach that focuses on issues of boundary definition and the effects of a leader's self-differentiation in a social system, both within and between families and family-like institutions. Starting with insights from studies of Graeco-Roman and Jewish households, systems thinking combined with Coser's propositions might also be able to add to the discussion, especially due to their focus on conflict. "The value of studying points of conflict lies in their tendency to bring to the surface otherwise hidden or taken-for-granted values and assumptions."[33] Direct evidence of conflict management within first century households might shed further light on Paul's own approach as "father in Christ" to the Corinthians, since the Corinthian ἐκκλησία, while worshipping a "God of peace" (14.33), was anything but peaceful itself, with discord being the primary issue addressed by their apostle-congregational parent. "Conflict is a process,"[34] so to understand conflict in a group such as the Corinthian congregation, it is essential to consider both the group and the conflict in dynamic, developing, boundary-setting terms. Then, when the otherwise stable environment of a social system is challenged, whether from within or without, it is possible to ask, "Why now?" A corner is turned upon the threat of change, thereby providing a greater understanding of the system's internal workings.

All this brings us back to the issue of the Corinthian church as a new, rather than an established, group. "If Paul seems to us to be over-paternalistic in his dealings with his churches this is a trait which he shares with many who have founded new movements."[35] It is precisely because the Corinthian congregation was so new at the time of Paul's first epistle that an understanding of his response to each situation of conflict becomes so crucial. As the parent-figure and founding apostle of the Corinthian ἐκκλησία, Paul was drawn into several conflictual situations as the third point of a triangle,[36] sometimes as scapegoat, often as a judge, rescuer, or even Christ-figure (see 1 Corinthians 1). In each instance, it is important to perceive which roles were open to him as the father/leader, and which ways he would choose to proceed.

"At the heart of the Corinthian correspondence are two things that demand attention: *what* is said and *how* it is said."[37] Mitchell and other socio-rhetorical scholars have rightly emphasized the deliberative nature of Paul's epistle, arguing that his wording and order of topics were strategically chosen by the apostle himself, with a cohesiveness to the overall argument for unity.[38] Not only does this imply some expertise in rhetorical forms (despite his own protests in 1 Cor. 1–3, such protestation itself being an ancient rhetorical tool), but also that Paul was committed to leadership "by means of persuasion whenever possible and commanded only when necessary."[39] In many ways throughout the epistle, the Corinthians themselves, as interdependent members of the body, were invited to help shape the process rather than develop even greater dependency on their "father."[40] Yet even as Paul called the Corinthians to join in decision-making about crucial areas such as intra-church discipline, at other times he himself clearly pronounced judgement (i.e. consider the different cases of litigating members and the incestuous man). How, then, and why did he choose certain moments to empower the Corinthians and other moments to show his authority?

There has not been offered a simple answer to this complicated question, for Paul himself seemed to deviate in his role almost unconsciously. Or perhaps these were not unconscious movements at all. A rhetorician worked hard to present a message that would have a desirable effect on the listeners/readers. But often such a process could involve *metamessages* which actually conveyed a far different reality than the one spoken openly. Hence, Paul's use of irony, "know-nothing" statements, and "imitation" arguments could carry within their forms very deliberate messages that would challenge, cajole, or persuade. Understanding this means understanding something of the skills involved in *negotiation*, an area which in recent years has been studied far more by those in conflict resolution and corporate management than by socio-historians or even socio-rhetoricians.

The Corinthian situation contained an "interweaving" of the members' perceptions, desires, fears, as well as Paul's response to them. Although at times he did invoke overtly his authority (which was not always recognized, of course, by all to whom he wrote), Paul more often than not invited his fellow saints into the conversation, giving way on several issues, while remaining utterly firm in others. His intensity of language and his language of intimacy show that even words can have body language! Examination of this "body language," Paul's subtle metamessages, could help reveal why and how Paul was able at times to concentrate on the process of Corinthians' handling of a particular matter (such as the case of litigation in chapter six) rather than the minutia of the situation itself. By focusing on the "how" of this situation (How are you Corinthians conducting yourselves in such matters?), he overturned and de-emphasized the "what" (the much-debated, largely unknown situation itself). Paul's responses to many of the conflicts in Corinth, his "conflict management" approach, will await discussion until part three of this thesis. However, it is possible and helpful to recognize from the start that Paul's responses only make sense when viewed against the backdrop of Paul's relational position in the social system that was the Corinthian ἐκκλησία.

Paul: A Threat to the System

Though he could not be present, Paul's letters bridged the gap between himself and his "children," inviting them to join in the dialogue. So much of Paul's writing was wrapped up in his personal relationship with the recipients and the occasional nature of his letters, so that "they have an intensely personal character which makes it, if not impossible, at least unwise to abstract what is said from the person and personality of the author."[41] His role as leader by necessity placed Paul in a social system that was marked by interdependency and interactions. His concern for the task of the gospel and his concern for his own relationship with his Corinthian brothers and sisters at times combined and clashed, resulting in different outcomes to different conflicts at different times.

Paul's handling of the problems in Corinth has been said by some to be "masterful, and should be a compulsory study in courses on management."[42] Yet, is this a fair statement? For many of the Corinthian Christians, Paul's attempts to change their world-view—to shift their paradigm—seemed to be a threat posing far graver danger than anything any of their individual members had done or were doing. Social systems then and now, in resisting major change to that which is known and predictable, "will often tolerate and adapt to trouble-making complainers and downright incompetents, whereas the creative thinker who disturbs the balance of things will be ignored."[43] Whether this was the case for Paul remains to be seen. Even in the Church's earliest days, it was recognized that "some things" in Paul's letters were "hard to understand" (δυσνόντά, 2 Peter 3.16), and resulted in distortions and criticisms of the apostle's message. This is not wholly surprising. Paul set up a standard that in some ways was destined to be rejected by many. M. Mitchell says quite succinctly that "Paul's rhetoric of reconciliation in 1 Corinthians was a failure."[44] Is this an accurate statement, obvious though it may at first appear? When and in what ways did Paul choose to make "effective and creative use of the suggestions for persuasion mapped out in the classical schoolbooks,"[45] and when did he not? The focus throughout this work will continue to be on the underlying dynamics of the Corinthian system, as well as Paul's boundary-defining responses.

For now, it is helpful to consider what has been said in this chapter. The basic assumptions and key principles of systems thinking have been outlined in brief, with particular attention given to the ways in which these principles may be applied appropriately to the Corinthian congregation. It has been argued that the ἐκκλησία may be considered in sociological terms as a family-like social system, and that Paul himself used familial terms when speaking to the Corinthians. This and other aspects of the apostle's response to the problems in Corinth will be taken up and examined more closely in the chapters that follow. For now, our attention must turn to a reconsideration of the problem itself, as the nature of the double dilemma of conflict is explored in light of relational networks in Corinth.

✧✧✧

NOTES

[1] Consider the A-G-I-L model of Parsons and Bales 1955, esp. 39. In terms of New Testament scholars using functionalist perspective and systems terms, see Meeks 1983.

[2] Cf. Broderick 1993, 7.

[3] Friedman 1985, 15.

[4] For a more detailed history of systems thinking and its applications in family and social group research, see Broderick 1993, 3–35.

[5] Klein and White 1996, 155.

[6] Not every part boasts an equal amount of influence, as seen in Chow's first principle.

[7] 1996, Appendix 1.

[8] Klein and White 1996, 17.

[9] Friedman 1985, 15 (emphasis mine).

[10] *Ibid.*, 36–39, for more on the 'laws' of emotional triangles.

[11] Klein and White 1996, 17–18.

[12] Cf. Broderick 1993, 123ff.

[13] Klein and White 1996, 156. E. von Glaserfeld's constructivist perspective is a starting point for this understanding of systems as heuristic devices and not 'the thing itself.'

[14] *Ibid.*, 175, citing Whitehead 1929, 11.

[15] Elliott 1993, 36.

[16] Klein and White 1996, 176.

[17] Klein and White 1996, 174.

[18] Cf. Malina and Neyrey 1996, appendix 2 (227–231), for a comparative table of salient features between modern western cultures and ancient Mediterranean cultures.

[19] Saller 1994, 95; cf. also Bott 1971; Burr 1979; Klein and White 1996; Zonabend 1996.

[20] Parsons 1951, 80–112, esp. chart 1 on p. 105.

[21] Broderick 1993, 54.

[22] Friedman 1985, 197.

[23] Broderick 1993, 52.

[24] *Ibid.*, 5.

[25] Dixon 1992, 161.

[26] Pogoloff 1992, 250.

[27] Meeks 1983, 74. This imagery of cohesion and distinctiveness is strengthened by Paul's metaphors: building (3.10–15), temple (3.16–17), and body (12.12–31 and elsewhere).

[28] Morgan, et al. 1981, 137.

[29] See Parsons 1951, 105, chart 1.

[30] Meeks 1983, 87–88, notes the 'adoption' qualities of baptismal language and shows precedents for it in Jewish and other adoptionist religions.

[31] Witherington 1994, 301.

[32] Barton 1986, 225. While Barton's focus is primarily on *intra*-church boundaries, his insights (and those of M. Douglas, on which he at times relies) may be quite relevant to this study.

[33] *Ibid.*, 225.

[34] Klein and White 1996, 209.

[35] Best 1986, 144.

[36] He has somehow become aware of the situation, probably by oral report, as the forcefulness of his opening exclamation, 'How dare you' (τόλμα), does not lend itself easily to a response to a written communique. Cf. Fee 1987, 230–231; also Orr and Walther 1976, 193, n. 1.

[37] Talbert 1987, xiii.

[38] Cf. Mitchell 1991 and 1989; also see Fiorenza 1987, Litfin 1994, Smit 1991, Talbert 1987, Witherington 1995.

[39] Witherington 1995, 46.

[40] Carpenter & Kennedy 1988, 27.

[41] Dunn 1994, 413.

[42] Goulder 1994, 54.

[43] Friedman 1985, 25

[44] M. Mitchell 1993, 303.

[45] Smit 1991, 216. Cf. also Mitchell 1991, 116–118, for more on Paul's rhetorical choices.

✧ CHAPTER THREE
Overlapping Networks

I argued in chapter one that the problem with previous studies of the Corinthian intra-church conflict has been their singular, linear focus: they have not accounted for the multifaceted nature of the tensions Paul addressed. While Theissen, Meeks, and others following a socio-historical approach have pointed to the previously neglected social dimensions of disputes in Corinth, their analyses often have remained on a fairly static level, focusing on dichotomies between "haves" and "have-nots" while neglecting the more complex interactions of persons in networking relationships. Mitchell's reading of Paul's letter as a unified, intentional and creative response to factionalism in the church is to be commended, although her focus on Paul's rhetoric and the political *topoi* therein leaves undiscussed the relational dynamics underlying Corinthian "factionalism." Similarly, despite the insightful connections made by D. Martin between ancient understandings of σῶμα and Paul's use of the term in 1 Corinthians, he still remains tied to a single "fault line" separating the different members of the ἐκκλησία, based on socio-economic status and differing perceptions of the body. Of all the approaches listed, it is Chow's social networks together with Petersen's insights on social roles which offer a more dynamic context for understanding στάσις in the church, while the limitations inherent in their own respective works invite further investigation into the Corinthian situation.

Building on this, it was suggested in the last chapter that systems principles could both complement previous research and elucidate the more perplexing aspects of the Corinthian situation and Paul's response. This, of course, does not imply a naive belief that systems thinking and "conflict management," with their twentieth century terminology, can be *applied* to the first century world of the Corinthian ἐκκλησία. Instead it is hoped that, as groups of people in any age display interdependent networking relationships which are affective, particularistic, and diffused (see *figure 2.d)*, systems principles may prove helpful in raising questions about boundaries, leadership and change that otherwise might not be asked. I remain, therefore, cautiously optimistic in my use of systems principles while always striving to remain grounded in a socio-historical approach.

One way in which systems principles can prove particularly helpful in the exegetical process regards clarification of the problem itself. What was happening in the church on a relational or systemic level that prompted apostolic response? What can be said about the conflict(s) in Corinth, and the lack of conflict between the church (and, more specifically, key members of the church) and the rest of the world? It would be easy, if misleading, to dive into an analysis of Paul's strategic response to the double dilemma in Corinth without first asking these important questions. While some scholars have traded the old argument about a theological dichotomy (e.g. between Petrine and Pauline camps) for a new and more sophisticated socio-economic "fault line" between the "haves" and the "have-nots," this pattern of linear, two-dimensional thinking still fails to account adequately for the complex relational patterns of first-century Roman Corinth.[1] I concur with Pickett that the interpersonal disputes in Corinth resulted from "an even more fundamental problem concerning perception" of the church itself,[2] as the Christian ἐκκλησία became seen as one more relational system among other associations and networks...and Paul, as one more leader among many others.

Therefore, it will be argued here that, from Paul's perspective, the Corinthian problem involved not only the *unity* of the church, but also its *identity*. A new paradigm was needed in which the church's members would view themselves together ἐν Χριστῷ as a unique and primary system with clear boundaries and clearly recognized leadership. The problem did involve issues of patronage, as Chow and Clarke have pointed out, but the patron-client relationship was only one of several relational networks intersecting the church and overlapping its boundaries. Likewise, though status differentials were indeed important components of the overall problem, we must not oversimplify the relational patterns of first-century Corinth and speak of the "haves" and the "have-nots" as two clearly defined and opposing "groups." Rather, in this chapter I wish to argue that there existed among the various church members a situation of confusion concerning the boundaries which should have marked them as distinct from other overlapping relational systems to which many in the church already belonged.

In short, from Paul's perspective, the church's boundaries were overly "porous."[3] In the midst of multiple lines of contact between fellow members of the church, we may ask which boundaries were considered primary by Christians, those which separated them according to the standards of other systems to which they belonged or those which drew them together ἐν Χριστῷ? In pursuing this line of enquiry, I am intentionally moving away from the notion of a single "fault line" separating the various Christians in Corinth, whether religious (e.g. Jew versus Gentile) or socio-economic (e.g. "haves" versus "have-nots").[4] Instead, I am here concerned with systemic issues of security, balance, belonging and change. It is precisely because members of the Christian church *also* belonged to other relational systems or networks—each with their own paradigmatic way of viewing reality[5]—that it is possible, and necessary, to examine their interactions (including disputes) in systemic terms.[6] To speak of the Corinthian problem solely in terms of "factionalism" is possibly to miss some systemic variables.[7] "Factions" in a narrow sense only account for one element in the multiplicity of relational systems in which Corinthian Christians existed, as the problem of a shared corporate identity arose and revealed itself in both internal disputes and outside influences. The key question for Paul, in terms of differentiation of the system as a whole, is: Where does the rest of society end, and we, ἡ ἐκκλησία τοῦ θεοῦ, begin?

In order to show that Corinthian intra-church conflict was directly linked with a multiplicity of relational networks, I first set the stage, as it were, by speaking briefly of the importance of networks of "belonging" in first-century Corinth. Through what channels did people relate to one another? After briefly considering households, I move into the various networks that existed in the πολιτεία, namely *collegia,* burial clubs, synagogues, cults, along with those which bound together citizens (through the ἐκκλησία and courts), young men receiving the *toga virilis,* or patrons and their clients (and masters and their slaves). It will be shown that relational patterns in first-century Corinth were by no means uni-dimensional, and that the same people could be connected to one another through more than one network. Then, it is important to show evidence of such networks in 1 Corinthians itself, especially in relation to the various disputes that arose therein. Who was connected to whom, and where did these persons fit in the complex interweaving patterns of relational networks? The final section offers a visual summary of all that has been said in this chapter while outlining the rest of the study. Particular attention is given to acceptable losses or "tension release valves" (to use Coser's terminology) set within the larger system of Corinthian society. Were conflicts *within* the Christian ἐκκλησία tolerated as long as they served to inhibit any real change from occurring *to* the larger system of relational networks in the πολιτεία?

In all this, I hope to illustrate that the Corinthian situation was far more dynamic than has often been suggested. Following this, chapters 4–5 will explore in greater detail the respective manifestations of intra-church conflict in 1 Cor. 1–6, focusing on key relational connections between (a) fellow members within the church, (b) members of the church and those outside its boundaries, and (c) members of the church and their various leaders, including Paul himself. Paul's own attempts to redefine "belonging" for those ἐν Χριστῷ, to reconfigure interrelationships in familial terms, and to re-establish his own authority will be considered in light of each problem and response. For now, having suggested that network theory is the most appropriate means of wrestling with the dynamics of conflict in Corinth (ch.1), and having asserted that systems thinking offers tools for examining relational networks (ch.2), it is time to turn to the issue of which networks operated in Corinth and in the Corinthian church.

Relational Networks in Roman Corinth

The Importance of Belonging

Any discussion about relational networks does well to include some thoughts on "belonging." For if, as M. Douglas asserts, "dirt is matter out of place," then "to belong" is above all else to be "in place," to be in order within accepted boundaries.[8] This is a theme well suited to first-century individuals in Corinth, since as recent contributions from cultural anthropology have shown, there existed a "collectivist, group-oriented" paradigm which permeated ancient Mediterranean society.[9] Marcus Aurelius states: "That which is not in the interests of the hive cannot be in the interests of the bee."[10] Alvarez-Pereyre and Heymann argue that this paradigm was also true within ancient Judaism: "The fact is that the individual does not live, has no meaning, outside a collective history."[11] Hence, the metaphor of the body was a popular one in rhetoric, especially in situations of στάσις: Plato, for example, asserts that the city is ordered best "whose state is most like that of an individual man...[so that] all of it feels the pain [of an individual member] as a whole."[12] As will be seen this meant something different for Paul than it did for Plato, in terms of rethinking versus reinforcing the societal status quo. The important thing to notice for now is the all-important connection between belonging and meaningful identity. Indeed, an individual who "acts unsocially" is likened to a severed hand or head, "lying at some distance from the rest of the body."[13] We must not underestimate the importance of belonging in the ancient world, as an individual's identity and worldview were shaped to a great extent by a sense of belonging to something greater than themselves. The forms this belonging took in Corinth will be explored in a moment.

It is helpful at this point to recall M. Douglas's reminder that "each culture has its own special risks and problems."[14] In a collectivist culture such as Paul's, one "special problem" was the multiplicity of relational systems in which many found themselves, so that a person could "belong" and thus be identified in different ways depending on the particular systemic context being viewed at any given moment.[15] For instance, the same person could be known in one context as the son of _____, and in another context as the tradesman from _____, and in still another context as a client of _____. More than this, the same person could carry multiple social roles in relation to another person, as Petersen has shown. As will be seen, this could cause special problems for those who were Christian ἀδελφοί.

The Household Network

The two primary systems in which individuals belonged, and through which they understood both their identity and place in the world, were the οἶκος and the πολιτεία. In distinguishing between these two systems, it is possible to speak of the respective realms of private and public life, but such characterisations are actually anachronistic. In reality, there existed a doorway—both figuratively and literally—between the household and the so-called public sector, so that "πόλις and οἶκος were less antithetical institutions than mutual and interdependent ones."[16] Just as in earlier years, the household had been the "fundamental constituent" of the Greek city-state, so, too, in the Roman republic, Cicero describes the *domus* (the Latin term used most often to translate the Greek οἶκος) as "the element from which a city is made, so to speak the seed-bed of the state."[17] Indeed, the οἶκος was the primary place of social "embeddedness" for people in first-century Mediterranean culture, and larger households even mirrored the public sector with "a citizenship of some kind" for members of the household.[18] Interestingly, it was in that membership that we see a significant difference between the οἶκος and the πολιτεία, for women, slaves and clients exercised rights in the household which would have been very difficult, if not impossible, to exercise in the public sector. In this way, the household was unique.

In the past, scholars often have made numerous erroneous assumptions regarding the first-century "household," sometimes equating it with "family," leading to misunderstandings and misrepresentations of Paul's familial language in the ἐκκλησία (which will be discussed in detail in ch. 4). These misunderstandings range between two extremes, the one focused on the absolute authority of the father figure and the other on an overly sentimental notion of family affection. In truth, "family" in Paul's time was as difficult (or more so!) to capture in a single phrase or concept as it is today.[19] Neither the Greek οἶκος nor the Latin *familia* or *domus* referred to what we might call "the nuclear family," *per se*. In fact, when Cicero spoke of the household (*domus*), he made it clear that he was referring to something distinct from, yet including, what we might term the nuclear family:

"The first association is that of marriage itself; the next is that with one's children; then the household unit within which everything is shared."[20]

Familia is defined in strict legal terms as "all persons subject to the control of one man, whether relations, freedmen or slaves, a household," while *domus* enjoyed a broader usage, referring to the physical house, relationships within the residence, or even one's native country.[21] Both terms for household can delineate a collection of persons set apart from society as a whole and bound by law and relationships for purposes of inheritance, intestacy, protection, economic stability, and the education of children. In the Gospels, the Greek οἶκος refers almost exclusively to a physical house (cf. Mk. 5.38, τὸν οἶκον τοῦ ἀρχισυναγώγου), while its usage in Acts reflects the same breadth of meaning as shown by *domus* which, not surprisingly, is used most often in the Vulgate to translate οἶκος. Indeed, in Acts 11.12 Peter speaks of entering "the house" (τὸν οἶκον) of Cornelius, then only two verses later mentions "his entire household" (πᾶς ὁ οἶκός σου, 11.14).

As illustrated in *figure 3.a* below, there existed within the household network a mixture of official legal authority (on the part of the *paterfamilias*) and unofficial influence (by other household members), creating a unique configuration of relationships.

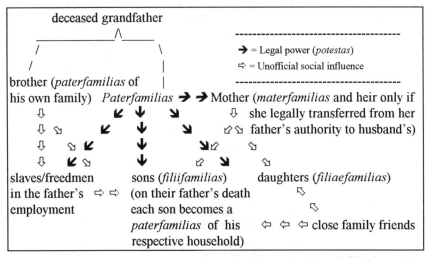

Figure 3.a–Household Relationships

The influence of the mother in the imperial era household, long believed to be virtually non-existent, has now been afforded greater weight. A wife/mother from a respected *domus* or *familia* could hold a "structurally central" position in the decision-making processes of the household into which she married and wield considerable influence over her children in terms of their education, marriage arrangements or vocational planning.[22] Uncles, other relatives, even household servants — by virtue of their regular relational interactions — could be said to have had some influence on the sons and daughters of the household. Indeed, it is now acknowledged that the social realities of the household system were far more complex than earlier studies of Roman legal theory suggested. Nowhere is this more evident than in the distinction between the *paterfamilias* as father and the *paterfamilias* as master.

The claim made by the Roman lawyer Gaius that "there are hardly any people who wield as much power over their sons as we do" (I. 557) has long been repeated in studies of the Roman family as part of an ongoing argument that the father, the *paterfamilias,* was often little more than a tyrant wielding power and discipline indiscriminately throughout his household. This "peculiarly Roman" notion of *patria potestas* has been used by some to minimize social differences between the children in a house and slaves (δοῦλοι) or household servants (οἰκονόμους).[23] In theory, for the children in such a house, as for the slaves, the father represented "the ultimate law."[24] Indeed, several scholars have pointed out that slaves were no worse off than children in *patria potestate* who had lacked the power of ownership or even the ability to choose a spouse or vocation without the father's approval.[25] As just mentioned, however, legal treatises do not tell the whole story.[26]

Despite individual exceptions, in general the master/slave relationship was "fundamentally exploitative."[27] On the whole, however, there existed within the immediate family a reciprocal, though asymmetrical, "loving devotion" that was absent from the master/slave relationship. "The father was considerably bound by *pietas* to his children and his wife, but not to his slaves."[28] This *pietas* or "dutiful respect" (cf. *Oxford Classical Dictionary*) towards a higher power existed "at the core of the Roman's ideal of family relations."[29] For younger children, this meant respect and devotion towards parents. As the children became adults, they "were expected to repay the care spent on them in their early dependence by looking after parents and other family members."[30] It is devotion much more than obedience that was the essence of *pietas,* as seen in Cicero's early description of *pietas* as *"benivolum officium"* or "well-wishing duty."[31] The Greek εὐσέβεια, often translated by the Latin *pietas,* clearly involves respect and awe rather than servitude, although its usage was almost always in reference to the divine or higher things.[32] *Pietas,* on the other hand, was expanded in meaning to see as its object not only higher powers, such as parents and patrons, but also spouses, siblings, and even one's children. In this way, Plautus speaks of a father saving his daughters out of *pietas* towards them.[33] In fact, Saller argues that there are actually more recorded instances of pietas on the part of parents than on the part of children towards parents, though he is careful not to infer too much from such findings.[34] Likewise, the *Herennium,* a first century rhetorical treatise, clearly promotes the "reciprocal aspect" of *pietas:* "There is a natural law, observed *cognationis aut pietatis causa,* by which parents are esteemed by children and children by parents."[35]

Just as *pietas* (εὐσεβεία) was a distinctive mark of the father/child relationship, so was the *verber* (whip or rod, ῥάβδος) a highly visible symbol of the master/slave relationship. Corporal punishment was, of course, part of the legal ammunition the *paterfamilias* had at his disposal over all in the household. However, Saller argues quite strongly that *verber* was reserved for slaves, while reasoned argument was used with grown children.[36] This was due largely to a connection in the Roman mind between whippings and the loss of *dignitas.*[37] Slaves had no recourse if their owners ordered a flogging; in a sense, the mere fact that they could be beaten at any time for any reason was itself a form of psychological assault. The rod served as an ever-present reminder that the slaves' bodies were not their own. They could not marry legally and relationships which they were allowed to have proved fragile things indeed, as an owner could transfer a slave's partner or children at any time.[38] In contrast, invocation of this power by the *paterfamilias* against his own children was quite uncommon. Similarly, the *vitae necisque potestas,* the father's dread legal power of life and death over all in the household, was in no way a "daily reality" with children, but rather a rare and unusual occurrence, as opposed to the more common torture and execution of slaves.[39] It is little wonder, then, that the slave's mind was depicted in Roman plays as "constantly preoccupied" with the thought of a possible beating (or worse).[40] Whatever individual stories have been circulated about caring masters, the fact is that many owners not only had the legal authority to use the whip or rod with their slaves, but actually used it. As notions of honour and shame were among the primary motivating tools for social compliance in the ancient Mediterranean world,[41] the "special potency of the symbolic act of beating for Romans hinged on its association with slavery."[42] For a free man to be beaten meant experiencing what Cato described as the "disgrace and greatest insult" (*dedecus atque maximam contumeliam*) of being no different than a slave.[43] This was *not* what most fathers wanted for their children, who were to be nurtured and taught reason by tutors as they grew. Limited corporal punishment was used for young children, since they were considered as yet unable to understand reason. However, once a child reached maturity, s/he would have outgrown the threat of corporal punishment. "Words, not the whip," were to be used with one's older children. [44]

Indeed, findings from tombstones and letters reveal that relations between parents and children were "usually affectionate."[45] In his role as "father" the *paterfamilias* was to his children the guarantor of their future inheritance (usually reserved for the sons, but at times daughters also became *sui iuris* upon the death of their father). No such promise awaited the servant or slave. Thus, while the father held a common *potestas* over all in the household, *pietas* and the whip served as identifying markers within the household, revealing more clearly who was a member of the immediate family and who was in a position of subjection. Thus, the image of the tyrannical family patriarch is now being read more realistically within the social context of complex interrelationships... although this in no way implies that the household was a democracy! Having said all this, the οἶκος was not the only relational network in Corinth, and so we turn to several others.

Corinth: A City of Contrasts

Intersecting the household network, yet distinct from it, was a collection of relational networks co-existing in the city. I say "collection of networks" because, for Corinth and other cities in the eastern part of the

Empire, the days of the self-sufficient Greek πόλις were long gone.[46] The bustling city of Corinth,[47] more than most cities in the eastern part of the Empire, was something of a "mixed bag" since its refounding by the Romans in 44 B.C.E. as *Colonia Laus Julia Corinthiensis*.[48] While it is true that "most Greek cities remained Greek in various respects,"[49] Paul's Corinth was also a Roman colony with a Roman imprint.[50] Likewise, while it was an urban centre where freedpersons, artisans, traders, and other "status inconsistents" (borrowing from Meeks) sought opportunities for financial and social advancement—however limited this possibility may have been[51]—Corinth was also an imperial colony where several residents enjoyed the ἐξουσία of Roman citizenship. "Corinth's history of faction"[52] may not be unrelated to these contrasts within its borders. However, as Coser has pointed out, conflict between two or more parties presupposes some kind of relationship, a means of interacting with one another. In Corinth, there were several possibilities for interaction.

The Network of Citizens: ἘκκλησΙα and Civic Courts

In anthropological terms, the classical Greek πόλις had served to "impose system on an inherently untidy experience" with a clear demarcation between the δῆμος (the people) who enjoyed the rights (ἐξουσία) of citizenship and those who did not.[53] Citizens were the ἐκκλήτοι, those who assembled together in the ἐκκλησία to deliberate the needs and problems of the city. However, with the ascendancy of the Roman empire, as "the *Urbs* became the *Orbis*,"[54] membership in the city ἐκκλησία became overshadowed by the more important mark of *Roman* citizenship. Bruce's assertion that the latter was understood as "a high social distinction in the Near East,"[55] is supported by Aelius Aristides' comments to Antoninus Pius in the second century C.E.: "For you have divided all the people of the Empire...in two classes: the more cultured, better born, and more influential everywhere you have declared Roman citizens and even of the same stock; the rest vassals and subjects."[56] While wealth and/or social status did not always go hand-in-hand with Roman citizenship, there is little doubt that this was often the case.

Corinth's political organization, like that of other Roman colonies, resembled that of the imperial capital itself, with senior magistrates or *duumviri* (Gk. στρατηγοί) assisted by *lictores* (Gk. ῥαβδοῦχοι).[57] In the πολιτεία itself or, more specifically, in the secular ἐκκλησία or council, fellow citizens could (and often did) vie with one another for power and primacy. Plutarch speaks of στάσις in terms of internal disputes amongst members of the ruling class, and not simply in terms of the more obvious jealousy (ζῆλος) felt by members of the lower classes towards their social superiors. Thus, conflict could take the form of *intra*-class disputes as easily as *inter*-class warfare.[58] Likewise, the *homonoia* speeches and writings of Dio Chrysostom were not directed solely to warring cities, but often concerned *intra-city* conflict. The same ἐκκλησία which provided a channel for possible κοινωνία between fellow citizens also acted as the battleground for their rivalries, disputes and mutual enmity. Benefactors competed with one another for honours such as hosting the Isthmian Games, financing the building of a new monument, or receiving the distinction of *socius et amicus populi Romani*.[59]

Another "legitimate sphere in struggles for primacy in πολιτεία" could be found in the court system.[60] Prosecutions were unlikely to be initiated by persons who were lower on the socio-economic scale, since the cost—both financially and in terms of the enmity produced by such proceedings—was too high.[61] Indeed, Epstein's study of enmity in the judicial process underlines the important role claimed by personal rivalries and ambitions in seeking prosecution. The courts could serve as a "release valve" (to use Coser's phrase) for competing citizens, for while prosecution was "one of the most destructive legitimate weapons available to Romans,"[62] it served to avoid other avenues of hostility which might have proven harmful to the city as a whole. Inasmuch as "the survival and prosperity of the entire community depended on the successful leadership of a disciplined and united aristocracy,"[63] citizens and people of influence could focus their aggression against one another through the court system. In theory, at least, these persons "would not tolerate *inimicitiae* when they thought vital state interests, especially the national security, were at stake," though Epstein notes how often they fell short of this ideal, as prosecutions often acted as a catalyst for open enmity between the parties involved and their relatives.[64] In any case, it may be said that in the ἐκκλησία and in the courts, Corinthian citizens found a network in which to interact and struggle.

The Collegia and Professional Guilds

With the advent of the vast Roman Empire, the sense of security and fellowship (κοινωνία) which people had found previously within the context of the city-state now had to be sought elsewhere within the larger whole. Thus, there arose "smaller local social units...whose foci [were] economic or cultural or, in a smaller number of cases, religious."[65] Indeed, κοίνον was an equivalent term for *collegium.* Trade guilds and other voluntary associations, or *collegia,* were among the most prevalent forms of societal interaction.

Their importance to studies of early Christian communities has been argued as early as Hardy, and recent years have witnessed a resurgence in interest concerning similarities between *collegia* (θίασοι) and ἐκκλησίαι, though it must be admitted that "we simply do not have enough evidence for early Christian organisations to match what is known about voluntary associations."[66] The fact that, despite some important differences, there were still many similarities between *collegia,* guilds and the ἐκκλησία,[67] may help explain Paul's reluctance (as we will see) to speak of the church in collegial terms. In fact, by his time, most *collegia* were suspect organizations. The reason for suspicion was quite simple. In earlier times, there were often connections between *collegia* and various political upheaval and campaigns for change, as noted by the Senatorial ban in 64 B.C.E.: "collegia quae adversus rem publicam videntur esse [constituta]."[68] Thus, even in republican times a qualification to the formation of a *collegium* was added, "dum ne quid ex publica lege corrumpant."[69] Undoubtedly in fear of the potential return of political instability which marked the latter days of the republic, first Julius Caesar, and then Augustus, proclaimed imperial bans on all *collegia* except for long-established (and, thus, well-investigated) ones:

"Cuncta collegia praeter antiquitas constituta distraxit." [Julius Caesar][70]

"Plurimae factiones titulo collegiinovi ad mullius non facinoris societatem coibant; igitur...collegia praeter antiqua et legitima dissolvit." [Augustus][71]

Despite imperial fears, however, measures to dissolve *collegia* were rarely enforced, and the various associations continued to grow in number,[72] with three basic types predominating: "the professional collegia, the *collegia sodalicia* (devoted to the worship of specific gods), and the *collegia tenuiorum* (clubs composed of the poor, allowing members to count on a proper funeral)."[73] Despite such categorisations, it may be said that most *collegia* shared common characteristics, particularly the emphasis on κοινωνία as visible in the common meal and religious affiliation and activity, which often was connected with the meal. "It is safe to assume that every *collegium* banquet was a religious occasion, since every banquet by definition involved sacrifice."[74] In fact, the more an association was viewed as a θίασος, or cult, the safer it was from imperial intrusion, as these strictly religious groups were deemed less "politically-inclined."[75]

In any case, besides the common meal and religious overtones, there are at least three other noteworthy characteristics shared by most *collegia*. One is the fact that, while there is some evidence for inclusion of slaves in some *collegia* (though even with these we do not know their level of involvement) as well as women patrons, indications are that *collegia* consisted mostly of male employers, managers, or workers in the same vocation.[76] Secondly, such associations were centred in particular areas of cities, so that "the collective identity of those engaged in the same business was reinforced by geography, and *vice versa*."[77] Inasmuch as many artisans and workers struggled to survive on the income they received, the social reinforcement and common identity they found with others "on the block" certainly acted as a strengthening agent.[78] Finally, while burial clubs often arose among the poorer people in a city like Corinth, since these were unlikely to belong to a worker's guild or *collegium* consisting of managers and patrons, burial privileges were also a common element among most *collegia*. Thus, membership in a *collegium* or guild could fulfil several needs, inasmuch as the association was like a miniature πόλις in an era when the πόλις of old had been swallowed up by the empire. For this very reason, collegial networks were both pervasive and (to imperial authorities) potentially dangerous.

Cults and Συναγωγαὶ

Religion permeated all of life in the first-century empire. Thus, religious activity was not limited exclusively to θίασοι, but was a vital part of households and *collegia* alike, with "formative rituals and cultural-linguistic codes" connecting individuals not only to the gods but also to one another.[79] Women, it was generally thought, were particularly susceptible to foreign cults with their "stealthy and secret rites."[80] In a pluralistic city such as Corinth, where visitors and merchants were regularly passing through, it is not surprising to find a plethora of temples to gods of various origins,[81] a fact to which Pausanius attests.[82]

Of particular interest is the existence of the Corinthian Asclepieium, a sanctuary of the god of healing.[83] I mention this because, besides the temple itself, the sanctuary also consisted of an *abaton,* or sleeping quarters, for those awaiting possible cures. It was in a similar residential site in Pergamum that Aristides stayed while suffering from a chronic ailment. In that period of incubancy, his life became intertwined with those of many friends and acquaintances in a series of networks that "functioned for him, one might say, as an extended...family."[84] The important point in this (and one to which we will return) is the crucial position Aristides occupied in these networks. Much like the hub of a wheel, he served as a focal point or connector for others in the networks: as a result of his own rhetorical gifts and personal characteristics, Aristides formed connections with fellow incubants or with those concerned for his own health. Just as the *paterfamilias* served as a linchpin in a household and just as a common vocation or interests drew persons together in a *collegium,* so in a religious system such as that found at the Asclepieium the combination of a common need/interest and a focal individual could connect different persons through a relational network, at least for a period.

Can we also speak of a distinctly Jewish network in Corinth, centred on the synagogue, in which Jews and proselytes interacted? At first glance, the answer might appear to be "no." Historically, there is a noticeable *lack* of sources confirming a Jewish presence in the city, although Philo does single out Corinth, along with the cities of Argos and Babylon, as a colony of Diaspora Jews.[85] Sociologically, Segal raises the more general query of whether Jews in the Diaspora can even be termed a "unified group, much less a social grouping."[86] However, besides Philo, a notable exception to the textual silence is, of course, the excavated lintel inscribed with the words [*Syna*]*gôgê Hebr*[*aiôn*], which "may belong to the oldest synagogue in Corinth."[87] There is also the Lukan account in

Acts 18.12–17 of the attempted prosecution of Paul before Gallio, the proconsul of Achaia. This latter passage is particularly intriguing, for it shows Gallio refusing to take part in the matter inasmuch as he perceived it to be *an internal affair amongst the Jewish community*, a matter about λόγου καὶ ὀνομάτων καὶ νόμον τοῦ καθ' ὑμᾶς (18.15). In this account, at least, the Jewish community is seen by an "outsider" as a semi-independent network, a πολίτευμα, "a corporation of aliens with permanent right of domicile and empowered to manage its internal affairs through its own officials."[88] We will return to this chapter in Acts at the end of this section, and to Paul's own account of a Jewish element in the church in the following section. For now, we may say that while our knowledge remains incomplete concerning *when* and *how* Jews came to be resident in Corinth, *why* they were in Corinth may be explained in terms of the same opportunities for advancement that drew others to the colony.

In speaking, then, of a Jewish network, two things should be noted. First, linkages between Jews in a city like Corinth were grounded in family or household relationships and "perpetuated by means of another network, one made up of prescriptions and prohibitions."[89] Feldman even lists examples of synagogues that were originally private houses and which often had entire sections of the house still reserved for private use by the donor's family.[90] The Jewish community was, to a great extent, a community of households, marking it as a fairly closed community. Even the Passover, the key ritual celebration of the year which reflected freedom from foreign oppression and rule, was a *household* meal.

Second, while several elements of Judaism—the Sabbath, festivals and ritual meals (e.g. Passover), a monotheistic faith, even the Temple tax —acted as identity markers to distinguish Jews from their neighbours, the synagogue itself was structured in such a way as to reflect existing collegial structures.[91] Like their collegial counterparts, synagogues usually were composed of men only,[92] although there was far greater diversity in the latter, both in terms of occupations and social status.[93] Above all, then, it appears that the Jewish community, of which the synagogue was a visible symbol, was determined not to draw undue attention to itself, an understandable stance given the unique position of its members as "resident aliens." The safety of the community and the continuation of their unique privileges (such as the Temple Tax) depended on members "fitting in" with others.

Networks of Dependence

While not formal associations, *per se,* the relationships linking patrons with their clients or masters with their slaves/servants were pervasive in the empire, weaving their way throughout other relational networks. Unlike the links which connected citizens or fellow tradesmen to one another, both the patron-client relationship and the master-slave relationship were marked by a *socio-economic dependence* between the respective parties.[94] Patrons could, and often did, have many clients, not only individuals but also associations or *collegia* which they supported. The network linking a patron and his various clients could, therefore, be quite extensive, even as a slaveowner could have many slaves. However, while the patron/client relationship clearly was uneven, there existed in it an element of reciprocity by which the client's "profuse expressions of gratitude then placed the benefactor under obligation to do something further for his client."[95] Indeed, despite similarities between the two types of dependent relationships, the chief difference between them regards the notion of ownership: while a client could be identified as "the friend of ____," a slave was actually the property of his or her master, and the latter's rights over the slave were total and absolute. Thus, although both types of dependent networks were ultimately grounded in the οἶκος, the expectation of loyalty between client and patron was often compared to that which existed between child and parent. Philo commented:

> "The fifth commandment, that about honour due to parents, conceals under its brief expression, many very important and necessary laws" which clearly mark "elders, rulers, benefactors and masters" as superior to "younger people, subjects, clients and slaves" *and deserving of their respect and obedience.*[96]

As Cato the Elder asserted, while "the foremost obligation is to a father, the next [is] to a patron."[97] Hence, even as the legal rights of the *paterfamilias* were balanced by the very real connections and potential influences between all household members (see *figure 3.a*), so, too, the rights of a patron in regards to his clients was balanced by an expectation of mutual loyalty and even devotion. While the slave always stood in the shadow of the rod or whip, this prospect was happily absent from the experience of most clients (and most adult children).[98] Pliny the Younger revealed a leniency on his part towards his household servants,[99] yet he said far more in regards to his role as patron: "my faith towards a client to be as precious to me as to my country, or, if that were possible, more so."[100] The question of loyalty between a client and patron is at the heart of the accusation against Pilate in John 19.12: Ἐὰν τοῦτον ἀπολύσῃς, οὐκ εἶ φίλος τοῦ Καίσαρος. Here, the suggestion on the part of Jesus' opponents is that by showing leniency towards Jesus, the "king of the Jews," Pilate was actually creating a new loyalty which conflicted with the relationship of *pietas* already set up between Pilate and his chief patron, Caesar.[101] Obedience on the part of a slave to a master was expected, and at times had to be forced or coerced, while loyalty between both parties in a patron-client relationship was an ideal.

Having said this, there is still no doubt that both networks of dependence were strictly hierarchical, with the emperor standing at the top of the pyramid as chief-patron to many clients, and then many of these being patrons to lesser clients, and so on.[102] There were, of course, friendships which bound together persons of similar rank, or between the children of fathers who had been ξένοι to one another.[103] "It was only where there were bonds between men or women of different formal status that the term 'patronage' (*patronatas*) was applied: between a freed slave and his former owner, between a Roman and his non-Roman 'client,' or between a powerful man and a corporation (*collegium*) or a town or community."[104] The fascinating thing to note here, and a point often ignored by scholars, is the dual social roles held simultaneously by a person in the patron-client network, inasmuch as *every patron was at the same time a client of someone higher up in the pyramid.* Thus, while Pliny the patron and governor was able to rebuke one who failed to attend a dinner with strong words couched in the language of friendship,[105] he changed his language and tone considerably when writing to his own patron, the Emperor Trajan, who is identified not as "friend" but as *domine.*[106] This is another key point of distinction between this network and the master-slave relationship, for a master was not simultaneously another person's slave, though he was likely a client to another.

A final brief point on patronage concerns the benefits to the client. As "an important buffer against the insecurity and hardships of life for members of the Roman lower classes,"[107] the patron-client relationship offered a sense of identity as well as practical assistance. Indeed, for the intentionally grateful client, one favour from a patron would usually lead to another.[108] The result was a homeostatic balance in which, as long as roles remained clear and loyalties were maintained—as long as everyone knew their position in the network and respected the balance—then the overall system remained intact. However, as seen in Pliny's comment above, the strong loyalty between a patron and his client(s) could take priority over the demands and responsibilities of other networks in the πολιτεία, if there was the perception of potential conflict between these loyalties/demands. Thus, *pietas* (εὐσέβεια) both undergirded the larger system and, potentially, threatened it.

Other Relational Networks

Inasmuch as networks are "a specific set of linkages among a defined set of persons," it is dangerous, though tantalizing, to describe various groupings of persons as "relational networks." Timing is a crucial factor in the formation or dissolution of any network, official or otherwise. However, at least two cases deserve our attention, insofar as they represent "groups" whose own position in the larger system was largely in flux. Young men receiving the *toga virilis* (with the privileges and ἐξουσία associated with this rite of passage), who found themselves at least partially out of the shadow of their elders and able legally to enjoy things which previously had been prohibited, could constitute a fairly cohesive and semi-independent network within which members shared an identity.[109] And while it would be saying too much to speak of a "network of women" in Corinth, it would be a greater mistake to ignore the impact of differing opinions about the "woman's role" among different segments of the city's population.[110] While women could be found at a Roman dinner party, in a strictly Greek cultural context their presence would have been "shocking and immoral."[111] This is quite interesting, since in theory at least, Greek philosophers often spoke of the virtues of men and women as being "one and the same,"[112] claiming that by nature "women are no worse than men."[113] The reality, however, is reflected more accurately in the proverbial thanksgiving to fortune (attributed to Socrates) that "I was born a man and not a woman," a saying that found its way into Jewish devotional thought, as well.[114] It was often only in θίασοι that equality between the sexes was promoted, as seen in an inscription concerning Zeus Panamaros: "The deity invites all human beings to a banquet, and sets the table for all together and equally."[115]

Confusion among Romans regarding women's roles is illustrated in architectural changes in the first-century C.E. While in the days of the Republic, "men and women went to baths segregated by gender, during the empire...these baths were rebuilt so that men and women bathed together nude."[116] Among those of higher status, there were questions about women's positions *vis-à-vis* men, so that while most women were "excluded from any leadership role" in both the court system and the secular ἐκκλησία,[117] widows who were beneficiaries of their husbands' wills could and did exercise considerable authority in the public arena.[118] Socio-economic factors, it appears, could seriously affect the way a woman was perceived by her male contemporaries. As noted above, it remains unclear whether there was any active involvement of women in the *collegia*, though there is little doubt that certain wealthy widows (or daughters) at times acted as patrons.

Jewish approaches to women's positions were even more varied, largely depending on where the synagogue or community being considered existed. In Egypt, for example, "women appear to have held central positions in religious life" and among certain groups they were seen as the equals of men. To this end, Philo notes that women in the Therapeutae were active members of the order and shared in both the worship and in the communal feast.[119] Elsewhere, opinions were mixed, as illustrated in the dialogue in the Mishnah between Rabbis Ben Azzai and Eliezer: while the former argues that a father "has the obligation to teach his daughter Torah," the latter warns against this.[120] Certainly, the Hebrew Scriptures offer notable examples of women leaders and heroes in Israel, including Deborah, Miriam, and Esther (and Judith, in the LXX). Interestingly, in the Babylonian Talmud, when a woman prophetess is shown to be superior to a male prophet, the reason given is not because of superior qualities of leadership or learning but because she is "more tender-hearted."[121] This perception may explain why, in terms of the education of children, it was the mother's duty to train them in their early years in the bases of morality, while later the father was responsible for their learning tradition.[122] On the other hand, there were opinions that women were "evil...scheming treacherously how they might entice man,"[123] with "venom worse than a snake's venom,"[124] and "a mouth full of blood."[125]

In the end, there might very well have been more heterogeneity among Jewish women than is sometimes assumed. While it would be unwise to assert that there were indeed women taking active roles in synagogue, nevertheless, it seems equally impolitic to demand the opposite, especially given the information cited above concerning the Therapeutae. If there was such inclusion for Jewish women, then as with their Gentile counterparts, it probably had more to do with socio-economic factors than with any kind of "liberated" understanding on the part of a community.

A Systemic Picture

Having outlined some of the key relational networks which existed in Roman Corinth, it is time to see how they all fit together. A "systemic" picture may begin to take shape, not a still portrait that remains static and unchanged, but a moving image which is always reshaping itself as time and other influences result in ongoing changes to the whole (see below).

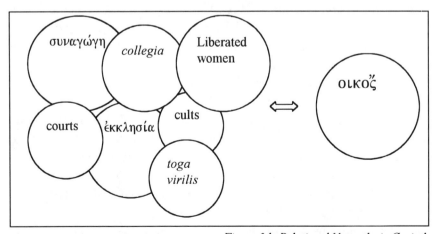

Figure 3.b–Relational Networks in Corinth

As seen above, it was possible for an individual to "belong" in more than one system at the same time. Time and circumstances were always shifting the balances that existed. A young son might have far less influence in the οἶκος than the household servant who is "over" him, but with time this son will overtake the δοῦλος in status and power, and ultimately might become the *paterfamilias* and have authority over all in the household. At the same time, this son might be at various points in life closely knit with other young men who suddenly find that "all things are lawful" for them, part of a *collegium* devoted to a particular deity, or vying with another in the court system or ἐκκλησία. We can speak of a poor Greek follower of Mithras who joins a burial club, or a wealthy Jewish shopkeeper, or a women patron of a *collegium* following the death of her husband. In other words, though there was overall stability through the very existence of these networks, changes within them and the overlapping of them meant an always-dynamic relational system.

Linear Versus Systemic Thinking

Two points should be made concerning the above illustration. First, variables which previously have been accorded such weight by other scholars, most notably the dichotomy between the "haves" and the "have-nots," are not discarded as much as *channeled* through the various networks. It is clear that certain relational networks were more likely to consist of persons of higher means and status. This was particularly true of the court system, since a social inferior was "not deemed to possess sufficient honour to resent the affront of a superior [who, for his part] can ignore the affront of an inferior, since his honour is not committed by it, though he may wish to punish an impudence."[126] However, as suggested above, the élite were just as likely, if not more so, to take *each other* to court as to seek prosecution against a social "inferior." The courts and the ἐκκλησία often became battlegrounds for in-fighting between those already possessing ἐξουσία. The συναγωγή, on the other hand, was likely to be more heterogeneous, with several points on the socio-economic continuum represented by the different members, even as in a professional *collegium* or trade guild there could be various levels of religious devotion and different religious beliefs. Thus, the networks in which people operated resulted in a more complex system of relational interaction than is sometimes suggested in the secondary literature.

Returning to the illustrations of linear versus systemic thinking in *figures 2.a* and *2.b,* and applying these principles to what has been described above, we can speak of interaction and conflict either in simplistic, purely hierarchical terms ...

The Emperor➔ the élite➔ lesser patrons➔ lower clients, servants

---

Figure 3.c–A Linear View of Networks

... or in more dynamic terms, accounting for a multiplicity of overlapping networks:

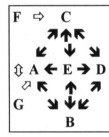

Here, we may say that E is patron to A, B, C and D, but at the same time, he is a fellow member of a cult with B and C that involves them in their own relationship. A, on the other hand, is a member of G's household, while C is the younger brother of F. F and G, not part of the patronage network pictured, are connected to each other as adversaries via the city's court system.

Figure 3.d–A Systems View of Networks

What is intriguing about the complex situation in *figure 3.d* is the implication that the delicate balance connecting individuals 'A,' 'B,' 'C,' 'D,' and 'E,' can be affected *by a conflict which does not even directly involve any of the members of that network.* The potential enmity between 'F' and 'G' would likely spill over into the relationships of those who are in their households.[127] Other potential outside influences include imperial bans or limits on *collegia*, or regulations within a religion (e.g. Judaism) against any form of intermarriage. Such influences could either draw closer together members of a particular network, drive them apart altogether, or create an atmosphere of suspicion and internal rivalries. Nero utilized a strategy of promoting a personal loyalty to himself on the part of his advisors while simultaneously instilling a distrust among the same persons towards each other.[128]

If we alter this illustration so that 'A,' 'B,' 'C,' 'D,' and 'E' are all fellow members of a *collegium,* and where F is connected to C as his patron while 'G' is the patron of 'A,' then we may see entirely different dynamics of interaction, especially if 'G' is then shown to be the younger brother of 'F,' the *paterfamilias.* In this case, while 'G' holds a position of ἐξουσία in relation to 'B,' he is not in such a position in relation to his brother 'F.' Thus, holding a position of ἐξουσία in one network does not equate ἐξουσία in another network.[129]

The second point concerning *figure 3.b* is that the passage of time and other factors external to the system can have an influence on both the balance of an οἶκος or networks of the πολιτεία and on the individual members. What effects did severe grain shortages have on the ἐκκλησία in Corinth and on separate households?[130] The economic "boom" in the first century following the birth of Roman Corinth certainly had an effect on the demographics of the city, and thus on membership in the various associations, religions, and networks.[131] Likewise, personal life changes such as the death of a *paterfamilias,* the acquisition of much-desired Roman citizenship, or the geographical move of an influential member of an associationc could also have repercussions on the networks in which these persons lived. Time and the changes that come with it create ripples throughout the entire system.

Acts 18

As a specific example of what is meant in this section by a "systemic picture" of Corinth, without yet turning to Paul's letter, we may examine the Lukan account of the origins of the Corinthian church in Acts 18:[132]

> After this Paul left Athens and went to Corinth. There he found a Jew named Aquila, a native of Pontus, who had recently come from Italy with his wife Priscilla, because Claudius had ordered all Jews to leave Rome. Paul went to see them, and, because he was of the same trade, he stayed with them, and they worked together; by trade they were tentmakers. (Acts 18.1–3)

Several things should be noted about this account. First, as convincingly narrated by J. Murphy-O'Connor, Paul's route from Athens to Corinth would have taken him through dangerous territory (cf. 2 Cor. 11.26), past the famed site of the Isthmian Games (cf. 1 Cor. 9.25), to a city that "had more business than it could handle...[where] cut-throat competition ensured that only the committed survived."[133] As a leather-worker in a city of visitors and traders, Paul would have been assured of a good deal of work.[134] Thus, it makes perfect sense that his first contacts would have been formed through a professional or vocational network. While it would be saying too much to suggest that Paul and his Corinthian hosts were fellow members of a formal guild or "κοίνον of tentmakers and leatherworkers,"[135] it is not unreasonable to assume that their "common trade" provided them with a sense of κοινωνία which could only grow and deepen upon discovering their other commonalities. The first thing to note from the Lukan account, therefore, is the professional network, whether formal or (more likely) informal, through which Paul found his way to Priscilla and Aquila's house.

However, a common trade was not all that Paul had in common with Aquila and Priscilla: they were also fellow Jews. The Claudian decree mentioned in the text is reported by Suetonius, whose mention of "Chrestus" has provoked much discussion that the problems were tied in with Jewish Christians:

> Since the Jews constantly made disturbances at the instigation of Chrestus, he expelled them from Rome.[136]

Luke notes that, as a result of this edict, Priscilla and Aquila came to Corinth to set up shop, although the fact that they did not make it their permanent home is evident from Paul's own pen (1 Cor. 16.19; Rom. 16.3). Concerning their socio-economic standing Theissen remarks that, based on their ability to travel, to welcome a houseguest for some time, and to host a congregation in their home, it is fairly certain that Aquila and Priscilla were "scarcely insolvent."[137] At the same time, it is equally fair to assume they were not among the city's élite, since "no individual with an Eastern name was recorded to have constructed or restored a building or have held any religious or civic position in the city."[138] Crispus, ὁ ἀρχισυνάγωγος, is pointed out as one who believed in Paul's message (18.8) and who was personally baptized by Paul (1 Cor. 1.14).

Also, Titius Justus, with whom Paul stayed after departing from Aquila and Priscilla's home, is one of many σεβόμενοι τὸν θεόν, "worshippers of God" or "God-fearers," listed in Acts.[139] A Roman who may or may not have been associated with the famed Titii family of potters in Corinth, Titius Justus opened his home to Paul, conveniently "next to the synagogue" (ἦν συνομοροῦσα τῇ συναγωγῇ).

It is interesting to note that the term, συνομοροῦσα (the periphrastic imperfect active of συνομορέω), is used only here in the New Testament. Its literal meaning is that his house "joined hard to" the synagogue or, as we might say today, they were "almost on top of each other." The image is of a joint boundary. While we cannot assume the author had anything other than the physical proximity of house and synagogue in mind as he wrote, yet "joint boundary" is also an appropriate image for what was occurring in the Lukan account in relational terms. After all, Paul by his own admission epitomized a man with several "joint boundaries": he was a Jew of the house of Benjamin (Phil. 3.5) and at the same time a Roman citizen (πολίτης) from Tarsus, "not an insignificant city" (Acts 21.39). He was, by trade, a leather-worker but understood his true vocation to be as an ἀπόστολος sent by Christ "to preach the gospel" (1Cor. 1.17). His joint boundaries made him "all things to all people" (1 Cor. 9.22). Likewise, Aquila and Priscilla were to Paul both fellow workers in their common trade (τὸ ὁμότεχνον, Acts 18.3), and also τοὺς συνεργούς μου ἐν Χριστῷ Ἰησοῦ (Rom. 16.3). They were his fellow Jews and fellow believers in Christ, friends of Paul "who risked their necks" for his sake (Rom. 16.3) and friends of Apollos, whom they instructed "more accurately" in the way of God (Acts 18.26). Similarly, Crispus was ἀρχισυνάγωγος and yet had a Roman name, and became one of the first Christian converts. Titius Justus was a Roman, a Jewish "sympathizer," and one who opened his house to the Christian missionary. Sosthenes was both a synagogue official (Acts 18.17) and (if it is the same person) Paul's companion and co-author of 1 Corinthians (1.1). Thus, even in these few references of persons named in Acts 18, it is possible to see multiple lines of contact between them, so that it is impossible to speak about them in one or two-dimensional terms (e.g. Jews and non-Jews).[140] In this account, we see the "joint boundaries" of several relational networks that, in effect, were "on top of each other.' If we return to *figure 3.d* and interpret 'E' as Paul, then his connections with, respectively, Aquila and Priscilla ('A,' putting them together, as in the account), Crispus ('B'), Titius Justus ('C'), and Sosthenes ('D'), are via the synagogue network as well as through the Christian community. Apollos ('G') is indirectly linked to Paul through Aquila and Priscilla ('A').

A final point should be made concerning conflict and overlapping networks in Acts 18. The author says that the Jews who came before Gallio were "united" (ὁμοθυμαδόν) in their attack against Paul. This is an interesting choice of words, inasmuch as it is a recurring Lukan term, appearing in Acts ten times out of a total of eleven times in the entire New Testament.[141] Until the account of Stephen's martyrdom, ὁμοθυμαδόν is used to describe the togetherness of the Christian believers in Jerusalem (1.14; 2.46; 4.24; 5.12; and again in 15.25), particularly in terms of their praying and decision-making. Following Stephen's challenging sermon, ὁμοθυμαδόν is used to depict the common purpose of those who oppose the Christian gospel and attack its messengers, including Stephen (7.57), Paul (18.12), and Gaius and Aristarchus, Paul's travel companions (19.29). Paradoxically, even as the opposition gains the same kind of unity as the Jerusalem disciples, ὁμοθυμαδόν is used once again in a positive sense, this time to describe the welcoming response of the Samaritans who want to hear more from Philip (8.6), unlikely heroes whose own series of networks barely intersect those of the Jews who oppose Paul. Thus, I would argue, the term ὁμοθυμαδόν denotes a linkage or unified network connecting those in Achaia who stood against (κατεπέστησαν) Paul; indeed, opposition to Paul was the very foundation for their network's existence. These persons operated as a kind of *ad hoc* network, noticeably distinct from the larger Jewish network centered around the synagogue, since not all the Jews were opposed to Paul, as the previous part of the account makes quite clear.

Thus, we see here a sub-system of the larger network of Corinthian Jews coming together for a specific time and purpose, not unlike the volunteer fire brigade mentioned by Pliny the Younger.[142] Indeed, it might be said that, from their perspective, the Jews of Achaia were attempting to put out a "fire' of potentially monstrous proportions and, therefore, they went to the proconsul (ἀνθυπάτος) in order to receive his support and approval in this matter. However, Gallio would have none of this, partly, as mentioned earlier, because he perceived their problem to be an internal affair best handled by themselves. Another more subtle reason for Gallio's position might have been his apprehension that this *contio*-like meeting between himself and the Jewish crowd could result in a disruptive *factio*, much like the situation at Prusa described by Dio Chrysostom, where the disorder caused by opposing networks in the town ἐκκλησία grew so intense that the proconsul there had to suspend further meetings of the assembly.[143] Gallio refused to recognize the network before him as anything but a united religious πολίτευμα which needed to handle its own affairs and not disrupt the larger πολιτεία. That which he could not see as an outsider to the synagogue network was that Paul's introduction of the gospel message into that previously stable system actually served to create two new networks, distinct from their "parent" network and in direct antithetical relation to one another: the Corinthian Christian community and the united Jewish opposition. The paradigm out of which Gallio responded to the situation before him—"this is an in-house feud between fellow members of a single network who, in turn, are but one part of a larger and more important imperial network"—was quite different from that held by Paul's would-be prosecutors, "Paul and his followers are not part of us."

Thus, in this one account of the founding of the Christian ἐκκλησία in Corinth, it is possible to see the various networks operating at the same time: the professional network through which Paul first encounters Aquila and Priscilla; the synagogue network out of which several of Paul's first converts came and which (according to Luke) operated in conjunction with the Christian mission until opposing Jews made a more visible boundary between the two necessary; the network of the newly-formed Christian ἐκκλησία itself; the network of Roman citizens in the secular ἐκκλησία, as represented by Gallio the proconsul; and, finally, the more informal (but no less influential) network of those united (ὁμοθυμαδόν) in their opposition to Paul. As these various networks intersect and overlap, it is Paul himself who is shown to be the focal point of the system: on the periphery of some of the networks (i.e. the synagogue or professional networks), in the very center of others (i.e. the Christian network), and the target of still others (i.e. his opponents). More will be said later about the long-term implications of Paul's position in the networks. For now, however, it is time at last to turn to Paul's own letter, and examine the evidence for overlapping networks in 1 Corinthians...especially in relation to the conflicts therein.

Relational Networks in 1 Corinthians

While strong cases have been made for a theological, or ethno-religious, or socio-economic basis underlying a given dispute, an exegetical danger arises when any one of these bases is then assumed to underlie *all* the issues addressed in the letter, as if congregational conflict in the first-century Corinthian ἐκκλησία was more unifaceted than in any other period. On the contrary, as we have just seen in the previous section, the interactional patterns of Roman Corinth were indeed quite complex, involving several overlapping and often-changing relational networks. This section (1) examines 1 Corinthians with an eye on the various overlapping networks mentioned above and, following this, (2) outlines the effects of such networks on the manifestations of intra-church conflict addressed by Paul. For the sake of clarity, I will draw upon the same categories of networks listed above, seeing if there is evidence for the presence and importance of networks in Paul's letter.

The Household Network

Even as the οἶκος was a crucial component in the organisation of Corinthian society, it was also foundational to the development of the early Corinthian church, both in terms of physical space and relational attachments. Concerning the former, W. D. Rordorf underlines the importance of the physical house in the beginnings of Christian worship: "Die ersten drei Jahrhunderte sind die Zeit der Hauskirchen."[144] At the end of 1 Corinthians, Paul passes on the warm greetings of his former hosts, Aquila and Prisca (Priscilla),[145] "together with the church in their house" (σὺν τῇ κατ' οἶκον αὐτῶν ἐκκλησίαν, 16.19). This echoes a similar greeting in Rom. 16.5 from Paul *to* Prisca and Aquila, καὶ τὴν κατ' οἶκον αὐτῶν ἐκκλησίαν. It has already been said that these two who were so dear to Paul's heart were probably a couple of some means, since "owning a fine house and, specifically, property was one of the leading indicators and symbols of wealth and status."[146] Indeed, Blue points to similarities between Paul's "recommendation" of Phoebe in Romans 16 and a Greek inscription from Corinth (dated to 43 C.E.) dedicated to a Roman woman named Junia Theodora. Both speak of the hospitality extended by these women, with Paul using the word προστάτις to describe Phoebe.[147] Meeks, following Judge before him, argues for this designation to be read as "patroness" or "protector" of many Christians, Paul himself being one.[148] It is immediately after his words about Phoebe in Romans 16.1–2 that Paul speaks in very similar terms of Prisca and Aquila (16.3–5). Even as Phoebe is described affectionately as both τὴν ἀδελφὴν ἡμῶν and a deaconess of the church, so Paul refers to Prisca and Aquila as "my fellow workers in Christ Jesus" (τοὺς συνεργούς μου ἐν Χριστῷ Ἰησοῦ). Likewise, even as Phoebe is acknowledged for her benefactions to "many" besides Paul himself, so, too, the apostle recognizes that his former Corinthian hosts deserve not only his appreciation, but also that of "all the churches of the Gentiles" (16.4). The point I am making here is that the similarities between Paul's respective descriptions (one directly after the other in Romans 16) of Phoebe, the patroness, and Prisca and Aquila, the hosts of a house church, suggest a similar status level between them, especially when other factors (such as the ability to travel) are added into the equation. I would add my opinion to that of Theissen, Blue and others who point to a correlation, albeit not always perfect, between οἶκος as physical house (as in Rom. 16.5 or 1 Cor. 16.19) and the higher socio-economic position of the owner of the house. This is not insignificant in terms of overlapping networks, when one considers that this same couple were also to Paul fellow Jews and fellow craftsmen.

Even more intriguing for our purposes here is the use of οἶκος-language in terms of household relationships. Twice in 1 Corinthians, Paul refers to the "household of Stephanas" (τὸν Στεφανᾶ οἶκον, 1.16; τὴν οἰκίαν Στεφανᾶ, 16.15). In the latter instance, the apostle even calls on his readers to "put yourselves at the service" (ὑποτάσσησθε) of the members of this household. This is a remarkable statement, since "the household of Stephanas" could very well have included slaves or household servants, not unlike "those of Chloe's household" (1.11).[149] The actual word used by Paul, ὑποτάσσησθε, is common in the *Haustafeln* of later post-Pauline literature, usually referring to the "submission" required of all within an οἶκος—whether wife, child or slave—towards the *paterfamilias*.[150] While not as immediately obvious, another use of this "household" terminology in 1 Corinthians is found in 15.24–28, which presents the image of all created things (even death!) being subjected to Christ who, ultimately, subjects himself to God who thus becomes πάντα ἐν πᾶσιν. It is more subtle, but even in the "hierarchy of heaven," the dutiful Son submits himself to the divine *Paterfamilias*.[151]

In two other extended passages in 1 Corinthians, the language of the οἶκος enters the discussion, notably in the opening chapters focusing on ἔριδες in the church (1.10–4.21) and in the section dealing with problems in the Lord's Supper (11.17ff.). Concerning the former, more about the details of the divisions as well as Paul's response will be said in the next two chapters of this study. For now, however, it is important to recognize that Paul's information about the intra-church tensions comes not from the church itself, but rather from another kind of relational system altogether, τῶν Χλόης. This enigmatic phrase in 1.11 has at times been translated as "Chloe"s household," although the phrase literally means "those of Chloe" and is more likely to point to slaves of Chloe (or freedmen) than to adult children in the household.[152] Theissen makes precisely this point in regards to 1 Tim. 3.12, where "children" (τέκνων) are clearly distinguished from others in the household, most likely the slaves/servants (τῶν ἰδίων οἴκων).[153] Whoever Chloe actually was, Christian or otherwise, she was known possibly as a patroness (like Phoebe)[154] and certainly as a head of an οἶκος (like Stephanas; see above).

What is intriguing about this sole mention of τῶν Χλόης is the placement of the phrase in relation to the following slogans of "belonging": Ἐγὼ μέν εἰμι Παύλου, Ἐγὼ δὲ Ἀπολλῶ, Ἐγὼ δὲ Κηφᾶ (1.12). Cotter argues that "there must have been some credibility to her name, or *why would he take care to identify his source as he does*, and then proceed to address the difficulty [reported to him] with no hint about the accuracy of the report?"[155] Why indeed, we may ask, unless there is another reason for the apostle's inclusion of τῶν Χλόης immediately before speaking about those who "belonged" to Paul, Apollos, or Cephas. Questions of "who belongs to whom" appear to be at the heart of the tensions in the opening chapters, as opposed to specific theological disagreements. Indeed, Pickett has argued that, despite the prevalence of the σοφία motif in chapters 1 and 2, Paul never actually refers to the *content* of this wisdom, much less the specific theological content behind the various slogans.[156] Again, inasmuch as these claims of personal affiliation on the part of different Corinthian Christians are the focus of much attention in the next two chapters, at this point I do not want to do more than suggest that it is noteworthy that Paul's information about divisions which apparently have much to do with personal affiliations came from those who themselves were affiliated with—belonged to— Chloe. Thus, we can see that the οἶκος enters into the conflictual story of chapters 1–4, both in terms of Paul's informants, the network of those who belong to Chloe, and those who claim to belong to Paul, Apollos, or Cephas.

In the passage on the Lord's Supper (11.17ff.), we see more signs of the presence of the οἶκος network in Paul's language about "having your own homes (οἰκίας) in which to eat and drink" (11.22). These are compared with the "have-nots" (τοὺς μὴ ἔχοντας), that familiar designation discussed at length above. Later, Paul urges the offenders directly: εἴ τις πεινᾷ, ἐν οἴκῳ ἐσθιέτω, and contrasts eating "at home" with "coming together" (11.34). Without saying too much at this point, what we see here in terms of intra-church conflict clearly has something to do with social distinctions that involved οἶκος networks which overlapped the boundaries of the Christian ἐκκλησία, which in turn included within itself both "haves" and "have-nots." What is crucial to see here is not simply the familiar dichotomy between those who have and those who do not, but to recognize that "the 'secure' or 'the haves' may not have been materially wealthy...but they did have a household which guaranteed them protection."[157] We do not immediately have to presume that all the people eating early were wealthy, but simply that they in some way "belonged" or tapped into the οἶκος network of the one hosting the communal meal, perhaps as fellow householders but also perhaps as ξένοι or household servants (who would not have had to stay behind and finish their work, as several suggest was the case for the "have-nots"). There were, it is likely, prior relationships between those who came early and the householder/host which had little to do with their shared faith in Christ. As Murphy-O'Connor and several others have demonstrated, even the physical layout of ancient houses, with their limited seating, encouraged a favouritism toward those who could come early to eat and meet with the host in the dining room. Christian ἀδελφοί who arrived late, on the other hand, were seated in an area outside the dining room.[158] Hence, Blue admits that "the house-church nature of early Christianity goes a long way in explaining some of the problems in the early Communities,"[159] inasmuch as the combination of relational connections through the οἶκος network and the architectural planning of the house together contributed to a favouritism that ultimately resulted in the potential σχίσματα addressed by Paul. Thus, while socio-economic factors were most likely involved in the problem, they entered the picture (as Paul himself stated) through the language of "homes" and "houses."

While much more could be said about these matters, it is important to state that the household network certainly appears in 1 Corinthians, particularly in relation to tensions over "who belongs to whom" and disappointing behaviour at the Lord's Supper. This brief overview does not even include the ways that Paul would translate the language of the οἶκος for his own purposes, as he reconfigured the internal relationships of the ἐκκλησία in terms of fellow ἀδελφοί (to be seen in chapter 4 below). However, the οἶκος is not the only relational network to be found in 1 Corinthians, and so we move on to the networks of πολιτεία.

The Network of Citizens: Ἐκκλησίαι and Civil Courts

There are at least two instances in 1 Corinthians in which it is possible to discern both the presence and the influence of political/citizen networks in the Christian church: in the quasi-political slogans of 1.12 (and the accompanying attraction to rhetorical sophistication), and in the problem of litigation in 6.1ff. First, recalling the fact that in the ancient world, there was a "constant flow...from family to politics and from politics to family,"[160] it is possible to see in the divisive slogans 'a cosmos of blood relations, clients and friends constellated around a few men of noble houses who contended for power against the backdrop of the class struggle.'[161] In this brief description, Welborn points to several networks (οἶκος, patron-client, and political networks) which operated alongside (and acted as channels for) divisions of status and class. While these likely were not actual formal groups in 1.12, it is clear that quasi-political allegiances were operating, some pro-Paul and some decidedly anti-Paul, in such a way as to undermine the unity of the church as a whole.

A clue as to the identity of those involved in such ἔρις is found later in Paul's reference to the wise, the powerful and well-born in the community (1.26), those who normally competed with one another within the secular networks of the ἐκκλησία and courts. Walbank notes that 'the Roman systems with its law courts and popular assemblies preceded by *contiones,* gave great scope for the demagogue.'[162] Judging from Paul's reaction to the ἔριδες in the Christian ἐκκλησία, it appears that several members brought in with them some of the patterns of the secular ἐκκλησία, elevating Paul and other Christian leaders to something like demagogues: "Was Paul crucified for you" (1.13)?[163] Pauls fears about possible σχίσματα in the Christian ἐκκλησία (1 Cor.1.10) bring to mind similar anxieties experienced by persons in the network of citizens, as seen in Cicero's warning: "Which house is so stable, which state so firm, that it cannot be completely destroyed by hatred and disagreement?"[164] We see further correspondence in Pliny's concerns following a controversial vote of the Senate, which he describes as but "the prelude and skirmish" of further *contentiones.*[165] There is also the link between the ecclesial in-fighting and members' admiration of πειθοῖ σοφίας (2.4). The prevalence of σοφία language in these opening chapters suggests a connection which was grounded again in the network of the secular ἐκκλησία, inasmuch as persuasion, "mainly in the form of oratory, but also by question and answer" played a large part in the Roman political system.[166] The focus on Apollos versus Paul (who, it should be noted, were not personally at odds with one another) in 3.4 and elsewhere suggests that rhetorical wisdom—a highly valued commodity in the political sphere—was a key issue.[167] Thus, in the situation of competing allegiances characterized by Paul in the slogans of 1.12, it is possible to find patterns brought into the Christian ἐκκλησία from those members who also operated within the network of the secular ἐκκλησία.

Even more evident is the influence of the network of citizens in the problem of litigating church members. In 6.6, Paul spells out the problem: ἀδελφὸς μετὰ ἀδελφοῦ κρίνεται.[168] There was nothing unusual about this to those who were personally familiar with the city's political system. The pattern in the πολιτεία was clear; "those who had the means (in terms of status and/or finances) made use of the courts as a means of attacking their political opponents."[169] Paul himself was caught in this cycle against his will, as he alluded in 4.1–4 to his own "trial" by the Corinthians. In this instance, ἀνθρωπίνης ἡμέρας literally means "by human day," and is contrasted with judgment on the Lord's ἡμέρα (cf. 3.13). His dismissal of such judgments against himself sound very much like Pliny's refusal to be bothered by "the enemies I brought upon myself" as a result of a case.[170] I do not wish to say any more at this time concerning the case of the litigating members (and Paul's response), other than to reiterate that the use of courts for dealing with problems between fellow Christians strongly suggests that at least some of those Christians remained present in, and influenced by, a network of citizens and influential peers.

The *Collegia* and Professional Guilds

It has already been noted that the early Christian ἐκκλησία has at times been compared with a *collegium,* in terms of its organization and practices (see *figure 1.c*). However, more relevant to the task here is the question of whether we can discern in 1 Corinthians hints of the *continuing involvement* of some of the church's members in the *collegia* and guilds. I would argue that at least two passages offer such hints: namely, the extended discussions on meals involving idol meat (1 Cor. 8–10), and the enigmatic issue of "baptism for the dead" (15.29ff.).

In terms of the idol meat controversy, several points may be made. First, the phrase in 8.10, ἐν εἰδωλείῳ κατακείμενον, is unique in the New Testament and almost certainly points to participation in a collegial or cultic banquet. It should be remembered, after all, that the shared meal was a common feature of *collegia,* usually including meat that had been sacrificed earlier to the local civic deity. While such feasts had in the classical period often been held in private houses (and sometimes still were)[171], more often than not in Roman times the venue had been moved to the temple precincts, where a dining room was available.[172] Thus, Paul's reference to a meal in "the temple of an idol" (8.10) and, later, to the invitations to such meals (10.27) mirror many recently-discovered invitations to collegial meals held in temple precincts, as seen below:

Chairemon requests your company at dinner at the table of the Lord (κύριος) Serapis, in the Serapaeum, tomorrow the 15^{th,} at 9:00 (*P. Oxy.* 110).

The god calls you to a banquet being held in the Thorereion tomorrow from the 9th hour (*P. Köln* 57).[173]

In a city where "there was tremendous incentive to want to fit in," it would have been very difficult indeed to refuse such invitations.[174] In the fellowship (κοινωνία) of these meals, many professional contacts were either made or strengthened. Inasmuch as Corinth offered possibilities for upward mobility to those who desired socio-economic advancement, participation in collegial banquets would have been not only common for Corinthians who were "on the way up," but necessary.[175]

Several other aspects of Paul's argument point to collegial involvement on the part of certain members of the church. Two terms which are rare elsewhere in the Pauline letters are, nevertheless, quite prominent in 1 Cor. 8–10: idolatry (εἴδωλων)[176] and knowledge (γνῶσις).[177] Concerning the former, the closest New Testament parallels to Paul's usage of idolatry language in 1 Corinthians may be found in Acts 15 and 21, which concern the decree of the Apostolic Council in Jerusalem on the co-existence of Gentile believers with their Jewish counterparts. The qualification was that the Gentiles abstain from εἰδωλόθυτον καὶ αἷμα καὶ πνικτὸν καὶ πορνείαν (Ac. 21.25; also 15.20, 29). Here, as in 1 Corinthians (cf. 1 Cor. 5.10–11 and 6.9), idolatry and sexual immorality (πορνεία) are linked together,[178] and viewed as particularly odious to Jewish believers. Immorality was understood to be common practice in the *convivia* (banquets) of *collegia* or similar associations (guilds, clubs, θίασοι), as participants "fed the flesh as well as the stomach."[179]

Concerning the second term, the contrast Paul draws between γνῶσις and ἀγάπη in 8.1 suggests the contrast between the collegial feasts graced with the oratory and γνῶσις of guest rhetors who would initiate the evening's conversation and the more modest communal meals of the Christians, which came to be known as ἀγάπη feasts.[180] This is supported by the other contrast Paul puts forward, between κοινωνία (a word associated with the *collegia*) in the body and blood of Christ (10.16) and κοινωνία with demons,[181] as well as the contrast between the τραπέζης κυρίου and the τραπέζης δαιμονίων (10.21). The "fellowship" language here provokes images of two different types of *gatherings*, and insofar as much of Paul's language—εἰδωλεῖον, γνῶσις, κοινωνία—reflects what is known of the banquets of the *collegia* and other public associations, it seems appropriate to suggest that here we see the network of associations overlapping that of the Christian ἐκκλησία.

The other probable reference to the *collegia* or guilds is found in the lengthy discussion on resurrection in 1 Cor. 15, particularly in the section concerning "bad company" (ὁμιλίαι κακαί, v. 33). About whom or what is Paul speaking here? Although the proverb cited by Paul originates with Menander,[182] in its context here the reference is certainly to a group of persons (τινες, 34) who are in a position to ask difficult questions of the Corinthian Christians concerning the fate of "dead bodies" (νεκροί, 29). Who else would be in such a position except for fellow members of a guild or *collegium* which, of course, was involved in the funerary arrangements of its members. This is not purely speculative, as the warning against "eating and drinking" in verse 32 and the admonition to "be sober" (ἐκνήψατε) in verse 34 clearly bring to mind once more the collegial banquets reviewed above.[183] Lattke appears correct in his assertion that the noun ὁμιλίαι ("company") "can almost be a substitute for κοινωνία."[184] The "bad company" must be more than random individuals the Christians might encounter; clearly, these are persons with whom they are connected, even as they are connected within the ἐκκλησία. Thus, it appears that fellow members of a κοίνον or guild were the source of the disturbances, as they were bringing more doubt than hope to those who were bereaved.[185] Indeed, it is precisely in the idol meat and resurrection controversies that we see an overlapping of several networks (see Appendix), but for now it is helpful to finish our brief listing of references to other networks in the letter.

Cults and Συναγωγαί

Because of the interweaving of religion throughout first-century life, it seems unnecessary to reiterate what has already been said about the cultic dimensions of the idol meat and resurrection issues. However, it is important to point out specific instances in 1 Corinthians where we see either semi-independent cultic or Jewish networks influencing and overlapping the Christian ἐκκλησία or a specific religious dimension to key disputes.

First, while Baur may have overstated the Jew-Gentile dichotomy, there is certainly some relevance to the issue of tensions between church members along ethno-religious lines.[186]   From the beginning of the letter, while discussing the ἔριδες surrounding key figures of the church, Paul refers to "Jews" and "Greeks" as distinct and largely independent relational groupings (I hesitate to say "groups" since I think this would take Paul's references too far), who share only a distaste for the Christian Gospel (1.18-25*)*.   It is interesting to note that Paul sees in the church's membership representatives of both ethno-religious groupings. Yet, though in one sense the two networks overlap in the ἐκκλησία, in another sense they are each distinct from 'the called' (1.24). A similar explicit reference to "Jews and Greeks" as networks separate from one another as well as from the Christian ἐκκλησία (in which representatives from both groupings co-exist), may be found in 10.32: "Give no offense to Jews *or* to Greeks *or* to the church of God" (also in 12.13).   Indeed, while Paul's focus on σοφία brings to mind qualities particularly important for those of Graeco-Roman background,[187] he never forgets the presence of a Jewish network.

It would be overly simplistic to refer to the issues in 1 Corinthians as Jewish (Petrine) Christianity versus Gentile (Pauline) Christianity. However, even as in Acts 18 Gallio lumped Christians and Jews together in one mix, together distinct from yet subsumed under the world of the empire, Paul seems to go to great lengths to do the opposite, to point to a specifically Jewish presence and influence and, then, distance himself and the church from it.   Much more will be said about this next chapter.   For now, however, it is worth noting Paul's more subtle references to the influence of a Jewish network on the ἐκκλησία: in his analogy of the temple (3.16-17),[188] his allusion to the Shema (8.4,6), his extensive use of the Hebrew Scriptures in the section referring to the idol meat question (9.8-9; 10.1-13), and his citation in the tongues/prophecy issue (14.21).[189] And while issues of σοφία and γνῶσις are associated more with Paul and Apollos (no Pauline-Petrine dichotomy here), when speaking of the idol meat issue, Paul refers once more to a contrast between himself and Cephas, albeit a contrast not directly linked with food laws (9.5).

Indeed, the suggestion that those "whose conscience is weak" (8.11) are Jewish Christians is supported by the story of Horace, who seeks a conversation with his friend Aristius Fuscus, only to be told by the latter that it is not right for him to speak on the Sabbath of the New Moon: "Would you affront the circumcised Jews?" Horace replies, "I have no scruples," to which his comrade asserts, "But I have. I am a somewhat weaker brother, one of the many...I will talk another day."[190] Here, "weakness" is associated with Jewish religious practice, although the "weak" friend is not Jewish himself, but wishes only not to offend those who are. The point of all this is that, though Baur may have argued too narrowly regarding a Jew-Gentile dichotomy, clearly there were religious sensibilities brought into the church by those who were still tied in (at least nominally) to the network of the synagogue—with its prescriptions and prohibitions, its concerns over circumcision and food laws—who came into direct contradiction in the church with those whose primary networks were within the *collegia* and cults. It is interesting to note Paul's reluctance to "change" the circumcised (7.18) or offend them (10.32), as well as his desire to take the collection to Jerusalem, the center for Jewish Christianity (16.1-4), and thereby retain the good favor of those in leadership there.

Networks of Dependence

Where in 1 Corinthians can we find evidence of networks of dependence? Chow's study of patronage suggests several instances where ties between patrons and clients may be inferred; the strongest case may be made for the situation involving the incestuous man (1 Cor. 5) as well as for the idol meat issue (8-10).[191] There are other references, as well, concerning masters and slaves.

First, regarding the case of the incestuous member, the aspect of the situation which Paul addresses directly and forcefully is the silence of the rest of the church's members in the face of so obvious a sin.[192] It seems likely, as Chow argues, that this silence was the result of the social position of the offender in relation to the rest of the members. If he was the patron of many of these fellow Christians, then it would have been difficult indeed to rebuke one who had so much influence over them.[193] The fact that he was not Paul's benefactor or patron is clear from Paul's harsh judgment (5.4-5). In terms of the context of this story, is there a possible link between the "untouchable" incestuous man and "some of you" who had become "arrogant" in Paul's absence (4.18)? Clearly, he challenged these "arrogant" persons (he repeats the descriptor) to see where true power (δύναμις) lay. In fact, it is probably an accurate reading of Paul's personal *apologia* concerning "the work of his own hands" (4.12; also ch.9) to interpret a reluctance on Paul's own part to become a client to any in the Corinthian church, in order to maintain an authority with all of them, to whom he was "father" (4.15). In connection with the idol meat question, it is not at all unlikely that the invitation to a collegial or cultic banquet would have come from a patron to his client(s), making a refusal even more difficult. For though patrons made a point of utilising the language of friendship, the subtle demand being made would have been clear to the "friend."[194]

As for masters and slaves, both clearly co-existed in the church (12.13), alongside freedmen (7.21-24), a fact that Paul acknowledged.[195] Those who arrived late for the Lord's Supper and "have nothing" (11.22) could very well be the slaves or servants of those who "go ahead with their own suppers" (11.21). "Only the elite had the leisure to go to thermal baths in the early afternoon and to begin their meals in mid-afternoon, a contrast to their poorer clients or slaves who lacked either the time in the afternoon or the resources to bring their own food."[196] Other things that were possible for those of higher status, such as the initiation of any form of legal prosecution, were automatically ruled out as possibilities for slaves. Such persons lacked the ἐξουσία enjoyed by their so-called superiors. While Paul relativises such differences in light of the Gospel, it remains clear that such differences still existed in the church.[197] Thus, it is interesting that Paul utilises the terminology of servanthood and slavery when he speaks of both himself and Apollos as faithful διάκονοι (3.5) and ὑπηρέται (4.1) in God's οἶκος. Paul's call for voluntary submission to those who themselves faithfully serve God (16.15-16) and the contrast he draws between a father and a master regarding his own position *vis-à-vis* the Corinthian Christians (4.21) will be explored in detail below.

Other Relational Networks

It was said above that it is difficult to point to a single relational network as *the* catalyst for each of the respective disputes in 1 Corinthians. There was often an interplay between different networks and social roles, as in the case of public banquets. What other networks are found in Paul's letter...and how do they contribute to the problems?

In contrast to the opinion of Fee and others concerning the issue of 6.12-20 (prostitution) as the demands of some Corinthians to be able to visit the brothels, Winter has offered a different and quite convincing argument that the context was actually the élitist private banquets (not unlike the collegial meals) in which gluttony and immorality often intermixed.[198] Thus, once again we might assert the strong possibility that those present included individuals from the network of citizens, patrons, and/or members of *collegia* or cults. The Corinthian slogan πάντα μοι ἔξεστιν (found in both 6.12 and 10.23) is particularly intriguing, insofar as that notion of "all things are permitted" is associated in other writers, such as Dio Chrysostom, with the person of higher status. As noted in Dio's *Orationes:* ὅτῳ μὲν ἔξεστιν ὃ βούλεται πράτειν ἐλεύθερός ἐστιν ὅτῳ δὲ μὴ ἔξεστιν ἃ ἐθέουσι ποιεῖν ("whoever is able/permitted to do whatever he wishes is a free man, and...whoever is not is a slave").[199] Winter remarks: "The free man and the élite in power do not have the restraints of those without social status."[200] It is precisely because those without status *could not* claim that "all things are permitted" and those who did possess higher status *would have little reason* to make such a statement that the most likely candidates for making that claim were those who only recently had received the ability to do "all things," namely those young men who had just received the *toga virilis.*[201] It is significant that the plea from Paul concerns fleeing fornication (πορνείαν, 6.18), not adultery (as would be true for the older, probably married, men). Also, the second person plural throughout this passage makes clear that Paul is addressing not one "young rogue," but several persons. Thus, in both private and public banquets, there appears to be a more informal network of those with little self-restraint, who only recently had discovered the delights of reclining at table.[202]

What can we say concerning a "network of women" in Corinth? First, it must be emphasised that there does not seem to be any hint in 1

Corinthians of an organised association of women in the same way as a Jewish or cultic network through the synagogue. It may also be said that while the existence of a group of ascetic charismatic prophetesses in the Christian ἐκκλησία, as suggested by A. Wire, is indeed possible, there is simply not enough internal evidence to suggest that this hypothesised group was the focus of Paul's arguments.[203] Nevertheless, what is clear is that since Paul's departure from Corinth (following his initial eighteen-month stay), problems had arisen which directly involved women in the congregation, both in the area of marital and sexual relationships (1 Cor. 7) and in worship (11-14). The question is whether it is accurate to speak here in terms of actual networks. In his admonitions on marriage and sexuality in 1 Cor. 7, Paul at various moments speaks to different sets of persons concerning different topics:

- to believing spouses on conjugal rights (vs.2–7),
- to the unmarried and the widows[204] on the question of chastity (vs. 8–9),
- to believing spouses on separation and divorce (vs.10–11),
- to husbands *or* wives with unbelieving spouses on questions of separation and personal witness (vs.12–16),
- to virgins and unmarried men on remaining unmarried (vs.25–35),
- to betrothed men on proper behaviour towards his fiancée (vs.36–38),[205]
- to widows on the issue of remarriage (vs.39–40).

The thing to notice here is that the issues raised by the Corinthians themselves in their written correspondence to Paul (ὧν ἐγράψατε, 7.1) involved not only the rights (ἐξουσία) of male members, but also those of believing wives, virgins, and widows (ταῖς κήραις). These last persons in particular might well have been operating as a semi-independent network, "a disruptive force," operating within the ἐκκλησία, as later seen in the period of the Pastorals (1 Tim. 5.3–16).[206]

Also, while "sexual relations between equal partners is a modern ideal, not an ancient one,"[207] it is remarkable to see the concern on both sides (the Corinthians and Paul) for the female members of the church. Although Paul probably moves one step further in his response than the Corinthians had anticipated—especially in regards to the ἐξουσία of women over their husbands' bodies (v.4) and protection from "easy" divorces on the part of their husbands (11)—it is significant that the issues were even raised at all! The fact that so much of the apostle's response appears to be directed towards the women in the congregation (10, 16, 25ff.) suggests that they were anything but a silent minority.[208]

Women also figure prominently in a key section on the worship of the church, namely 1 Cor. 11.2–16. Discussion on the prophylactic veils has been fraught with controversy, not the least of which has focused on Paul's attitude towards prophesying women.[209] What is important to see here is that the point in question is not *whether* women should be able to pray and prophesy in the public worship, but *how* (veiled or unveiled). Certainly, as we have seen already, despite the "biological and spiritual polarities" which often separated women from men in Paul's day,[210] there was a tendency in some associations—some θίασοι, συναγωγαι, and *collegia*—to de-emphasize gender differences and encourage active participation by all. However, the rarity of such occurrences would have made the Christian ἐκκλησία even more attractive "to upwardly mobile women whose education or economic position ('achieved status') exceeded their hereditary social position ('attributed status')."[211] Once again, then, status does indeed seem to enter into the equation, although the focus remains very much tied to gender and not class distinctions.

Finally, the combination of a subtraction and an addition point to a network of women influencing the church and contributing to the problems therein. The subtraction in question refers to 12.13, in which the familiar "neither/nor" baptismal formula appears to be missing a clause ("neither male nor female"), at least when compared with the earlier and more complete version found in Gal. 3.28. While many commentators have passed over this difference without comment,[212] we must at the very least raise a question as to why the third main division between first-century human beings should be left out in this message to Corinth. Could it be that women had gained enough prominence and authority in the congregation that the issue was not as relevant here as earlier in the Galatian churches? Rather than surrender to empty speculation, it is best to proceed to the addition mentioned above, the controversial verses at the end of 1 Cor. 14. Concerning these verses, 34–35, it has already been suggested that they are the result of a non-Pauline interpolation.[213] Whether one holds to this position or not is unimportant for our purposes here, where the crucial thing is to notice that if Paul is indeed the originator of these verses, then he is responding to a problem involving a group of women who would not stay silent in the church's worship but were instead causing disruptions and disorder. If, on the other hand, the verses are the result of an interpolation, it shows that such a set of women were an issue at least to the interpolater. In either case, vs. 34–35, whether interpolated or original, point to a problem in which some women in the congregation are clearly at the centre.

Thus, we may speak of some kind of a network of women, whether they were smaller groupings of wives or widows, patronesses or prophetesses. The conflicts discussed certainly involved related issues of status, but the focus is still on gender distinctions and societal roles, not on wealth or class or status, per se. Most interesting is the fact that questions on marital and sexual relations were discussed, in part at least, in light of other distinctions and networks such as master-slave and Jew-Greek (7.17–24; 12.13). Here, too, we can see the interplay of many different relational systems and the overlapping of many different boundaries.

A Return to the Familiar

What remains, then, to be said about the Corinthian problems? First, as intimated from the start, conflict was not always the result of the continued involvement of church members in other networks; sometimes the real problem was a lack of tension between persons, as in the case of the incestuous member (1 Cor. 5) or the young men (probably) enjoying the various pleasures of a banquet (1 Cor. 6). Here is where we return to Paul's "double dilemma," for the apostle was not simply confronted with quarrelsome church members but rather with norms that were accepted without question because they were so familiar. In speaking purely of physical space, Osiek and Balch have pointed out that "for perhaps the first century and a half, there were probably no structural adaptations for Christian worship, but rather the adaptation of the group to the structures available."[214] What was true of physical structures appears to have been equally true of the social and relational structures of the fledgling Christian community. It seems apparent, as well, that Paul's departure served as a catalyst for a systemic return to the familiar on the part of church members, to the homeostatic balance of the οἶκος and πολιτεία.

We have seen the likelihood of the more familiar roles of slaves and masters, or clients and patrons, taking de facto precedence over a common calling in Christ.[215] This should not be surprising, given the fact that Peter and even Barnabas are said to have returned to old patterns of Jew-Gentile segregation when a delegation from Jerusalem arrived in Antioch, resulting in Paul's stern rebuke (Gal. 2.11ff.). Likewise, in the Corinthian case of the Lord's Supper, "custom must have its way,"[216] even if that meant the well-to-do ate first without waiting for their Christian brothers and sisters. Likewise, the pressure on some church members to eat meat offered in the pagan sacrifices was great, precisely because the opportunities for social advancement that likely would be thrown away with an outright refusal were considerable.[217] Even where conflicts and disputes *were* occurring in the church, the fact is that the motivation and weapons were often those of the "outside" world, such as litigation and divorce. Thus, Barclay's assertion that there was little hostility between the believers in Corinth and persons outside their ranks should come as little surprise, given the fact that many members probably remained firmly entrenched in the relational networks in which they previously existed.[218]

In presenting these overlapping networks, then, the systemic principle of homeostatic balance has been implicit throughout the chapter. The chief problem facing Paul was not simply factionalism, per se, but rather the tendency on the part of many Corinthians to give priority to the claims and roles of their other, pre-existing networks rather than to those of the Christian ἐκκλησία. "Holiness means keeping distinct the categories of creation."[219] However, the danger in Corinth, as Paul saw it, was the lack of clear distinctiveness for the church. As will be seen in the coming chapters, his emphasis on "correct definition, discrimination and order"[220] in the church points to a concern on Paul's part that his fellow believers were becoming more and more like "ordinary people" (3.4), especially now that his physical absence prevented him from reminding them on a day to day basis of their unique and primary calling in Christ.

The Corinthian problem was a multifaceted one, in which the church could end up becoming one more *collegium* or θίασος among many, even as Paul himself was in danger of becoming one more παιδαγωγός among many (4.15). It was the uniqueness of the church, and the uniqueness of his position in it in relation to the Corinthians, that was at stake.[221] Thus, as we will see, the apostle did not get bogged down in the minutia of each problem which arose in Corinth; his concern was not "What is the reason one member takes another member to court?," or "Who is the more impressive leader, himself or Apollos?" Throughout 1 Corinthians, Paul seems to have grasped the fact that "the issues under dispute were not the [fundamental] issues."[222] The crucial issue underlying both the factionalism and the indifference in the Corinthian church—the cancer that could destroy the Christian "body"—was the ease with which the members kept a foot in more than one world.[223] At one point, Paul remarked, "What have I to do with those outside?" (5.12), but for Christians who were at the same time Jews, Gentiles, citizens, benefactors, masters, slaves, patrons, clients, men, women, householders, members of cults or *collegia*, persons of higher status and persons of lower status. All these people distinctions between "inside" and "outside" were not easy to make. Theirs was a world of multiple networks...but Paul was calling them to something not of this world.

NOTES

[1] Cf. Martin 1995.

[2] Pickett 1997, 41.

[3] I admit to a play on words here, as many of the Roman-style buildings constructed in first-century Corinth used the Corinthian sandstone, or πόρος, often taken from the ruins of old Greek structures (cf. Engels 1990, 62). Even so, the Corinthian church was built using the "material" or members of pre-existing, and often still-existing, social structures. As a result, the boundaries of the church were far from closed to surrounding social elements.

[4] Cf. Brown 1997, 526.

[5] Cf. Murphy-O'Connor 1983, xix.

[6] Friedman notes that a system's constituent parts will function differently outside the system, making it important to define *which* system is being considered at any given moment in order to understand the position and function of a part/member *in that system* (1985, 15).

[7] Here, I part from Mitchell, for the very term "factionalism" can suggest an "us versus them" paradigm which may still miss the interactions and even collisions of multiple systems.

[8] Douglas 1966, 40.

[9] Malina and Neyrey 1996, 227–230. Their argument breaks down when ancient "collectivism" is contrasted sharply with modern Western "individualism." This view of the latter and the consequent argument that moderns "represent themselves and their opinions alone," remains unconvincing in light of social realities of peer pressure, the need for social recognition, the desire to belong, and "it's not what you know but who you know." This does not necessarily contradict Geertz's statement concerning the "rather peculiar idea" of twentieth-century Western culture (1976, 225). While the value placed on individualism in the ideological consciousness of the modern West may indeed result in more of an "unwillingness to enter the private lives of others" or a tendency towards "broad, shallow relationships," the fact remains that modern persons continue to operate out of, and even think paradigmatically in terms of, social networks, albeit in more subtle forms and often unconscious ways than in the ancient world.

[10] Marcus Aurelius, *Med.* 6.54. Cf. Livy's *Hist. of Rome* 2.32.9–12, whose off-hand remark that there exists in his time *concordia* among the Romans in a way that was not true in the past, is counter-balanced by the pleas for ὁμόνοια by rhetors such as Dio Chrysostom.

[11] Alvarez-Pereyre and Heymann 1996, 163.

[12] Plato, *Rep.* 5.10. For a much more detailed account of the use of σῶμα imagery in the ancient world, see D. Martin 1995, or chapter 1 above.

[13] Marcus Aurelius, *Med.* 12.35–36, although the author admits that God's goodness allows for a person who has been thus severed to "return again and grow onto the rest and take up his position again as part" of the whole.

[14] Douglas 1966, 121.

[15] Cf. Morgan, et al. 1981, 137, who speak of "a large matrix of systems, all of which influence one another." Cf. Engels 1990, 97: "nexus of social relationships."

[16] Strauss 1993, 11; citing Marilyn Arthur, the author states that "the πόλις was defined as the sum of its individual households or οἶκοι."

[17] Cicero, *De off.*, 1.54. Cf. Rouselle's description of the family as "the essential foundation of all social life" (1996, 292).

[18] Cotter 1994, 370. Thus, Pliny writes that, "for slaves the household takes the place of city and commonwealth" (*Ep.* 8.16).

[19] Even within our own cultural and temporal context, the task of defining the "modern western family" is problematic at best. Some family analysts often resort to the now almost-outdated definition used several years ago by census takers: namely, the unit of parent(s) and dependent child(ren) living within a single domicile, i.e. the residential nuclear family. The limitations of this definition in today's multi-variegated society are fairly obvious. In some areas, this "ideal" family may be the exception rather than the rule. Cf. also Broderick 1993, 52.

[20] Cicero *De off.* 1. 53. Cf. also Gardner and Wiedemann 1991, 3; Dixon 1992, 4.

[21] Cf. the *Oxford Latin Dictionary*, 46, 54. According to the third-century jurist Ulpian in the *Digest,* familia could refer to a collection of slaves belonging to a married couple; the slaves belonging to each respectively; freedmen under a patron; a business; kin network for the purpose of funerals or commemorations; and agnatic relationships, that is "the kin originating from the same house, and related by blood

through males." An interesting distinction between *domus* and *familia* concerns lineage and inheritance, inasmuch as the former could refer to a matrilineal line and the latter could not. Cf. Saller 1994, 76, 85.

[22] Hallett 1984, 5, using terminology introduced by cultural anthropologist N. Tanner.

[23] Consider Veyne's description of children as those "who were moved about like pawns on the chessboard of wealth and power [but] were hardly ever cherished and coddled" (1987, 18). Cf. also Watson 1987, 46ff.; Gardner and Wiedemann 1991, 5.

[24] Rouselle 1996, 270. As Malina and Neyrey succinctly put it: "It is the duty of children to treat a father honourably" (1996, 166). Note the case of Orestes and Clytemnestra, cited by Cicero, *Inv.* 1.13.18–14.19; *Rh. Her.* 1.10.17; *Inst. Orat.* 3.11.4–13.

[25] Dixon 1988, 26–27; see also the *Digest* 23, 2.2; and Gaius, *Institutes*, 1, 48 ff.

[26] Saller argues that "the nearly absolute legal powers of a father over his children [cannot be read] as a sociological description of family relationships" (1994, 115).

[27] Saller 1991, 165. Cf. Barclay 1991, 178: "The whole institution of slavery was inevitably built on an underlying structure of fear and compulsion (however effectively masked this might be)."

[28] *Ibid.*, 151. Cf. Dixon 1988, 28, where she speaks of "typically fatherly behaviour" towards his children including "anxiety, forgiveness, indulgence, involvement in [their] education." Hallett has recently shown the strong bonds between fathers and their daughters (1984).

[29] Saller 1994, 105.

[30] Dixon 1992, 25.

[31] Cicero, *Inv.* 2.161.

[32] Cf. *TDNT* VII, 175–185, esp. 178. Interestingly, the Greek term does not appear in the undisputed Pauline writings, while it is a prevalent term in both 1 Timothy (2.2; 4.7–8; 5.4; 6.3–6, 11) and 2 Peter (1.3–7; 2.9; 3.11), as well as in Acts (3.12; 10.7; 17.23). Interestingly, while in 1 Timothy the term is always used in a positive sense, referring to piety to God or godliness, in one of only two occurrences in 2 Timothy, there is a strong warning against those who hold to "the outward form of piety" (μόρφωσιν εὐσεβείας) while denying its power (δύναμιν, 3.5).

[33] Plautus, *Poenulus* 1137.

[34] Cf. Saller 1991, 149, n. 9.

[35] *Herennium* 2.19, cited in Saller 1994, 113.

[36] Cf. 1991, 151–154.

[37] While the physical pain induced by a flogging could be great indeed, it was the psychological assault on the slave's "personal space," that proved most painful.

[38] Although tombstones reveal that many slaves separated from their families continued to keep their familial ties, the obvious difficulties were great. Bradley notes the great distances often involved (1984, 59).

[39] In Jewish families, the mother's word was also required for the sentence of death to be carried out. Cf. Philo, *Spec. Leg. II*, 232.

[40] Saller 1991, 153.

[41] Cf. Osiek and Balch 1997, 38ff.; Malina and Neyrey 1996, 176ff.; the latter point to subtle but important gender distinctions in what exactly constituted honour or shame (177–178).

[42] Again, cf. Saller 1991, 153.

[43] Cf. the account found in Aulus Gellius 10.3.2–17.

[44] Testation, the father's ability to decide on transmission of the patrimony following his death, has been seen as "the most potent power in the paternal arsenal." Saller 1994, 119.

[45] Saller 1994, 131.

[46] This notion of the city's self-sufficiency is mentioned by both Aristotle (*Pol.* 1.1252a26–1253a3) and Plato (*Rep.* 2.369B–372A). Concerning the classical Greek era, Herman (following Redfield) notes: "After the rise of cities, men became something different from what they were before," for the πόλις "devised new points of reference for interpreting the world" (1987, 159). The πόλις became for the Greeks "the natural form of human society." Cf. Stambaugh's article on "Cities" in *ABD,* I, p.1044.

[47] Strabo noted the importance of the city's strategic position as a primary reason for its commercial success (*Geog.* 8.6.20), a position supported by Witherington, who remarks that Corinth was "a center of trade…a manufacturing center…a major tourist attraction…and a center for religious pilgrimage" (1995, 9). For details, see Murphy-O'Connor 1983.

[48] Osiek and Balch point to Corinth's "considerable, enduring Roman character" (1997, 30), the result, no doubt, of Caesar's resettlement programme and the continuing commercial links with aristocratic families in Rome. Cf. Williams 1994, 33; also Millar 1995, 108.

[49] Applebaum 1989, 155.

[50] In terms of its architecture, Corinth boasted the only amphitheatre in Roman Greece, and Corinthian columns reflected Italian and not Greek design (cf. Engels 1990, 62–69; also Williams 1994). Cotter notes that Latin, as well as Greek, was found on Corinthian coins, unlike those at Sparta or Athens (1994, 357). Cf. also DeMaris 1995, 671; Spawforth 1994.

[51] Cf. Engels 1990 and Romano 1996. For more on Roman Corinth, see Hays 1997, 2ff.; Murphy-O'Connor 1983; Stambaugh and Balch 1986, 157–158; Williams 1994.

[52] Welborn 1987, 110; who cites Herodotus 5.92; Strabo *Geo.* 8.6.23; and *1 Clement* 47.1–4.

[53] Cf. Douglas 1966, 4, who speaks of the systemic functions of separation, purification, demarcation, and the punishment of transgressors.

[54] Turcan 1996, 17: the void left by the death of the city-state "was favourable to the formation of marginal groups" such as the various *collegia* and professional guilds which are the focus of the next sub-section.

[55] From Bruce's article on "Citizenship" in *ABD,* I, p.1048–1049.

[56] Ael. Arist., *To Rome* 59–60. Cf. Gill 1994, 107. Walbank likewise cites Polybius, whose contempt for the masses must be read within the context of his own position as a member of an upper-class Achaean family (1995, 203). Similarly, Pliny the Younger shows this distinction when he states that certain Christians would be

sent to the capital for separate treatment from the rest, *quia ciues Romani erant* (*Ep.* 10.96.4). Cf. Williams 1994, 33, who speaks of certain aristocratic Roman families who could not, by law, operate the lucrative businesses which they promoted through freedmen resettlement programmes.

[57] The latter term literally means "rod–bearers" (cf. Acts 16.38), and it is quite possibly a significant term for Paul, as seen in this study. Cf. Murphy-O'Connor 1983, 7.

[58] Plutarch, *Praec. rei pub. ger.* 20. Bowersock comments: "It was hard to encourage an aristocracy, when the aristocracy was divided within itself" (1965, 104).

[59] Cf. Schürer 1973, 316. Kent records the interesting account of L. Castricius Regulus, who was president of the Games sometime around the beginning of the Common Era and refurbished all the facilities for the occasion and even financed a banquet for all the city's residents (1966, 70). For more on the role of benefactors, see Winter 1994, 26ff.

[60] Winter 1994, 120; cf. also Jones 1978, 99.

[61] Consider Petronius, *Satyricon*, 14: "Of what avail are laws to be where money rules alone, and the poor suiter can never succeed?"

[62] Epstein 1987, 126.

[63] Raaflaub 1996, 291.

[64] Epstein 1987, 12.

[65] Feldman 1996, 587. Epstein notes that the result of this was the prevalence in Roman politics of "factions, loose organisation of politicians, united primarily by personal bonds rather than ideology" (1987, 80). Cf. also Dixon 1992, 31.

[66] McCready 1996, 62. For earlier comparisons, see Hardy 1906, 129ff.; Malherbe 1983, 87–91; Meeks 1983, 77–80. More recent works include: Kloppenborg and Wilson's edited compilation of articles on voluntary associations (1996), as well as Gathercole and Hansen's forthcoming book, especially chapter 1.

[67] As already noted above in *figure 1.c.* Not unlike the ἐκκλησία, membership numbers in a single *collegium* "ranged between thirty and forty but rarely went beyond one hundred" (McCready 1996, 61). See also Murphy-O'Connor 1983a, 161ff; also, Osiek and Balch 1997. Another important similarity is the common meal shared by participants.

[68] Asconius, *In Senatu contra L. Pisonem* 8.

[69] *Dig.,* 47.22.4.

[70] Suetonius, *Caes.* 42.

[71] Suetonius, *Aug.* 32. Later, Trajan, in the midst of a reign distinguished by "tranquility and good order," urges Pliny, governor of Bithynia, to take great care in allowing the formation of a *collegium* of firefighters at Nicomedia, since "it is to be remembered that these sort of societies have greatly disturbed the peace of your province in general" (factionibus esse vexatas, Plin. *Ep.* 10.34). Yet again, concerning disturbances at Pompeii, the historian Tacitus writes: "Collegia quae contra leges instituerant dissoluta" (*Ann.* xvi, 17).

[72] Hardy remarks that "inscriptions prove to us the existence in immense numbers, and in every part of the empire, of *collegia* of every sort and kind, with regard to only a very small minority of which there is any sign that they were licensed either by the senate or by the emperor" (1906, 132).

[73] Stambaugh and Balch 1986, 125.

[74] Cf. Gathercole and Hansen's upcoming work (pp. 15–16), which speaks of "hundreds of *collegium* inscriptions which make no reference to religious activity whatever."

[75] "There is no ban on assembly for religious purposes," *Dig.* xlvii, 22, 1, 1.

[76] See Gathercole and Hansen's upcoming work, p. 11. Cotter (1994, 364) notes, "whether or not women patrons of professional *collegia* were also considered members is not clear."

[77] *Ibid*, 12.

[78] Cf. Hock 1980, 34. See also Murphy-O'Connor 1983, 175–178.

[79] Pickett 1997, 33, esp. n. 77.

[80] Plutarch, *Mor.* 19. For this reason, he adds, a married woman should worship only her husband's gods and "shut the door against all queer rituals and outlandish superstitions."

[81] Cf. Furnish 1984, 15–19, who notes the presence of Greek, Roman and Egyptian cults.

[82] Pausanius, *Des. of Greece* 2.2.8.

[83] See Wiseman 1979, 487–488.

[84] Remus 1996, 164.

[85] *Leg. ad Gaium* 281–282.

[86] Segal 1990, 92: "Group commitment [among Hellenistic Jews] was built in quite different circumstances."

[87] Cf. Murphy-O'Connor 1983, 79.

[88] From Murphy-O'Connor's article on "Corinth" in *ABD* I, p.1138. Cf. also Munck 1967, 178.

[89] Alvarez-Pereyre and Heymann 1996, 167.

[90] Such a synagogue (or prayer house, προσεῦχη, to refer to the building as distinct from the membership, the συναγωγοῖ) was not a Sabbath-only worship building as much as a focal point for the Jewish community, thus serving at various moments as the communal meeting place, study hall, guest house, community dining room, centre for outreach (in the form of a *patella* or soup kitchen), and even a place for the dedication or manumission of a slave. Cf. Feldman 1996, 597–599.

[91] "The influence of Greek culture on Jewish life…in the Second Temple period and subsequently is today an accepted fact among most historians" (Applebaum 1989, 30). This is seen in the use of titles for synagogue officials which were also used by leaders of pagan associations and cults. Ἀρχισυνάγωγος is such a term (cf. Feldman 1996, 588). Another title—πάτηρ συναγωγῆς—had "no Jewish roots but apparently [was] taken over from pagan Hellenistic and especially Roman sources and particularly from mystery cults, where it denotes an initiate of an advanced degree" (*Ibid.*, 596).

[92] Among the ἀρχισυνάγωγοι listed in the inscriptions, three were women (cf. Brooten 1982). Despite the suggestion by some that such a title was given to the wives of male ἀρχισυνάγωγοι, Feldman insists that "there is no clear evidence" the title was purely an honorary one (1996, 591). Of course, this does not mean in effect that the title denoted active leadership either, but perhaps represented a substantial

financial donor. For more on the question of women's roles in the Corinthian synagogue, see Matilla 1996.

[93] Murphy-O'Connor suggests that Diaspora Jews were "found in the whole range of occupations from the most prestigious to the most degrading," thus proving to be something of a "microcosm of the empire as a whole" (1983, 80). The diastratic structure of Jewish communities (as well as churches) has been noted by Theissen 1992, 214ff.

[94] Gardner and Wiedemann remark that the "inferior" identified himself with the master or patron who provided much-needed "material and social existence" (1991, 39).

[95] Winter, 1994, 46; cf. also Chow 1992; Clarke 1993; Marshall 1987 (esp. 157–164).

[96] Philo, *Decal.* 165,166 (emphasis mine); see also *Spec. Leg. II*, 227.

[97] As cited by Aulus Gellius 5, 13.

[98] Cf. Saller 1994, 133–153. More will be said about this in the coming chapters.

[99] Pliny, *Ep.* 1,4: far from producing greater devotion on the part of his slaves/servants, "a long course of mild treatment is apt to wear out the impressions of awe."

[100] Pliny, *Ep.* 1,19.

[101] Cf. Malina and Neyrey 1996, 163.

[102] For more on the nature of social pyramids, see Herman 1987, 153.

[103] Herman 1987, 152–153, who notes that the ancient Greek world had been "interlaced with a web of informal alliances which were not congruent with the offical foci of power of the city-states themselves."

[104] Gardner and Wiedemann 1991, 166.

[105] Pliny, *Ep.* 1,15: *Heus tu!* exclaims the host, *promittis ad coenam, nec venis.*

[106] See, respectively, Pliny *Ep.* 1,13; 1,14; and Book 5 (letters with Trajan).

[107] Dixon 1988, 20.

[108] A particularly interesting case concerns Pliny, who profusely thanks the emperor for "condescending" to give him prior advice, only then immediately to ask for more help, *quod nunc quoque facias rogo (Ep.* 5, 56,1).

[109] Despite the obvious anachronisms, the latter may be compared with modern youth who, on their eighteenth birthday, find themselves legally allowed to buy and drink alcohol.

[110] Dubisch remarks that first-century studies often have not taken fully into account "the significance of gender in a wider, more complex social and cultural web." Cf. also Chance 1994, esp. 148–149.

[111] Cotter 1994, 360. Consider Nepos, *Lives* 5–6: "In Greece things are far different."

[112] From Plutarch's *Moralia,* "The Bravery of Women" (242F). On the other hand, the same writer speaks of mourning as "womanish and unbecoming to decorous men," since it is not only "feminine" but also "weak and ignoble" ("A Letter of Condolence" 112–113).

[113] Crates, *Ep. Hipparchia* 28–29: "The Amazons...have not fallen short of men in anything."

[114] Cf. Diog. Laer. *Lives of Eminent Philosophers,* "Thales" 1.33. Distinctions are also made in this prayer between human beings and animals and between Greeks and barbarians.

[115] As cited in Boring, et al. 1995, 467–468.

[116] Osiek and Balch 1997, 115.

[117] Cotter 1994, 367: "In this aspect, Roman conventions were no different than what one could expect to find anywhere else around the Mediterranean."

[118] Cf. Pomeroy 1996, 251, whose focus here is on the Therapeutae. See more below.

[119] Philo, *On the Contemp. Life* 8.68; 11.83–84. It is interesting to note the similarities between this familial community who have left behind "possessions, brothers, children, wives, parents, kinsfolk, friends and fatherlands" and Christ's disciples as described in Mk. 10.29; Mt. 19.29; Lk. 18.29 (and 14.26).

[120] *Sotah* 3.4. Elsewhere, Eliezer's own wife is presented as learned (*Shabbath* 116a–b).

[121] *Megillah* 14b, edited circa 500 C.E.

[122] Alvarez-Pereyre and Heymann 1996, 165. Cf. also the Babylonian Talmud, *Qiddushin* 31b, in which Rabbi Tarfon speaks with great respect concerning his mother, who raised him and taught him. Likewise, Rabbi Joseph even describes his mother in terms of the *Shechinah*, the Divine Presence.

[123] Cf. *Test. of Twelve Patriarchs, Test. of Reuben* 5.

[124] Ben Sira, *Ecclesiasticus* 25.15; later, verse 24 states that "from a woman sin had its beginning, and because of her we all die."

[125] Taken from the Talmud, *Shabbath* 152a, arguably the most negative statement about women in rabbinical literature; cf. Boring, et al. 1995, 201, n. 8.86.

[126] Pitt-Rivers 1977,10.

[127] Cf. Epstein 1987, 92: "The convicted man's sons and friends were duty-bound to take revenge [on the one who initiated the prosecution]."

[128] As noted by Suetonius, *Life of Nero*. This strategy, hardly unique to Nero, has been employed by many leaders and despots throughout history, from Machiavelli to Hitler.

[129] Cf. Foerster's discussion on ἐξουσία and ὕβρις in *TDNT* II, 562–563.

[130] In a recent work, Winter draws attention to the evidence for a shortage (1999, 9).

[131] Cf. Williams 1994, 45–46.

[132] This does not imply an unquestioning acceptance of the historical accuracy of this account. I am well aware of textual discrepancies between the Western and Alexandrian traditions, as well as the evidence of considerable redactional work. However, inasmuch as the issue here is not historical reliability of the passage but rather an illustration of the complexity of first-century networks, it seems appropriate to use it.

[133] Murphy-O'Connor 1996, 258. The author notes that the well-known proverb, "Not for everyone is the voyage to Corinth" (Horace, *Epis.* 1.17.36) was originally not about the city's sexual distractions, as Strabo suggests (*Geogr.* 8.6.20), but rather about the intensity of commercial competition therein.

[134] Cf. 1 Cor. 4.12, mentioned above in *2.3.2*; also, see Hock 1980 for more on Paul's work.

[135] The root term, κοίνον—"common" (cf. Mk. 7.15,18; Acts 10.15, 11.19; Rom. 14.14) —was often associated with collegia (Gk. θίασοι), which is particularly interesting when one considers the importance of κοινωνία, in Paul's thought, as

seen especially in Romans and the Corinthian correspondence. Unfortunately, the apostle's prolific use of the κοινων- word group has usually been associated only with the LXX and not with collegial usage (cf. Hauck's article in *TDNT*, III, 789– 809, esp. 800–804.). Waltzing notes that κοίνον was even used as an equivalent to *collegium;* hence, a κοίνον "of swordmakers" or "of workers" (1895, 4.94,191,210; cf. Gathercole and Hansen's upcoming work, p. 3).

[136] Suetonius, *Claud.* 25, dated c. 49 C.E. The comment about "Chrestus" has often led to speculation that Jewish Christians were somehow at the heart of the controversy. For a more detailed discussion about this this edict, see Lampe. A similar edict against Jews is attributed to Tiberius: "Foreign religions, the Egyptian and the Jewish religious rites, he suppressed, and...the Jewish youth he dispersed, under pretense of military service, into provinces of unhealthy climate" (Suet. *Tib.* 36).

[137] Theissen 1982, 90.

[138] Engels 1990, 71.

[139] Lydia, the "dealer in purple cloth" from Thyatira is another (16.14). Cf. also 13.43, 50; 17.4, 17. In all of these passages, the "God-fearers" are listed as a group distinct from, yet always together with, "the Jews." While Kraabel (1979) is correct in asserting that the term itself is unique to Acts and not found anywhere among over 100 synagogue inscriptions, there are still several texts from both pagan and Jewish writers that draw distinctions between Gentiles who clearly convert to Judaism, undergoing either circumcision or proselyte baptism (concerning the latter, more will be said in a moment) and those who simply honour the Jewish customs and rites. Josephus, for example, makes reference to "those who worshipped God" and contributed generously to the Temple alongside "all the Jews of the habitable world." (Jos. *Ant.* 14.110). Cf. also Jos. *Ant.* 20.195 (concerning Nero's wife) and Jos. *Contra Apion* 2.282. Epictetus makes a less favourable distinction between those who through baptism prove themselves true proselytes and those "only acting the part" (cited by Arrian *Disc.* 2.9.19–21). Cf. also Petron.37; Juv. *Sat.* 14.96–106. Recent evidence from two early inscriptions lists among a set of financial donors, "Joseph a proselyte...Joseph a proselyte son of Eusebios," as well as Emmonios and Antoninos, who are specifically labelled "God-fearers." This is the strongest inscriptural evidence that σεβόμενοι τὸν θεόν was distinguished from a proselyte (cf. Feldman & Reinhold 1996,142).

[140] This does not count those other Corinthian Christians listed in Romans 16, some of whom were probably of higher social status (e.g. Erastus, Gaius). For an excellent summary of those Corinthians known by name, see Theissen 1982, 94–95.

[141] The only other non-Acts appearance is in Paul's prayer for the Romans: "...that you might live in harmony with one another, in accordance with Christ Jesus, so that together (ὁμοθυμαδόν) you may with one voice glorify the God and Father of our Lord Jesus Christ" (15.5–6). There are echoes here of LXX passages such as Ex. 19.8 ("they all answered as one") and Numbers 27.21 ("both he [the priest] and all the Israelites with him"). The word is found quite often in Judith, usually in terms of corporate prayer: "They cried out in unison, praying fervently to the God of Israel" (4.12). It is also a favourite term in Job, where among its varied uses is

Job's lament that God "is not a mortal, as I am, that I might answer him, that we should come to trial together" (ὁμοθυμαδόν, 9.32).

[142] Pliny, *Ep.* 10.33.

[143] Dio Chrysostom, *Or.* 43.2–11; 45.7–9; 50.3–4. Cicero likewise warns against such "crowd politics" (*Flacc.* 7/15–18, see also Millar 1995, 111–112). Cf. Pliny, *Ep.* 10.34, in which Trajan warns against the formation of fire brigades, lest *hetaeria eaeque breui fient.*

[144] Cited in Blue 1994, 124. Also referring to the work of R. Krautheimer, Blue outlines three stages of development for the early Christian period: the first stage (roughly 50–150 C.E.) is marked by house churches, private homes of members that were used for the local Christian assembly. The second stage (c. 150–250) witnessed the massive increase in numbers of Christians and, as a result, the renovation of members' private houses specifically for the purposes of the Christian communities. This is the era of the *domus ecclêsai,* which should be rendered as "community center" or "meeting house" (127). The final stage (250–313) is marked by the switch from renovated houses to larger buildings, some private and some public, before the age of basilicas.

[145] Cf. Bruce 1985, 45, who notes that Paul's choice of *Prisca* instead of *Priscilla* (as in Acts) "is in line with his habit of referring to people by their formal names (in his letters)."

[146] Blue 1994, 156. Theissen concurs: "Reference to someone's house is hardly a sure criterion for that person's high social status; but it is a probable one" (1982, 87).

[147] The term itself is found only here in the New Testament, although προΐστημι occurs in Rom. 12.8, 1 Thes. 5.12, and the Pastorals. For προστάτης (masc.), see 1 Clem. 36.1; 64.

[148] Meeks 1983, 60, 79.

[149] For more on slaves in the οἶκος, see Theissen 1982, 84–87; Dixon 1992, 35.

[150] For ὑποτάσσω in reference to wives, see Eph. 5.24; Col. 3.18; Tit. 2.5; 1 Pet. 3.1,5. In reference to a child's obedience, see Lk. 2.51 (a fascinating use of the term, since it comes immediately after the episode of the "disobedient" adolescent Jesus justifying his absence from his parents with a claim to "his Father's" higher call to obedience). In reference to the subjection of household slaves, see Tit. 2.9 and 3.1.

[151] There is, of course, the other occurrence of ὑποτάσσεται in 14.32, which does not fit the "household pattern" mentioned above, but does share the common element of a desire for order in the relevant system. In the worship of the church, as opposed to the discipline of the church, the *paterfamilias* imagery is not as prevalent. I am intentionally abstaining from reference to 14.34, which I would regard as a non-Pauline interpolation. For more on this last point, see Payne 1995 and 1998; Hays 1997, 55–59; Osiek and Balch 1997, 117.

[152] Cf. Theissen 1982, 57 (also 92–94), who notes that if "those of Chloe" had been adult children, they would instead have used their father's name, even if he was deceased. See also Fee 1987, 54.

[153] *Ibid.*, 86.

[154] Cf. Cotter 1994, 368.

[155] Cotter 1994, 352 (emphasis mine). It seems reasonable to accept the opinion that "Chloe's people" were somehow outside the situation addressed by Paul, not representing the congregation officially in the same way as those who bring written correspondence to Paul. See Fee 1987; Hays 1997; Pickett 1997 for more detailed discussion of the question of the identity of τῶν Χλόης. Mitchell's argument, at times overstated, that the περὶ δέ formula should not be read as always introducing the written material to Paul, does not change the fact that Paul did receive some report from persons who appear to have been "out of the loop," as it were, of recognised leadership.

[156] Cf. Pickett 1997, 38; for a contrary view, see Davis 1984, who views Paul's "wisdom" language in the context of Jewish sapiential traditions.

[157] Winter 1994, 203.

[158] "The Christian confession and the design of Graeco-Roman houses were at odds with each other" (Osiek and Balch 1997, 199). See also Murphy-O'Connor 1983.

[159] Blue 1994, 121.

[160] Cf. Strauss 1993, 12.

[161] Welborn 1987, 91.

[162] Cf. Walbank 1995, 222. This distrust of οἱ πολλοί does not alter the fact that Polybius had great respect for the Achaian political system as a whole.

[163] "The different cliques seem to be more interested in the characteristic features of leaders they venerate than the theologies represented by them" (Pickett 1997, 40).

[164] Cicero, *De Amic.* 23. In the same way, Polybius, speaking in terms of Achaian politics, warns that the people are "like the sea when strong winds blow over it."

[165] Pliny, *Ep.* 6,13.

[166] Cf. Millar 1995, 111: "The use of words…was central to the political process" (p.109). Pliny reveals his own "exquisite happiness" upon hearing news that two young speakers looked to him as their *rectorem* and *magistrum* in oratory, emulating his style (*Ep.* 6,11).

[167] Consider Pogoloff 1992, 196: "Two Hellenistic speakers who essentially agreed with one another could easily become sources of division without ever intending to."

[168] The fact that this was not simply one isolated case appears fairly certain from verses 7 and 8, in which Paul broadens his appeal to a larger audience, who are "defrauding believers" (ἀλλὰ ὑμεῖς ἀδικεῖτε καὶ ἀποστερεῖτε, καὶ τοῦτο ἀδελφούς). The last term is plural, and implies more than one believer defrauding another individual believer.

[169] Welborn 1987, 107. Cf. Epstein 1987, 97: "The Roman courts provided the most convenient outlet for conducting private warfare." See Winter 1991, esp. 571–572.

[170] Pliny, *Ep.* 3, 9: "However, it is but for a short season" (*ad breve tempus*). Likewise, Paul's calls for unity and not σχίσματα echo Plutarch's injunction to "not join any party, but conduct one's affairs without party spirit" (*Prec. Statecraft* 10).

[171] Consider, for example, the invitation to "the table of the Lord Serapis in the home of Claudius Serapion," likely a priest of Serapis. (*P. Oxy.* 3.523). See 1 Cor. 6.12–20.

[172] Cf. Witherington 1995, 192. Winter views the most likely context as the Isthmian Games, referring to the example of Lucius Castricius Regulus (1994, 171).

[173] As cited in Boring, et al. 1995, 148 and 420–421. Concerning the banquets in honour of Serapis, Tertullian symbolizes the extravagances of such feasts with the vast amount of smoke rising from the incense, enough to "call out the firemen," he laments, "yet about the modest supper–room of the Christians alone is a great ado made" (*Ap.* 39.15ff.).

[174] Consider the Pauline principle of "Don't ask if you don't want to know" (10.25–30), a reasonable and highly pragmatic suggestion in the case of shopping for meat–since Christians could distance themselves in their visit to the marketplace by asserting that they were only crossing into the public sector and not into the network of the pagan cults themselves–a more difficult situation arose when an invitation to a meal was received by a Christian, since even the invitation would contain overt references to a specific pagan deity. Tertullian, likewise, goes to great lengths to justify a Christian's participation in different kinds of festivals, both civic and private (such as celebrations of the *toga virilis*), arguing that "it will be lawful for us to be present at some ceremonies which see us doing service to a *man,* not to an idol" (*On Idol.* 15–16, esp. 16.10ff.).

[175] Cf. Witherington 1995, 201; earlier, Orr and Walther had asserted that participation in collegial meals dedicated to a pagan deity "seems to be an ordinary social possibility for inhabitants...of Corinth" (1976, 232, n.10).

[176] While "idolatry" or "idol" is mentioned at least 14 times in 1 Corinthians, and again in 2 Cor. 6.16, references in other undisputed Pauline letters are limited to 1 Thes. 1.9, Gal. 5.20 and Rom. 2.22.

[177] The apostle refers to "knowledge" no less than 12 times in 1 Corinthians (1.5; 4.19; 8.1,7,10,11; 12.8; 13.2,8; 14.6,7,9) and another 7 times in 2 Corinthians (2.14; 4.6; 6.6; 8.7; 11.6; 13.6), while elsewhere in his letters the term can only be found 6 times total (Gal. 4.9; Rom. 2.20; 11.33; 15.14; Phil. 3.8; 4.5).

[178] Another significant parallel is found in Rev. 2.14–21, where the writer accuses the church at Pergamum of presently having members (ἔχεις ἐκεῖ) who at the same time accepted "the teaching of the Nicolaitans." Here, too, we see the familiar combination of idolatry and πορνεία.

[179] On the link between sexual and culinary pleasures at the *convivia,* cf. Tacitus, *Agr.* 21; also see Quintilian, *Inst. Or.* 2.2.14–15, for a warning to young boys, to stay away from such feasts lest they be entrapped sexually by the older men reclining at the table. For more on the "unholy trinity of eating, drinking and immorality," see Booth 1991, 106; Winter 1998, ch. 4; and Witherington 1995, 13–14, 191–195.

[180] Cf. Tertullian, who asserts: "Our feast explains itself by its name...ἀγάπη, i.e. affection" (*Ap.* 39.15).

[181] The argument, of course, is that those who involve themselves in the rites of pagan deities get far more than they expect; for more on Paul's response, see Oropeza 1999; Willis 1985; Witherington 1995, 186ff.

[182] ΘΑΙΣ frag. 218.

[183] A common inscription on tombs (this one from Aphrôdisia) reads: "As long as you live, be happy, eat, drink, live high [well], embrace others. For this was the End ."

[184] See Lattke's article in *EDNT* II, 510, n.3. Cf. also *Ac. Thom.* 139 for similar usage.

[185] That there were differences between Greek, Roman, and Jewish inhabitants in the manner in which they lay their dead is clear, and these differences might well have contributed to the "heightened concern" among members of the Christian ἐκκλησία in which both groups were represented. See DeMaris 1995, 671, who adds that "early Roman Corinthia provides ample evidence of an emerging preoccupation with the dead and the world of the dead" (665). Cf. Kloppenborg 1996, 20–23, for the responsibilties of *collegia* in funerary arrangements; see also Wedderburn 1987, 287–293. Regarding the Jewish concern for "the decent burial of the dead," cf. Josephus, *Contra Apion* 2.27.

[186] As Barrett notes (citing T. W. Manson), we can see these tensions most clearly in the observance of food laws and in the judicial rights of the community, and in the questioning of Paul's apostolic status (Barrett, 1968, 44). More recently, Stanley has argued that Paul's references to "Greeks," not "Gentiles," points to "a history of interethnic (not interreligious) conflict between people who defined themselves as 'Jews' and 'Greeks' in the cities of the eastern Mediterranean basin" (1996, 123-124). Stanley argues that Paul's own situation as a Jew in a Greek city gave him a sensitivity to the issue.

[187] It is interesting to see a parallel to Paul's distinction between divine and human wisdom in the speech of Socrates at his trial, where the philosopher speaks of a "wisdom greater than human wisdom" (Plato, *Ap.* 20 DE, 23 A).

[188] Paul's statement here is remarkable, considering that he speaks of the assembly of Corinthian Christians as the true temple, in which dwells God's presence. For a similar claim by a first-century Jewish group, see 1QS 8.5-9.

[189] Again, the nature of these allusions and citations will be noted in chapter 4 on belonging.

[190] From Horace, *Sat.* 1, 9.60-72.

[191] Chow's connection between patronage and the so-called rite of baptism for the dead relies far too heavily on the largely unchallenged theory that such a rite actually existed in Corinth, despite the lack of evidence concerning such a practice. For a different, and far more plausible interpretation of the enigmatic 15.29, see Winter 1999, or chapter 5 below.

[192] The suggestion by some that the practice described was actually a form of prostitution wholly acceptable to the Corinthians but odious to Paul lacks credibility, particularly in light of Paul's assertion that not even the pagans do such a thing (ἥτις οὐδὲ ἐν τοῖς ἔθνεσιν, 5.1). He even prefaces his comments with the climactic qualitative pronoun ὅλως. Despite Jewish understanding of a sexual relationship between a man and his stepmother as "an outrageous crime" (cf. Jos. *Ant.* 3.274; see also Lev. 18.8), at least one rabbi, Akibah, offered a "legal loophole" as it were, in the case of some proselytes. This shows that the practice, while exceptional, did exist, and that Rabbi Akibah did not want this to bar a person from the synagogue network. The question, of course, is why?

[193] For slaves, there was the even more difficult position of sometimes being the objects of their masters' desires. Rouselle remarks: "*Paterfamilias* scattered their seed around their households, creating tangled webs of kinship and giving rise to

incestuous relationships between themselves and the daughters they had by their servants, between half-brothers and sisters born of those unions, and between their legitimate sons and illegitimate daughters" (1996, 294).

[194] "Roman 'friendship' was based upon the exchange of very real *beneficia*, goods and services required by the parties involved: 'I give so that you may give,' *do et des.*" (Gardner and Wiedemann 1991, 168). Thus, Seneca warned "that I should not receive an unworthy person...into the most sacred rights of exchanging benefits," a key to friendship (*On Benefits*, 2, 18.5).

[195] The interpretation of μᾶλλον χρῆσαι as "make use of" has been strengthened through the finding of an apocryphal Jewish biography (dated sometime between the first and third centuries C.E.), which speaks of Joshua's relation to Moses: "he used [χρῆσθαι] the servitude, knowing him whose servant he was...he loved one who was God's servant, and was his servant of his own choice." We can see here that Moses acted both as patron and client, for he was "over" Joshua but at the same time he served the LORD. Paul's use of ὑποτάσσησθε in 16.16—that the Corinthians should submit themselves voluntarily in service to the οἶκος of Stephanus precisely because the latter "had devoted themselves to the service [διακονίαν] of the saints" (16.15)—echoes the claim that Joshua served [ὑποτάσσειν] Moses of his own choice [προαίρεσις]. Cf. Boring, et al. 1996, 412.

[196] Osiek and Balch 1997, 199.

[197] "What early Christianity did was to insist on a humanised and nonabusive relationship between owner and slave, but it did not change the structure" (Osiek and Balch 1997, 192).

[198] Cf. Winter 1997b; *contra* Fee 1987, 250-251.

[199] Dio Chrys. *Or.* 14.13; on the phrase πάντα ἔξεστιν, see *Or.* 3.10.

[200] Winter 1997b, 80. The need for self-restraint, therefore, was emphasised by several ancient philosophers, as seen in Xenophon *Cyr. 8.30* (cited by Winter).

[201] Winter 1999, ch.4, sections 3-4. For more on the toga, see Plutarch *Mor.* 37C.

[202] Cf. Booth 1991, 106-108. Pliny thus speaks of the need for a young man to be trained first in good manners and "moral improvements" and only then in eloquence (*Ep.* 3.3).

[203] Cf. Wire 1990. For a balanced criticism of her points, see Witherington 1995, 174f.

[204] The term τοῖς ἀγάμοις, unique in the New Testament to 1 Cor. 7, is a masculine plural and clearly differentiated from "widows" (feminine plural).

[205] I concur with Fee that the "father-daughter" interpretation, though possible in light of the active role of the *paterfamilias* in a daughter's marriage plans, is less likely than the "fiancée" reading, which is supported both internally by the third-person plural imperative γαμείτωσαν (see Fee 1987, 352), as well as by the earliest commentators (cf. Chrys. *Hom. 1 Cor.* 19); Methodius, *Banquet of Ten Virgins* 14.

[206] Cf. Winter 1994, 62, 72-75. See also Dixon 1988, 47, who remarks on the security of widows who could live well without being a financial burden on the church.

[207] Osiek and Balch 1997, 116.

[208] In speaking against the foreign practice of polygamy, Gaius Sallust, a contemporary of Paul's, wrote that none of those foreigners' wives "has the position of a partner; all are held equally cheap" (Sallust, *Jugurthine War* 89.7).

[209] For differing views on the passage in question, cf. Wire 1990 and D. Martin 1995. The question of whether this passage is a non-Pauline interpolation—based on the otherwise smooth transition from v. 2 to v. 17 as well as on questionable terminology and style of argumentation—has not carried as much weight as similar arguments over 14.34–35.

[210] Osiek and Balch 1997, 111.

[211] Cf. Hays 1997, 53.

[212] Cf. Hèring 1962, 130; Conzelmann 1975, 212; Fee 1987, 606; Witherington 1995, 258. The same silence concerning any distinction between 12.13 and Gal. 3.28 is found in Clement of Alexandria's second-century work *Pædagogus* 1.6, although the author is quick to remark earlier on the equal virtue of men and women in God's eyes and the irrelevance of gender distinctions in the eschaton (1.4, citing Lk. 20.34).

[213] Payne, in particular, has utilised text-critical tools in order to show that certain ancient manuscripts most likely did not contain the verses in question (1995, 1998). He also remarks: "In 1 Corinthians Paul consistently champions the cause of the down-trodden. Only here [in vv. 34–35] is unqualified silence demanded, and only here is it demanded of a specific social group" (1995, 246).

[214] Osiek and Balch 1997, 33.

[215] Osiek and Balch 1997, 192: "Did baptism of slaves bring about a different relationship with a Christian owner? Aristides suggests that it did...but did their roles change? The rest of the evidence suggests they did not."

[216] The speaker cited here, of course, is Plutarch, from his *Table-Talk* (616D–617A), in response to his brother's assertion that "the dinner is a democratic affair." This is true, Plutarch responds, when the guests are young, not of high learning and status.

[217] Consider the position of Erastus, ὁ οἰκονόμος τῆς πόλεως (Rom. 16.23), which would have placed him often in the situations described above (cf. 2 Tim. 4.20; also Acts 19.22). Hays argues that there were other considerations, as well, such as the fact that "such occasions were among the few opportunities many people would have had to eat meat" (1997, 42).

[218] Cf. Barclay 1992, 57.

[219] Douglas 1966, 53.

[220] *Ibid.*

[221] For Paul, "the issue was not the distinction in purity between Jews and Gentiles," or any other distinctions found in the οἶκος or πολιτεία, "but church unity." He "would not tolerate any distinctions among the saved within the Christian community" (Segal 1990, 230).

[222] Cf. Friedman 1985, 203. Earlier, the author notes: "Efforts to bring about change by dealing with symptoms, rather than the process [of how to live together in unity], never will achieve lasting changes in an organic system. Problems will recycle unless the balancing factors...shift" (202).

[223] Cf. Hays 1999, 396, who notes that the Corinthian Christians, far from having an over-realized eschatology, instead "employed categories of self-understanding derived from a decidedly non-eschatological Graeco-Roman cultural environment."

✧ CHAPTER FOUR
Identity Crisis

In response to claims that conflict in Corinth was the result of status differentials, gender-related issues, or religious disagreements, I have argued in the previous chapter that the situation was far more complex than any uni-focused analysis can convey. Several factors—several overlapping networks—contributed to the problems in the church. To describe socio-economic status, for example, as *the* factor is to ignore or underestimate the many relational links by which individuals were connected to one another and ordered their relational universe. Thus, to reduce the situation to "haves" versus "have-nots," as if these were two formal opposing groups, would be to oversimplify the more dynamic social reality which existed in first-century Corinth. Rather, it can be said more accurately that status differentials AND gender-related issues AND religious disagreements AND several other factors all contributed to the Corinthian intra-church conflict, as members brought in with them distinctions present in their various other relational networks.[1]

In chapters 4 and 5, we move from discussion about the relational basis of the Corinthian problem—multiple overlapping networks—to a more detailed analysis of Paul's responses to specific intra-church conflicts in 1 Cor. 1–6. Although we shall see that Paul's "conflict management" strategy was no more one-dimensional than the situations he faced, yet it is also possible to point to the apostle's consistent focus on issues of *differentiation*. This will be seen in his attempts to redefine both the church's unique identity (in relation to other networks) and his own unique position (in relation to the Corinthians and other church leaders). Paul's utilisation of familial imagery in his reconfiguration of relationships within the Christian ἐκκλησία is of particular interest, since this remains a point on which many commentators have long been silent.

This present chapter explores Paul's response to the ἔριδες involving key figures in the Christian community, as found in 1 Corinthians 1–4. It has been suggested above that the key issue *as Paul saw it* concerned not doctrinal differences as much as personal allegiances. Commentators seeking to define a clear theological basis for the factionalism in 1.10ff. are left, in fact, in the realm of conjecture.[2] While the potential for σχίσματα between fellow members was the immediate issue in question (1.10–11), and while other specific issues of contention would later be addressed (as we shall see in Chapter 5), an examination of Paul's argument in 1 Cor. 1–4 reveals his awareness of two fundamental systemic problems: *the tendency of many members to regard the church as simply one more network in their relational world, and the inclination of some to view Paul as one more leader among many.* Thus, behind issues of disunity lay a deeper problem of confused corporate identity, in which the key question was not "Who was thinking what?" but rather "Who belonged to whom?"

The following three sections represent one attempt to examine the problem and Paul's response using a systemic methodological approach. The first major section explores the question of an "identity crisis" in the church, with particular attention given to the apparent inadequacy of baptism to serve as a sufficiently clear identity marker for the Christian network and Paul's conscious or subconscious reliance on the Septuagint usage of ἐκκλησία. The second section focuses on Paul's use of the cross as a primary identity marker/boundary for the church. The final section examines Paul's reconfiguration of internal relationships along familial rather than collegial lines, thereby redefining his own position in relation to other leaders and the Corinthians themselves. Here, the apostle's prolific use of ἀδελφός language, as well as his less frequent but well-placed "servant" and "father" images, will be considered.

It is in no way suggested that this is the only way to approach 1 Cor. 1–4, or that these features (baptism, cross, ἐκκλησία) are the only ones which may be examined. I have chosen my particular approach for two reasons: First, far from being an artificial construct of my own design, I believe the chapter outline offered above follows Paul's own pattern of focusing on relational issues of "belonging" and group perception (3.23), and therein linking key images such as baptism and the cross with issues of corporate identity (1.13). Second, although terms such as ἐκκλησία and ἀδελφός are familiar ones in the Pauline corpus, here in 1 Corinthians the apostle specifically utilised them as terms of definition and differentiation, i.e. the church as a sanctified, set-apart assembly (1.2), and the "brethren" as those who are in agreement (1.10) and *not* defined according to the standards of their networks of belonging (1.26). Thus, while this is by no means the only approach to take in exploring 1 Cor. 1–4, it is one which is grounded in Paul's own language and literary order, as well as one which considers in greater detail the systemic nature of his choice of wording.

Rethinking the ἐκκλησία

Points of Anchorage

By addressing himself to τῇ ἐκκλησίᾳ (singular) τοῦ θεοῦ τῇ οὔσῃ ἐν Χριστῷ Ἰησοῦ (1.2), and not to "the various Christian house church*es* in Corinth,"[3] Paul made it clear that, from his vantage point in the system, the church as a unit still existed and was not yet destroyed totally by σχίσμα.[4] Indeed, his call to unity *before actual schism could occur* finds a parallel in Plutarch's admonition "not to join any party, but conduct one's affairs without party spirit, and with word and deed work toward unity."[5] Paul, concerned for the Corinthian Christians, challenged them to seek unity precisely so that there would be no σχίσματα among them.[6]

However, at the same time Paul acknowledged the ἔριδες which existed within the Christian network (1.11). For Paul, ἔρις was "one of the dominant characteristics of humans without Christ (Rom. 1.29; 2. Cor. 12.30; Gal. 5.20)," and yet here he regretfully linked it to his Christian ἀδελφοί,[7] whose "divided loyalties and ecclesiastical preferences"[8] illustrated the incongruency between their ontological reality ἐν Χριστῷ and their relational reality in the ἐκκλησία.[9] Even as a "divided team" is an oxymoron, so, too, is a "divided church." Yet this was the sad reality that Paul faced. Though the Corinthian Christians were neither apostates nor outsiders, their behaviour was that of σαρκικοί, making them no different than anyone else outside the boundaries of the church (1 Cor. 3.3–4). Trajan remarked that "whatever title we give them…men who are banded together for a common end will all the same become a political association before long."[10] Indeed, the different allegiances within the Christian ἐκκλησία were not unlike those of the secular ἐκκλησία, where individuals "were united primarily by personal bonds rather than ideology,"[11] and where one important measure of a leader was the kind of rhetorical eloquence which appears to have been a large part of the debate concerning Apollos and Paul (3.1–4).

Whether Paul liked it or not, he and Cephas and Apollos (like Aristides in Pergamum) respectively had become "points of anchorage" for different persons within the one Corinthian ἐκκλησία (1.12).[12] The slogans in 1.12 suggest that "belonging" to the Christian ἐκκλησία appears to have meant less than "belonging" to figures such as Paul or Apollos or Cephas.[13] Paul's term εἰμί, when linked with the genitive, conveys a relationship of possession or ownership.[14] The NRSV's translation of 1.12 as "I belong to..." brings this out more clearly than the NIV's "I follow..." Paul and the others named could be regarded as patrons, if you will, but not necessarily in the more narrow sense of direct economic dependence. As Petersen has shown, even as Paul was a client to Philemon in the financial sense, he was also a patron to Philemon in the spiritual sense.[15] In the οἶκος network the language of belonging usually referred to the relationship between parent and young child (as contrasted to an adult son or daughter) or between master and slave.[16] Hence, as suggested already, the close proximity of the 'ἐγὼ εἰμί slogans to the phrase τῶν Χλόης might very well imply that the attention given by church members to focal individuals like Paul the founder, Apollos the eloquent, or Cephas the pillar, simply revealed them to be little more than slaves or unreasoning children, not unlike "those of Chloe." Such a situation showed how childish the Corinthian Christians had become in the time since Paul's departure (3.1–4), allowing "ideas of order and hierarchy out of other spheres of life" to infiltrate the ἐκκλησία.[17]

An Identity Crisis

Herein lay the Problem behind the problem. Paul's challenge, οὐκ ἄνθρωποί ἐστε (3.4), reveals his conviction that the underlying issue in Corinth was not division itself, *but the fact that the Corinthians' divisiveness pointed to their inabililty to see the unique and special unity that was theirs* ἐν Χρίστῳ. Indeed, as D. Martin asserts, it was Paul's working assumption "that identity is established by participation in a larger entity."[18] *Who* we are is grounded in the reality of *whose* we are, i.e. to whom or to what do we belong as members? Was the Christian community in Corinth simply another relational network—another cult or *collegium* or political gathering—or did belonging to the church mean something more? Paul faced not only a crisis of unity, but also a question of identity. This is particularly evident in the fact that Paul's opening remarks about intra-church conflict are connected to baptism, arguably a key identity marker for the church.

"Every system has a boundary which separates it from things outside."[19] Within the walls lies a castle and within a combination of fences and hedges lies a family's property.[20] One such "fence" for the church (though by no means the only one), was Christian baptism, which distinguished those who "were being saved" from "the perishing" (1.18). At the same time, baptism served as an "entrance gate" into this Christian community. The key for Paul was that through this gate, one would enter a *new* and unique network in which distinctions of gender, ethnicity and socio-economic status were no longer relevant. We can see this paradigm in two other Pauline letters. In Gal. 3.27–28, Paul noted that those who were baptised εἰς Χριστόν "clothed themselves with Christ." As a visible sign of Christian faith (cf. vs. 23–26), baptism marked one as having come out from the old reality and become one (εἰς) in Christ (cf. 1 Cor. 12.13). The movement of a believer "towards a new orientation" through Christian baptism at the same time meant "movement away from an old orientation" such as societal distinctions of ethnicity and status.[21] Interestingly, Paul's words concerning baptism occur in the midst of a discussion on the status of Christians as "children (υἱοί) of God through faith in Christ Jesus" (3.26) and "heirs according to the promise" (3.29). Such familial imagery will be considered below. Likewise, in Romans, Paul presented baptism as a dramatic sign of entrance into new life through death to the old. "Do you not know that all of us who have been baptised into Christ Jesus were baptised into his death?" (Rom. 6.3) The imagery is quite striking; for Paul, baptism into Christ Jesus meant freedom from the dominion of sin and death, and freedom to consider oneself "alive to God in Christ Jesus" (Rom. 6.11). The old world with its old distinctions had little meaning inside the boundaries of the new community in Christ. "This means seeing baptism as having rather radical consequences. The common life in Christ, into which one was baptized, implied a unity and a solidarity which questioned religious, cultural, and social conditions of the ordinary world order."[22] Christian baptism was not unlike Jewish proselyte circumcision in that one who before was considered outside, part of the old order, was now inside, sharing the common identity of those within.

Returning to 1 Corinthians, we see that for Paul, even the boundary between Jew and Gentile lost its significance within the Christian network (1 Cor. 12.13). As seen already, the Corinthian church began its life as something of a mixed breed, with both Jewish and Gentile elements. Inasmuch as the Diaspora itself was "an inherently untidy experience" for many Jews, their rituals and laws served "to impose order on the system" and, thus, bolstered their shared sense of identity.[23] Yet, "as Christianity grew on Corinthian soil it became more and more a Gentile community,"[24] thereby provoking questions such as the one concerning food offered to idols, a major focus of Paul's attention in 1 Cor. 8–10, signifying that a Jew-Gentile dichotomy was still very much present in the "one body into which all were baptised" (12.13).[25] Similarly, the combination of Roman names (such as Paul and Justus) and Greek names (such as Sosthenes) among Corinthian Christians brings to mind the differences between things Roman and Hellenistic, another particularly delicate issue in Corinth. However, for believers, the boundaries and distinctions accepted in other networks in Corinth were no longer to be considered primary in their claims. The "old written code" (Rom. 7.6) which was a crucial boundary marker for the Jewish covenant community was itself rendered irrelevant *as a boundary marker* for those in the Christian ἐκκλησία. That which was all-important was the reality of God's mercy to both Jews and Gentiles (Rom. 1.16).[26] Even circumcision, that "most distinctively Jewish rite of transfer of status,"[27] Gentile to Jew, lost its significance for all those, Jew and Gentile alike, who were among "the called" (1 Cor. 1.18).

Christian baptism, then, was to be a "bridge between past and present, from the old order with its distinctions of ethnicity and social status to the new order of Christian community."[28] Problems arose, therefore, when the loyalties and distinctions of other networks continued to infiltrate the Christian community. Herman notes that the κοινωνία of the secular ἐκκλησία or πόλις could be lost amidst the many personal rivalries and competing ξένοι alliances which existed therein:

Networks of alliances linked factions from several cities and radiated from the great empires located at the fringes of the world of cities, creating a system of external friendships that could offer rewards—wealth, fame, position—even more tempting than those of the city itself.[29]

In systemic terms, the question was: in which network would persons find their primary place of belonging? Similarly, the danger for the Corinthian church was that the κοινωνία of its members, indeed the uniqueness of their bond in Christ, could be lost amidst lesser allegiances to various "focal individuals." In 1.16, Paul clearly stated that among those whom he had baptised were "the household of Stephanas" (τὸν Στεφανᾶ οἶκον), who were among the first converts in Achaia (16.15). This does not have to mean that only four or five persons were now loyal to Paul. The baptism of the head of an οἶκος often meant the baptism and Christian "belonging" of his whole household (cf. Acts 16.33). The newly Christianised head of the household "thereby had a ready-made group of supporters," not formal groups, *per se*, but different relational linkages within the network of the church.[30] If by baptism Stephanas looked to Paul as a "spiritual patron," then those under him—relatives, slaves, servants, clients, even certain friends—might well have looked to their patron's own spiritual patron with some deference.[31] The common thing about such "focal individuals" was that they enjoyed a "right to honour" among a particular cross section of the church,[32] implying, of course, that the opposite was also true: the fact that *some* aligned themselves with Paul suggests that *others* certainly did not! Even these competing affiliations were not set in stone, for as various persons like Prisca and Aquila moved out of the system (or as others like Apollos entered the system), the allegiances and alliances would shift, but the overall equilibrium based on this competition, and not on Christian κοινωνία, would remain.

In later passages in 1 Corinthians where baptism is mentioned, it is possible to see further influences from outside the boundaries of the church. In the analogy with Moses and the Israelites in 10.1ff., Paul argued that those who were "struck down" (10.5) had been idolaters, positioning one foot in the world of יהוה and one foot in the world of other gods and allegiances. Likewise, in 12.13ff. Paul showed that old societal distinctions which should have lost their significance still threatened the "one body" into which all were baptised. The only other report of baptism in 1 Corinthians concerns the enigmatic reference to being baptised for the dead (15.29): Ἐπεὶ τί ποιήσουσιν οἱ βαπτιζόμενοι ὑπὲρ τῶν νεκρῶν; εἰ ὅλως νεκροὶ οὐκ ἐγείρονται, τί καὶ βαπτίζονται ὑπὲρ αὐτῶν; While this passage has been compared with 2 Maccabees 12.43—"For if he were not expecting that those who had fallen would rise again, it would have been superfluous and foolish to pray for the dead" (ὑπὲρ ἀναστάσεως διαλογιζόμενος)—neither passage elucidates the practices to which they refer. Was Paul speaking about a Corinthian practice of which we are unaware? DeMaris answers in the affirmative, arguing for evidence of "a distinctively Corinthian practice,"[33] while Winter disagrees and calls for an alternative way of reading the text.[34] What is clear, however, from a reading of the surrounding epistolary context (15.29–34) is that the concerns raised by certain Corinthian Christians no doubt arose through their encounters with other people who had "no knowledge of God" (ἀγνωσίαν θεοῦ, v.34). Indeed, Paul's warning that "bad company ruins good morals" (15.33), as well as his reference to a Corinthian slogan ("Eat and drink, for tomorrow we may die," 15.32), reflect the language of the *collegia* in which many members probably continued to operate. As already noted, most voluntary associations, not simply the so-called burial guilds, included among their duties the arrangement of funerals for their members (although this is certainly not all that they did).[35] Most likely, concerns about death and dying from outside the ἐκκλησία were brought into it by those members who likewise belonged to other networks. [36] The resurrection faith was to differentiate those of "a sober and right mind" (15.34) from those who had "merely human hopes" (15.32), yet Paul's extended argument on resurrection, and specifically on the nature of the resurrected body, suggests that the same questions outside the ἐκκλησία were being raised inside the ἐκκλησία.[37] Whatever the precise meaning, therefore, of οἱ βαπτιζόμενοι ὑπὲρ τῶν νεκρῶν, the fact remains that even here we can see that discussion on baptism (and resurrection faith) is in the context of Christian distinctiveness or, rather, the disappointing lack of distinctiveness.

Thus, it may be said concerning some Corinthian Christians, that their sense of belonging was found not within the entire company of those ἐν

Χριστῷ, but rather with a few others in the church who affiliated themselves with a particular leader[38] or shared common membership in other overlapping networks (such as various *collegia*). Baptism, the very marker which was meant to be a sign of the identity and unity of the Christian ἐκκλησία, had itself been co-opted by those "still behaving according to human inclinations" (3.3) and thereby became another mark of segregation and competition. Many Christians who should have understood themselves as "those of Christ" instead saw themselves as "those of Paul (Apollos, Cephas)," and in doing so, proved that the Christian church was not that different from the competitive network of the secular ἐκκλησία. Though Paul chose to use that very term, ἐκκλησία, in describing the neophyte Christian community, a different understanding of the term was needed. Indeed, a new paradigm of identity was needed, one which would challenge the Corinthians to see one another and their leaders in a new, yet not unfamiliar, way.

Belonging in the New Testament

Here, we consider Paul's attempts in 1 Cor. 1–4 to alter the systemic paradigm which the Corinthians had regarding their own communal life, with particular attention given to Paul's definition of the Christian system in terms of a set-apart, sanctified community of belonging. As already shown, "belonging" was crucial to the identity of an individual or group; this is evident throughout the New Testament, where individuals were often defined in terms of their belonging to something bigger than themselves. Individuals in the Gospels or Acts were often designated by their *household* connections (Jesus, son of Joseph, Lk. 4.22; cf. 3.23ff. and Mt: 1.2ff.; "the son of Timaeus," Mk. 10.46; James the son of Alphaeus, Lk. 6.15), or by their *city/region* of origin (Jesus of Nazareth, Mk. 1.24 and elsewhere; Saul of Tarsus, Acts 9.11). At times, persons were described in terms of *occupation* (Matthew the tax collector, Mt. 10.3; Cornelius a centurion, Acts 10.22), *religio-political affiliation* (Simon, τὸν καλούμενον Ζηλωτὴν, Lk. 6.15), or some combination of factors (Lydia, πορφυρόπωλις πόλεως Θυατείρων σεβομένη τὸν θεόν, Acts 16.14). Indeed, certain individuals are identified *only* by their systemic position, such as "the centurion's servant" of Luke 7. Similarly, a change in life could be indicated by a change in designation, sometimes indicating both continuity and discontinuity with one's former life. Thus, Peter and Andrew, the fishermen (ἁλιεῖς) become "fishers of men" (ἁλιεῖς ἀνθρώπων, Mk. 1.16–17 NIV), and James and John, formerly designated only as the sons of Zebedee were nicknamed by Jesus as the "Sons of Thunder" (Βοανηργές, ὅ ἐστιν Υἱοὶ Βροντῆς, Mk. 3.17).[39] Even the move from the Hebrew שָׁאוּל to the Roman cognomen *Paulus* in Acts 13.9 coincides with a change in mission from being a preacher to fellow Jews (ἄνδρες ἀδελφοί, υἱοὶ γένους Ἀβραάμ, 13.26) to an apostle to the Gentiles (13.46). In these and many other cases, we see that individuals' identities were often clearly designated in relational terms: to what network(s) did they belong?

If there are any doubts that both "belonging" and the distinctiveness of the Christian community within the larger system of the Corinthian πολιτεία are central themes in Paul's letter, they are quickly dispelled with even a cursory reading of the apostle's opening words. From the beginning, Paul's words make it clear that the church's members, though they dwelt in Corinth, were actually to see themselves as part of a larger system of Christians "in every place" (πᾶσιν τοῖς ἐπικαλουμένοις τὸ ὄνομα τοῦ κυρίου ἡμῶν Ἰησοῦ Χριστοῦ ἐν παντὶ τόπῳ, 1.2). In comparison with other Pauline letters, this terminology—"together with all those..." (σὺν πᾶσιν)—is unique to the Corinthian salutations,[40] and immediately suggests the importance of "belonging" as a theme of this letter. Those who would "call on the name of the Lord Jesus" (1.2) were to see themselves as called into the κοινωνία of God's Son (1.9). The context of this κοινωνία, Paul said, was within the boundaries of the Christian "church": ἡ ἐκκλησία τοῦ θεοῦ τῇ οὔσῃ ἐν Κορίνθῳ (1.2).

It may be asked, however, why we should focus attention on the term ἐκκλησία at all, especially since it is not explicitly prevalent in these chapters. Why not, instead, move immediately to Paul's words concerning the cross in 1.17ff.? Two reasons may be mentioned. First, Paul himself began this letter not simply by speaking of ἡ ἐκκλησία, but also by *qualifying* what this network, this ἐκκλησία, actually was to be. As we examine his "temple" imagery, his emphasis on "sanctification" and "set-apartness," we keep coming back to the fact that these other explicit terms and images refer ultimately to the ἐκκλησία. While Paul would use many images to describe the church (i.e. body, temple, field, etc.), it was still "the church of God in Corinth" to which he was pointing. It may be argued that the ἐκκλησία was implicit throughout Paul's discussion in 1–4, even as it would become more explicit in ch. 14. Second, it is precisely because the term ἐκκλησία is not unique to 1 Corinthians that it is all the more important to understand what Paul meant when he used the term in this systemic context. *Why* did he qualify the church immediately with terms of "set-apartness" and "holiness," even as he qualified his apostleship from the start (1.1–2)? It is often noted that Paul probably was thinking of the LXX use of ἐκκλησία when he used it, but what exactly does this mean? Was there one generic usage on which he likely relied? These are the kinds of questions that will be explored in this section, and which I believe deserve some exploration.

We have already considered the secular ἐκκλησία as a relational network in Corinth and one which intersected with the Christian network. Indeed, it may be argued that the Christian communities which Paul did designate from the outset as ἐκκλησία are ones in which the issue of distinctiveness from the world was particularly relevant.[41] In the case of 1 Thessalonians, problems of repression and persecution from outside the church led Paul to remind the Christians there that God's will was ὁ ἁγιασμὸς ὑμῶν (4.3). They were, Paul asserted, υἱοί φωτός and υἱοί ἡμέρας (5.5), to be distinguished from "those who sleep" (5.6) and engaged in πορνεία (4.3ff.). In the case of Galatians, the situation was much more like that in Corinth, where views and practices deemed important "outside" the church were being incorporated into the life of the ἐκκλησία. Thus, to the Christians there as in Corinth, Paul differentiated his gospel from any other gospel κατὰ ἄνθρωπον (Gal. 1.11).[42]

Outside of the salutations, however, ἐκκλησία is used rather infrequently in the other undisputed Pauline letters, as already mentioned. In 1 Corinthians, on the other hand, it appears (in one of its various forms) no less than 22 times. Only Acts (21) and Revelation (20) come close to this high usage in the New Testament. Much has been said about Paul's choice of ἐκκλησία as a designation of the Christian community, but the point that remains largely undiscussed is why Paul would use the term so much in this particular letter to a conflict-challenged community. In contrast to Witherington's comment that Paul chose a "familiar term" in using ἐκκλησία, the argument here will be made that the apostle had, either consciously or subconsiously, a more specific meaning derived from key passages in the Septuagint.[43] In particular, the importance of the term in Chronicles, Ezra-Nehemiah and Psalms will be noted.

The Use of ἐκκλησία in the LXX

As early as Schmidt, it was noted that ἐκκλησία was one common translation of the Hebrew root קהל, referring to the gathered community and more specifically, either implicitly or explicitly, to "the assembly of the LORD."[44] The noun ἐκκλησία is actually quite rare in the Torah, where instead we more often see συναγωγή (Gen. 28.3; 35.11; 48.4) or some variant of the verb form ἐκκλησίασον (Lev. 8.3; Num. 20.8; Deut. 4.10; 31.12,28).[45] The people could be gathered for the purpose of battle (Judg. 20.2; 1 Sam. 17.47), dedication and sacrifice (1 Kin. 8.14, 65) or, especially in the Psalms, praise and worship (Ps. 21.26; 34.18; etc.). The most notable ἐκκλησία, perhaps, is the gathering of the tribes "as one man" at Mizpah (13 km north of Jerusalem) for the purpose of waging war against one of their fellow tribes, Benjamin (Jud. 20.2; 21.5,8).[46] In the Psalms, the ἐκκλησία is always the setting for the Psalmist's praise and thanksgiving (21.26; 34.18; 39.10; 106.32; 149.1), and in one intriguing passage, the ἐκκλησία is the assembly of heavenly beings or υἱοί θεοῦ, also described as the "holy" or "set-apart ones" (88.6–8).

It is only later, in Chronicles and Ezra/Nehemiah, that we find the most frequent usage of ἐκκλησία, and it is here that we may argue for the greatest correlation with Paul's use of the term. In these books, ἐκκλησία almost always refers to the people gathered together *with godly kings or leaders for godly purposes*, usually for the purpose of *restoration or renewed sanctification*. This statement deserves further elucidation. We see this pattern emerge with the return of the ark from Kiriath-jearim by David (1 Chr. 13.2). Here, David addressed "the whole assembly (ἐκκλησία) of Israel" with an entreaty, not a command, to send abroad πρὸς τοὺς ἀδελφοὺς ἡμῶν, that all may come together and and bring the ark back *en masse*. David's pleas fell on fertile ground, for it says that this plan pleased παντὸς τοῦ λαοῦ (13.4). Again, during the dedication of the temple by Solomon (2 Chr. 6.3; cf. also 1 Kings 8), the king turned and blessed πᾶσαν ἐκκλησίαν Ισραηλ, and later he and the entire ἐκκλησία held a festival of celebration (2 Chr. 7.8). Other instances include the triumphal meeting under Jehoshaphat (2 Chr. 20.5, 14), when the assembly was strengthened for battle, assured by the godly king that the Lord was μεθ' ὑμῶν (20.17). In a similar way, members of the ἐκκλησία were present for the return of a true king, Joash, to the throne (23.3), as well as for the restoration of temple worship under Hezekiah (29.28, 31–32; 30.2, 13, 23–25). The term ἐκκλησία is similarly used in Ezra and Nehemiah to speak of the community gathered together under their godly leaders for the purpose of prayer, repentance, and the restoration of temple worship (cf. Ez. 2.64; 10.1,12,14; Neh. 5.13; 7.66; 8.17; 13.1). Interestingly, the only occurrence of ἐκκλησία in the prophets is also found within the context of a call for restoration and sanctification: "Blow the trumpet in Zion; sanctify a fast; call a solemn assembly; gather the people. Sanctify the congregation" (ἁγιάσατε ἐκκλησίαν, Joel 2.15–16). Here, too, the ἐκκλησία was to be holy, set apart.

This emphasis on the sanctified or restored ἐκκλησία was often conveyed through holiness language, so that what was sanctified was set apart or marked off by boundaries from that which was profane or common.[47] In the Torah, God was said to be δεδοξασμένος ἐν ἁγίοις (Ex. 15.11), as contrasted with other gods (θεοῖς), and his Name likewise was holy and not to be profaned (Lev. 22.2). The Sabbath also was ἅγιον, so that work which was appropriate on other days was forbidden on the day set apart for rest and in honour of the Lord (Ex. 31.14; 35.2).[48] Nazirites were considered holy during the period of their vows, during which time they would "separate themselves" from the rest of the people (Num. 6.5–8). The sacrificial offerings were "holy to the Lord" (Ex 30.10) and even that which was left of the grain offering was reserved for the priests only to eat (Lev. 2.3). The "tithe of the land" was to be considered holy, treated in a different way than the other ninety percent which belonged to the owner of the land or flock (Lev. 27.30–32).

The most prevalent usage of holiness language, however, concerned the "holy place," the Tabernacle (Num. 7), and the utensils and oil used within it (Ex. 30.25ff.). Similar language was later used of the Jerusalem Temple (1 Kin. 6.16).[49] Even so, the Israelites were to see themselves as holy, ὅτι ἅγιος ἐγὼ κύριος ὁ θεὸς ὑμῶν (Lev. 19.2; also 11.44–45; 20.7; 21.7 and elsewhere). It is because God has separated these people from other peoples that they were to consider themselves ἅγιοι (Lev.

20.26), even as God separated clean from unclean animals (Lev. 20.25). Despite the fact that a distinction was made between the priests and the rest of Israel (Lev. 20), together all the people were described as "a priestly people, a holy nation" (βασίλειον ἱεράτευμα καὶ ἔθνος ἅγιον, Ex. 19.6).

Thus, while in the πολιτεία of Paul's day, the ἐκκλησία was associated with the assembly of citizens who had ἐξουσία and privileges denied to those outside their network (again, see *3.3.2*), in the Septuagint it referred instead to the sanctified assembly. Particularly in Chronicles and Ezra/Nehemiah, where ἐκκλησία is most prevalent, the emphasis was on the commitment or recommitment of the set-apart people under a godly leader. In one particularly interesting case in 2 Chronicles, ἡ ἐκκλησία refers to a network of people assembled with Jeroboam, their *recognised* but unofficial leader, against the authorised king, Rehoboam:[50]

καὶ ἦλθεν Ιεροβοαμ καὶ πᾶσα ἡ ἐκκλησία Ισραηλ πρὸς Ροβοαμ λέγοντες, ὁ πατήρ σου ἐσκλήρυνεν τὸν ζυγὸν ἡμῶν καὶ νῦν ἄφες ἀπὸ τῆς δουλείας τοῦ πατρός σου τῆς σκληρᾶς καὶ ἀπὸ τοῦ ζυγοῦ αὐτοῦ τοῦ βαρέος οὗ ἔδωκεν ἐφ' ἡμᾶς καὶ δουλεύσομέν σοι (2 Chr. 10.3–4).

The promise made by Ιεροβοαμ καὶ πᾶσα ἡ ἐκκλησία Ισραηλ to follow Rehoboam if he would only lighten the load laid on them by Solomon echoes the earlier promise made by the people to Rehoboam's grandfather, David: "We are yours, O David; and with you, O son of Jesse!" (1 Chr. 12.19; see 11.1–13.14). However, this is where the similarities between these two assemblies end, as seen below.

First, in the opening scene of the Rehoboam incident, the people of the ἐκκλησία were still prepared, at least in theory, to follow the king's leadership; yet, their call to Jeroboam may have indicated a degree of ambivalence on their part that is missing from the David tale. Were the people weighing their options at that point?

Second, while David had agreed to "knit his heart" to the people if they were coming to him εἰς εἰρήνην (1 Chr. 12.18), Rehoboam and his young advisors stood aloof from the ἐκκλησία, forming another relational system distinct from them. Indeed, there are at least three intersecting networks that may be discerned in the Rehoboam story: the ἐκκλησία, later described simply as "all the people" (πᾶς ὁ λαός, 10.12) or "all

Israel" (πᾶς Ισραηλ, 10.16), linked unofficially here with Jeroboam; the older advisors who had worked with Solomon and now were part of Rehoboam's court; and the younger advisors, who are described as having grown up with the king. Rehoboam is a point of anchorage in this array of systems/networks, yet his actions and words allowed a gulf to grow between himself and the ἐκκλησία, with the latter forming a response in reaction to whatever the king decided to do.

Third, Rehoboam's decision to act on the advice given to him by his young advisors reflects his preference of their more familiar "wisdom" over the proven success rate of his father's one-time advisors. Indeed, by segregating the two networks in this way, instead of having representatives of both sets of advisors in one body before him, the king essentially set up a conflictual situation in which any decision he made would inevitably be connected with the choice of one relational system over another. His strategy, in essence, promoted disunity even before a decision was reached and put before "the people." This is in marked contrast with David's decision to form a covenant with πάντες πρεσβύτεροι Ισραηλ (1 Chr. 11.3) and his chiefs gave him strong support for his kingship (11.10). *Fourth,* upon hearing the king's ill-chosen proclamation, the response the ἐκκλησία gave, εἰς τὰ σκηνώματα σου Ισραηλ νῦν βλέπε τὸν οἶκόν σου Δαυιδ (10.16), was nothing less than a rejection of the recently-established paradigm of Davidic monarchy (represented by the οἶκόν) in favour of their more familiar pattern of tribal confederation (represented by the tents or σκηνώματα). I have devoted some space to this passage, precisely because of the unique way in which it supports the argument that the ἐκκλησία was the assembly of persons committing themselves to the Lord in connection with a respected leader.

The question remains, however, whether this kind of usage in the Chronicles and elsewhere in the LXX was on Paul's mind when he used the term in 1 Corinthians. Certainly, it would be saying far too much to insist upon specific scriptural echoes each time the apostle referred to ἐκκλησία. However, at the same time *he could hardly have been unaware* of the features in biblical usage of ἐκκλησία shown above. Indeed, elsewhere (2.9) Paul cited a passage ("it is written") that does not directly correspond with any known text of Hebrew Scripture. In that instance, it has been argued by several scholars that Paul was either quoting from memory, thereby making mental mistakes in his citation, or drawing upon a source for the scriptural citation now lost to us.[51] The point here is that we do not need to argue for or against the apostle's reliance on LXX renderings of ἐκκλησία solely on the basis of actual citations or clear allusions or echoes. Thus, in the following discussion, while it would be unwise to overstate the case, I believe that we can point to an awareness, *conscious or subconscious*, on Paul's part when he used ἐκκλησία.

A Sanctified Congregation

Turning, then, to 1 Corinthians, we can see how many of the occurrences of ἐκκλησία seem to echo the twin Septuagint themes of the *whole* assembly gathered together, i.e. the unity of the community, and the *sanctified/restored* assembly, i.e. the set-apartness of the community.[52] This is first apparent in 1 Cor. 1.2, where Paul speaks of the church of God (τῇ ἐκκλησίᾳ τοῦ θεοῦ) as ἡγιασμένοις ἐν Χριστῷ Ἰησοῦ, and then further adds that these members were "called to be saints" (κλητοῖς ἁγίοις). We may note here the correspondence between the term ἐκκλησία and "holiness language."[53] The term ἡγιασμένοις, the perfect passive participle of ἁγιάζω—a word group unique to the Greek scriptures and subsequent ecclesiastical writings—occurs only in 1.2 and in two instances in Acts (20.32 and 26.18).[54] The language of holiness and "church" appear together again in the case of the litigious members, as Paul criticised the Christians for failing to take their grievances before "the saints" (τῶν ἁγίων, 6:1), and distinguished οἱ ἅγιοι (6.2) from those who "are of no account in the church" (τοὺς ἐξουθενημένους ἐν τῇ ἐκκλησίᾳ). Later, in 6.11, he spoke of the Corinthian Christians as those who had been "washed, sanctified (ἡγιάσθητε) and justified," set apart both from their former life and from the rest of the world. Also, in 10.32, ἡ ἐκκλησία τοῦ θεοῦ is distinguished from both the "Jews" and the "Greeks."[55]

Paul conveyed a similar sense of strong boundaries between church and outside networks through his temple imagery. Beginning with the agricultural image of the church as a field (3.6–9), Paul moved into the imagery of a building (θεοῦ οἰκοδομή), the foundation of which he himself, by the grace of God, laid (3.9). This, in turn, led him to use what Hays describes as the "audacious metaphor" of the Temple for the

Christian assembly (ναός θεοῦ, 3.16–17).⁵⁶ The term ναός is significant, as it refers not simply to the temple enclosure, ὁ ἱερός, but to the sanctuary itself, the Holy Place in which God dwells (οἰκεῖ). In a similar way, Paul claimed that "God's Spirit dwells (οἰκεῖ) in you" (plural, 3.16).⁵⁷ Such imagery is all the more remarkable when one considers that the Jerusalem Temple was still standing at the time Paul wrote these words. Indeed, the only other contemporaries of Paul to speak of their community in similar terms were the sectarians at Qumran, as seen in 1QS 8.5–9 (predating Christianity). There, the Council of the Community is described as "a House of Holiness (קדש) for Israel," "a Most Holy Dwelling Place for Aaron," "a House of Perfection and Truth in Israel." For both the Qumran sectarians and the members of the Corinthian ἐκκλησία, a paradigm shift was occurring, as they respectively were challenged to look *not* to the familiar Jerusalem Temple as the "place where the glory of God resides," but rather to their own unique and set-apart community.⁵⁸

In 6.18–19, Paul again used temple imagery, asserting that unlike other sins committed "outside the body" (ἐκτὸς τοῦ σώματός), sins of sexual immorality were εἰς τὸ ἴδιον σῶμα. The last phrase has been erroneously translated in the RSV as "against his own body," conveying a sense of the personal consequences of sexual sins. However, the context of the verse suggests instead a collectivist or systemic reading. For while verse 16 speaks of an individual believer joining his body with that of a prostitute (all words here are in the singular),⁵⁹ in the verses that immediately follow, Paul changes to the plural when he asks the church members: "Do you not know that **your** (ὑμῶν, plural) body (σῶμα, singular) is a temple of the Holy Spirit within **you** (ὑμῖν, plural), which **you have** (ἔχετε, plural) from God, and that **you are** not **your own** (ἐστὲ ἑαυτῶν, plural)? For **you were bought** (ἠγοράσθητε, plural) with a price; therefore **glorify** (δοξάσατε, plural) God in **your** (ὑμῶν, plural) body (σώματι, singular)" (6.19–20). It is not simply that sexual immorality somehow affects the physical body of the individual involved, but rather that such sin has harmful consequences for the entire Christian community, the Body of Christ and God's holy Temple.⁶⁰ Such an interpretation obviously differs from that of Fee and others, who argue that the "distributive singular" be read out of the text ("where something belonging to each person in a group is placed in the singular"),[61] thus emphasising that "one's own body" (as in 7.4) is the concern here. This is accepted by several scholars despite the fact that the temple imagery used earlier in 3.16 clearly concerns the collective group, and that "the members of the body" of 6.15 directly corresponds to the phrase in 12.14, 27, where a collectivist meaning is understood. In a related passage by Musonius Rufus, the author suggests that it is possible for one to commit immoral sin and yet "it affects none of the people around him."[62] Paul, however, argues systemically that the actions of church members (whether taking a fellow believer to court or a prostitute to bed) do indeed have an effect on "the body itself" (τὸ ἴδιον σῶμα). Thus, the ἴδιον in verse 18 is part of an important programme of redefining the ἐκκλησία as the sanctified and set-apart community.

For Paul, then, the Corinthian ἐκκλησία was to be marked by a sanctification that was not its own. Because the church's members had been "bought with a price" (6.19–20), they belonged first and foremost to God (3.23) and, therefore, were together a holy and distinctive congregation. Yet, the Christian ἐκκλησία was still very much connected to other societal networks. As a "church in the marketplace," a physical withdrawal was not possible.[63] An example of this difficulty is found in 1 Cor. 14.20–25, where Paul argued that any ἄπιστοι καὶ ἰδιῶται who were present during worship and witnessed the orderliness and edification of members through the use of prophetic words (as opposed to a cacophony of γλῶσσαι) would acknowledge the distinctiveness of the Christian ἐκκλησία.[64] The church's conduct in worship would reveal its identity as ἐκκλησία.

Thus, it might be little surprise to find that the most prevalent use of ἐκκλησία in 1 Corinthians occurred in passages dealing directly with the church's worship (10.32; 11.16, 18, 22; 12.28; 14.4, 5, 12, 19, 23, 28, 33–34). Here, we see a greater parallel with the use of ἐκκλησία in the Psalms than with, for instance, the Rehoboam incident. Ironically, it was precisely in the Corinthian worship gatherings, when the Christians "came together as the church" (συνερχομένων ὑμῶν ἐν ἐκκλησίᾳ, 11.18) that so much internal conflict revealed itself, i.e. in questions about the Lord's Supper (chs. 10–11), spiritual gifts (ch. 12), and order in the church's worship (ch. 14). It is noteworthy that in 1 Cor. 14, where the use of ἐκκλησία is most prominent, the term was linked with the notion of "building up" (οἰκοδομή), a concept fairly unique in religious talk of the time.[65] Yet it is consonant with the implicit notion in the Psalter that the Psalmist's praise (22.25—LXX 21.26), thanksgiving (35.18—LXX 34.18), or news of deliverance by God (40.9—LXX 39.10) somehow strengthened the entire ἐκκλησία. However, while in the Psalms, the ἐκκλησία was usually the background for the Psalmist's praise or thanksgiving, Paul's use of the term in 1 Corinthians challenges *all* in the ἐκκλησία to listen to one another and encourage one another. An example of this is found in 14.5, where Paul calls for priority to be given to prophecy over glossalalia, ἵνα ἡ ἐκκλησία οἰκοδομὴν λάβη.[66] The same word which in 2 Cor. 10.8 is used to speak of Paul's own authority "which the Lord gave for building up (οἰκοδόμην) and not for tearing down," is found throughout 1 Cor. 14—in verses 3, 5, 12, 26—all pointing to encouragement for the sake of the whole ἐκκλησία. Other forms of οἰκοδόμη are likewise found in 8.1; 10.23; 14.4,17. Interestingly, Paul added that a believer could be emboldened by the bad example of a fellow church member; he or she would be "built up" to do wrong (οἰκοδομηθήσεται, future passive, 8.10).

What is important in this is that, while many of the uses of the οἶκος word group so prominent later in the Pastorals are missing in 1 Corinthians,[67] what is very much present in this letter is a concept of "building up" directly connected with the gathered worshipping community. Again, as in the Psalms, the sanctified and set-apart community would be edified (from the Lt. aedificabitur, for οἰκοδομηθήσεται, 8.10) by the words and worship of all its members. While Paul's role as "master builder" was unique (see more in *4.4.5*), each and every Corinthian Christian was called to take notice of how s/he ἐποικοδομεῖ the living temple that was the ἐκκλησία (3.10). Thus, the prominence given to the term ἐκκλησία in passages dealing with the distinctiveness of the worshipping community, particularly in 1 Cor. 14, suggests that Paul likely was aware of the word's usage in the Psalms.

Earlier, I devoted some space to the Rehoboam incident, not because Paul makes clear reference to the passage (which he does not), but because of the potential light it sheds on *several* aspects of the nature of the ἐκκλησία as understood by the Chronicler and possibly shared by

Paul. I have already argued that Paul acknowledged the need for the Christian ἐκκλησία to be a sanctified community, and that he saw the assembly as most clearly ἐκκλησία τοῦ θεοῦ when they were gathered together for worship. Beyond this, there are in 1 Corinthians a few other possible "echoes" of the use of ἐκκλησία in Chronicles/Ezra/Nehemiah. First, the importance of the godly leader as integral to the unity and spiritual renewal of the entire ἐκκλησία appears to have been a major issue for Paul throughout the letter. Not only do we see ἐκκλησία mentioned in the immediate context of both μιμηταί μου γίνεσθε passages (cf. 4.16–17;10.32–34), but Paul also clearly defined God's appointed leadership roles ἐν τῇ ἐκκλησίᾳ: first apostles, second prophets, third teachers, etc. (12.28). God appointed these ministries, Paul asserted, to encourage order and unity in the church.

Related to this, in the LXX occurrences of ἐκκλησία, it is always the *entire* community or *all* the people that is represented by the term. While Paul may not specifically have had in mind the Rehoboam incident in 2 Chr.10, he certainly appeared to address a similar systemic issue: the possibility of a divided ἐκκλησία, cut off from the officially appointed leader. Was Apollos the Corinthians' Jeroboam? Certainly, the Corinthians were willing to consult Paul on certain matters (7.1), but were they willing to follow his advice or admonitions on these or unwritten issues? While Rehoboam distanced himself from the people of the assembly, listening instead to a "wisdom" that was hardly wise, Paul instead appears to have followed the examples of David and other wiser kings in attempting to call the Corinthians away from worldly σοφία and back to a covenant with God. Like David, and clearly unlike Rehoboam, Paul reached out to all the church's members and not simply to "those of Paul" (1.12). The *combination* in 1 Cor. 1–4 of the call to sanctification *and* acknowledgement of Paul's own leadership is a pattern that was present throughout Chronicles/Ezra/Nehemiah, suggesting that *it is a viable possibility* that Paul was somehow drawing upon these stories as he defined the system for his fellow believers in Corinth.[68] At the very least, the Septuagint offered a tradition concerning the ἐκκλησία that allowed Paul to utilise and define the term in a similar way for his own congregation.

As a final note on Paul's attempt to redefine ἐκκλησία for the Corinthian network, it is important to recall that the church was to be seen by its members as something distinct from the σαρκινοί (3.1), yet at the same time open in some way to both ἰδιῶται καὶ ἄπιστοι (14.23). Ἡ ἐκκλησία was distinguished from Ἰουδαῖοι καὶ Ἕλληνες, yet it contained within its boundaries both Jews and Greeks, as well as representatives from several other Corinthian networks (12.13). When Paul called for the mutual "encouragement" of the members of the ἐκκλησία, it was because, in his paradigm, the church IS one.[69] Yet the diversity of membership which marked the Christian network—something "new in pagan society"[70] —made it quite difficult to maintain a clear corporate identity and boundaries, especially when baptism proved inadequate as a unifying and distinguishing mark. As seen in 1 Cor. 12.12–13, Paul clearly did not dispense with baptism, but in 1.17ff., he quickly set out to deepen the Corinthians' understanding of the initiation rite by pointing beyond it to an even deeper identity/boundary mark.

Redefining Boundaries

Radical Change

This section builds on the previous one, answering the question: What was to be the primary identity marker of the Christian network, and how would those within be differentiated from those outside? Morgan, et al., differentiate between two types of change in a system: *first-order change* is that which is acceptable to those within a network or system, for it involves minor changes that are familiar and not threatening to the integrity or balance of the overall structure of the system. *Second-order change*, however, is that which threatens to alter the actual homeostatic balance of the entire system.[71] Thus, in answer to the query, "did baptism of slaves bring about a different relationship with a Christian owner," Aristides suggests that it did; slaves were then called brothers and sisters without distinction. But did their roles change? "The rest of the evidence suggests that they did not."[72] For those in the ἐκκλησία whose lives had been shaped by the accepted boundaries of the Graeco-Roman social world, "masters [and slaves] made uneasy colleagues."[73] Corinthian slaves (or women or gentiles or clients, etc.) were initiated into the Christian network through baptism (first-order change), but the internal ἔριδες addressed by Paul suggests that real change, radical change, second-order charge, was still needed in the Christian ἐκκλησία.

It has been noted that in the opening verses of 1 Corinthians, Paul asserted that those within the boundaries of the Christian network were defined as "set-apart ones" (1.2). He spoke of their κοινωνία of Christ (1.9), yet contrasted this ideal with the dismal reality of quarrels and internal alliances (1.11ff). With 1.17ff., Paul began a new line of thought and introduced a markedly different way of viewing common membership in the one church:

> οὐ γὰρ ἀπέστειλέν με Χριστὸς βαπτίζειν ἀλλὰ εὐαγγελίζεσθαι, οὐκ ἐν σοφίᾳ λόγου, ἵνα μὴ κενωθῇ ὁ σταυρὸς τοῦ Χριστοῦ. 18 Ὁ λόγος γὰρ ὁ τοῦ σταυροῦ τοῖς μὲν ἀπολλυμένοις μωρία ἐστίν, τοῖς δὲ σῳζομένοις ἡμῖν δύναμις θεοῦ ἐστιν. 19 γέγραπται γάρ, Ἀπολῶ τὴν σοφίαν τῶν σοφῶν καὶ τὴν σύνεσιν τῶν συνετῶν ἀθετήσω. 20 ποῦ σοφός; ποῦ γραμματεύς; ποῦ συζητητὴς τοῦ αἰῶνος τούτου; οὐχὶ ἐμώρανεν ὁ θεὸς τὴν σοφίαν τοῦ κόσμου; 21 ἐπειδὴ γὰρ ἐν τῇ σοφίᾳ τοῦ θεοῦ οὐκ ἔγνω ὁ κόσμος διὰ τῆς σοφίας τὸν θεόν, εὐδόκησεν ὁ θεὸς διὰ τῆς μωρίας τοῦ κηρύγματος σῶσαι τοὺς πιστεύοντας· 22 ἐπειδὴ καὶ Ἰουδαῖοι σημεῖα αἰτοῦσιν καὶ Ἕλληνες σοφίαν ζητοῦσιν, 23 ἡμεῖς δὲ κηρύσσομεν Χριστὸν ἐσταυρωμένον, Ἰουδαίοις μὲν σκάνδαλον, ἔθνεσιν δὲ μωρίαν, 24 αὐτοῖς δὲ τοῖς κλητοῖς, Ἰουδαίοις τε καὶ Ἕλλησιν, Χριστὸν θεοῦ δύναμιν καὶ θεοῦ σοφίαν.

The cross—ὁ σταυρός—was offered here as the primary identity marker for those in the Christian ἐκκλησία. The introduction of the cross at this point is interesting, since it appears to move the discussion away from the apostle's concern over the ἔριδες. Indeed, Conzelmann speaks of *"die ringförmige Komposition"* of 1.18–3.23, in which "3.18–23 leads back to the starting point."[74] Yet, others have since argued that there is continuity between this "digression" on the message of the cross and the divisive spirit which Paul was confronting in earlier verses.[75] In essence, this "digression" on ὁ σταυρός answered the unspoken query, "If Christians were the set-apart ones, from what were they set apart?" For Paul, the cross created a new, all-encompassing dichotomy that effectively reconstituted the Corinthians' relational universe, replacing the more familiar dichotomies of Jew and Greek (1.22–24), foolish and wise (1.26–27), weak and strong. Instead of multiple *overlapping* networks (see *fig.*

3.b above), now there were only two *mutually-exclusive* ones: "those who are perishing" (ἀπολλυμένοι) and "those who are being saved" (σῳζομένοι). The message of the cross was the instrument of "second-order change," as it were, by which these two networks were distinguished one from another.[76] In order to understand this Pauline paradigm, it might be helpful to consider the way Paul used ὁ σταυρός in 1.17ff. in light of its use in his other letters.

The term σταυρός is surprisingly rare in the undisputed Pauline letters, found only three times in Galatians (5.11; 6.12, 14), twice in Philippians (2.8; 3.18), and twice in 1 Corinthians (1.17–18). Likewise, the various forms of the verb σταυρόω are also fairly uncommon in Paul, concentrated mostly in Galatians (3.1; 5.24; 6.14) and 1 Corinthians (1.13,23; 2.2,8; also 2 Cor. 13.4).[77] Within these letters, however, there is strong continuity in Paul's use of σταυρός-σταυρόω. While later in Ephesians and Colossians, the power of the cross to reconcile disparate peoples (i.e. Jews and Gentiles) would be emphasised (Eph. 2.16; Col. 1.20; 2.14), in the earlier Pauline letters, the stress was on the power of the cross to create a distinct and wholly separate network. Thus, in Galatians 5.2–15, the cross is pictured as a σκάνδαλον to those still clinging to the need for circumcision, and the two networks are viewed in mutually exclusive terms: to seek justification by the Mosaic Law was to "sever oneself" (καταργέω) from Christ and, implicitly, from the community of those who were ἐν Χριστῷ (5.4). In light of this exclusivity, Christians in that church were warned by the apostle against "biting and devouring one another" (5.15). Unity here was linked with their corporate identity, as a network connected with, yet distinct from, both Judaism and other contemporary relational networks.

What is noteworthy about the Galatians argument is the fact that it sets up a clear contrast between those who "boasted" (καυχάομαι, 6.13) about fleshly things like circumcision (i.e. those who wanted "to make a good showing in the flesh," 6.12) and Paul himself, who boasted of nothing "except the cross of Christ" (6.14). This is even more clear in Philippians, where the apostle contrasted the Christians, whose "citizenship is in heaven" (3.20) with those whom he designated as "enemies of the cross of Christ" (3.18). In this latter passage, it is less clear who is meant by Paul's designation, and we need not assume that

Jews or Judaizers are necessarily the intended referents. What is important in both Galatians and Philippians is the fact that people's responses to ὁ σταυρός revealed the relational world to which they chose to give primary allegiance…and these worlds did not overlap. Thus, in aligning himself with the crucified Christ, Paul "died to the flesh" (Gal 2.19–20).

In 1 Cor. 1.22–24, Paul again spoke of the cross as an offense to Jews, but here he expanded his image to include "Greeks," as well. For the latter, ὁ σταυρός was, quite simply, "foolishness." Although there is some truth to Conzelmann's assertion that the dyad "Jews and Greeks" was a convenient Jewish form of classifying humankind,[78] we have already seen above that there were real networks of Jews and Greeks in the Corinthian church.[79] Despite the fact that the situations in the two churches were not identical, even as in Galatians 5.4, Paul used καταργέω to describe the end of those who put their trust more in circumcision than in the cross, so in 1 Cor. 2.6, Paul spoke of those who were clinging to the wisdom "of this age" as people who were "doomed to perish" (καταργέω). Paul used similar terms and imagery precisely because, though the specific issues might have differed, the underlying reality in both situations was an acceptance of outside standards over and against the standards of the Christian network. The cross stood, as it were, at the crossroads of their relational worlds: they could continue to cling to a world and a *Weltanschauung* that was known and acceptable to them, or they could embrace the identity of those for whom Christ had died.[80]

The cross, therefore, served as a *divider,* marking those who looked to the crucified Christ as "the power and wisdom of God" (1.24) as wholly set-apart from those whose faith still rested on σοφία ἀνθρώπων (2.5). Thus, Paul's language in 1 Cor. 1.18–3.23, like that of the Corinthians themselves, was a language of differentiation, yet the boundaries to which he called attention were altogether different from those familiar to members of his congregation. Language common to *collegia* was noticeably absent from Paul's descriptions of the ἐκκλησία, while many terms Paul did employ when speaking of the Church (i.e. "elect," "beloved," "saints") are sought in vain among associations.[81] Those who accepted the message of ὁ σταυρός were identified with a new status: they who once "were pagans" (12.2) had crossed over the threshold from "the world" to God (2.12), from the "unspiritual" to the "spiritual" (2.14–15), from "this age" to the age to come (3.18), from "slavery" to "freedom" (7.22), from "the perishable" to "the imperishable" (15.42).[82] Jew and Gentile, free and slave alike, would be included in one of two categories which Paul presented in light of the cross: "the perishing" or "those who are being saved" (1.18).

The cross was also a *unifier* for those within the Christian network.[83] In this way, Paul appealed to the cross when facing the competing allegiances within the ἐκκλησία (1.13). Moffatt notes that the divisive spirit in the ἐκκλησία was the result of a failure of self-perception: the Christians did not recognise what it truly meant to belong to this network.[84] Yet, if it was Christ—and not Paul or Apollos—who had been crucified for the Corinthians, then that was their common ground. The slogan "I belong to Christ" was not to be claimed by any one subgroup, but instead served as the fundamental cry of unity for all for whom Christ died.[85] For the Christian ἐκκλησία, then, the cross represented "the elimination of all distinctions of status and an other-regarding behaviour which 'builds up' the community."[86]

The "Vicious Circle"

In many ways, the ἔριδες in the church represented an attempt on the part of many Corinthian Christians to return to the more familiar boundaries and distinctions of their other relational networks, thereby avoiding the radical implications inherent in a κοινωνία with others whom they previously knew only in separatist terms. One way of visualising what has been discussed (though by no means the only one) is the model of the "vicious circle," as seen in *figure 4.a.*

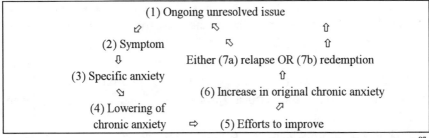

Figure 4.a—The Vicious Circle[87]

The underlying, unresolved issue (1) was confusion regarding the unique identity and solidarity of the Christian ἐκκλησία. Having crossed the threshold into a new community ἐν Χριστῷ, some of the Corinthians continued to act as if former distinctions remained in force within the ἐκκλησία, resulting in the ἔριδες surrounding various focal individuals/leaders (2). This created an anxiety among at least some (Chloe's people?) which led to the issue being brought to Paul's attention (3). By focusing only on a specific issue (i.e. the superiority of Apollos as leader),[88] the underlying issue of the nature of the Christian network would seemingly fade into the background for the Corinthians (4). Indeed, if Paul had responded only to the specific issue in question, for instance by supporting those who "belonged" to him instead of to Apollos, the result would have been temporary relief in that one area (5) but with a simultaneous return to the forefront of the underlying question of corporate identity confusion (6). By pointing to the cross, something wholly outside the conventional wisdom of either "Jews or Greeks," Paul avoided falling into the Corinthians' own patterns at point (7a) and instead challenged them to break through to a new paradigm (7b) and begin to understand their corporate identity as more than "one more network among many."

Far from being a purely modern concept, this "vicious circle," as Friedman describes it, has played out in various ways throughout the ages, perhaps most evidently so in the wilderness account of the Israelites' various attempts to return to the familiar by forcing Moses to defocus on the call of Yahweh and instead to get bogged down in one debate after another, whether over water, food, or something visible to worship.[89] Paul might well have used Friedman's term "natural" (at least in the sense of "merely human") to describe the response of those Corinthians who would do anything to avoid facing "the moment of truth, the critical turning point."[90] Because of his unique position in the system, it was in many ways up to Paul to break through the resistance and set up a pattern which could then be imitated (4.16; 11.1), even as he himself imitated Christ, whose cross stood at the "critical turning point" and challenged all who would stand in its shadow.

Thus, the ἔριδες which were seemingly impossible to confront through normal means (such as initiation into the ἐκκλησία through baptism) could only be disarmed through an instrument totally outside the familiar patterns. The cross that divides created new distinctions, and *within* those distinctions—the perishing and the being-saved—lesser distinctions lost their meaning. Paul utilised the message of the cross to effect a "paradigm shift" in how the Corinthians viewed themselves collectively: no longer in terms that perpetuated what he saw as unhealthy internal divisions and conflicts but, rather, in terms that drew together all who belonged to the Crucified One.[91] God's self-disclosure in the cross essentially placed "all human pretensions to power and wisdom under judgment...establishing a radically new norm and context for life in this age."[92] By invoking a second-order change in the system through the message of ὁ σταυρός, Paul effected a paradigm shift for members of the Corinthian ἐκκλησία, thereby relativising distinctions between "Jews or Greeks, slaves or free" (12.13) even as he strengthened the boundaries between members of the ἐκκλησία and those "outside" (ἔξω, 5.12–13). We turn now, therefore, to the question of how Paul envisioned relational patterns for those "inside," focusing on his use of language from the network of the οἶκος.

Reconfiguring Relationships

A Different Relational Paradigm

As mentioned already, Paul was hardly an objective, outside consultant in the Corinthian situation. On the contrary, as one of the focal individuals for church members (1.13), Paul had to address not only the question of the church's identity, but also his own position in the church *vis-à-vis* both the members of the Christian ἐκκλησία AND its other focal individuals (e.g. Apollos). In this second half of the chapter, the focus is on Paul's attempts to differentiate himself and reconfigure the overall pattern of relationships in the ἐκκλησία using familial/household imagery. Observing Paul's own pattern of usage, the following subsections examine respectively his prolific use of ἀδελφός language, which begins in 1.2 and extends throughout the letter; his various "servant" terms in relation to himself and Apollos, which are concentrated in 3.5–4.2; and his single but intentionally-placed self-descriptor of πατήρ in 4.14ff., underlining the uniqueness and primacy of his relational position in the ἐκκλησία while introducing the "family matters" which follow in 1 Cor. 5ff. Before examining these terms, it might prove helpful to answer some general preliminary questions.

First, it may be asked why there is a focus here on familial language at all, especially when scholars often have passed over such language in favour of Paul's more obvious and overt usage of "body language," a common motif in speeches and writings which can be traced "as far back as 900 B.C.E."[93] It might be easy to think that the σῶμα Χριστοῦ was a constant theme in the Pauline writings but, in fact, such imagery is almost exclusively confined to 1 Corinthians and Romans 12.[94] Even in 1 Corinthians, with the exception of a brief mention in 5.8, the term σῶμα does not appear at all until chapter 6 (1 Cor. 6.13–20; 7.4, 34; 9.17; 12.12–27; 15.35–57).[95] In the first four chapters, Paul instead draws upon other systemic images to describe the Christian ἐκκλησία, including a plant/field (3.9), a building (3.9ff.), and the temple (3.16). Together, these images denote both the church's separateness from other systems and unity among its constituent parts, since it was Paul's contention that "God transforms and saves a *people*, not atomised individuals."[96] But, as we shall see, the apostle's most pervasive systemic imagery was drawn not from inanimate, agricultural, or human physiological models, but rather from a social model in Paul's midst: the family. Meeks has noted that the terms "brother" and "sister," while used by other New Testament writers, "occur far more frequently in the Pauline letters than anywhere else in the earliest Christian literature."[97] Within the undisputed letters, one-third of the variant uses of ἀδελφός occur in 1 Corinthians alone![98] As we shall see, household relationships in Paul's time offered him a dynamic and complementary set of systemic images which he used throughout his letter. It is precisely Paul's copious employment of family imagery, most particularly in direct connection with situations of intra-church conflict, that commends its study here.

It must also be emphasised that despite the pervasive use of familial terms in 1 Corinthians, "family" *per se* was not set up as a model for the church, in the way that the body was a model, i.e. the σῶμα Χριστοῦ. In this sense, it is appropriate to draw a fine line between marking Christian interrelationships as familial in quality and seeing the church itself as a family. Paul never spoke in 1 Corinthians of the "family or household of

Christ" and, indeed, only in Gal. 6.10 did he even use οἶκος terminology directly for the church, referring there to "the family of faith" (τοὺς οἰκείους τῆς πίστεως). Furthermore, there is a lack of emphasis on members' own οἶκοι in 1 Corinthians, especially when compared with the Deutero-Paulines and 1 Peter, where considerable attention is devoted to issues of household management.[99] As will be seen more clearly in the next chapter, matters "outside" the life of the Christian community itself held little interest for the apostle in 1 Corinthians, whose concern was more with how fellow Christians lived in fellowship with one another.

Finally, questions can also be raised concerning the uniqueness of Paul's familial language. Even if he did refer to himself as πατήρ in 1 Cor. 4.15, was not the head of a trade guild also referred to as the "father" of its members, or a rabbi the "father" of his pupil?[100] And did not his prolific use of ἀδελφοί find its echo in many philosophers, including Plato, Xenophon and Plotinus?[101] Perhaps the most obvious parallels to Paul's "brother" language are found once more within Judaism, not only in the Septuagint,[102] but also among the Essenes (Jos. *Bel.* 2.122) and even in New Testament passages where fellow Jews are referred to as ἀδελφοί.[103] Paul himself even spoke at one point of the Jews as "my brothers" (τῶν ἀδελφῶν μου, Rom. 9.3). What, then, set Paul's Christian familial imagery apart? The answer to this question lies in a more detailed analysis of the apostle's sibling, servant and father terminology.

Ἀδελφοί μου ἀγαπητοί

As noted, Paul's most pervasive household image was that of sibling, both in direct address and as a descriptor for members of the church.[104] Paul's other self-descriptors—founder, planter, master-builder, father—will be discussed in this section at various points, but a focus on any of these alone runs the danger of becoming skewed if not viewed within the context of his more prolific use of ἀδελφός imagery, which runs like a thread throughout the entire letter. In this subsection we will examine both *how* and *why* Paul utilised his brother/sister terminology, especially in connection with intra-church conflict. In *figure 4.b* below, all the various occurrences of ἀδελφός terminology are arranged into five categories, represented by the table's five columns. As we shall see here, the vocative ἀδελφοί is quite prominent in 1 Cor. 1–4, as well as at later points in the letter. Thus, greater attention will be given to the first column at this time. At the end of this subsection, we will discuss possible reasons for Paul's use of sibling terminology.

It should be said at this point that the significance of Paul's pervasive use of sibling langauge is only recently receiving careful attention by scholars. In his most recent work, D. Horrell has examined the ἀδελφοί language in both the undisputed Pauline letters and the later epistles, i.e. Ephesians, Colossians, and the Pastorals (cf. Horrell 2001 in the bibliography below). Horrell uses a developmental approach, exploring how the prevalent use of an egalitarian ἀδελφοί terminology in the authentic letters gives way to the language of a more hierarchically structured community by the time of the letters to Timothy and Titus. He argues persuasively, and rightly, that we cannot lump all the letters— undisputed and disputed—together when we speak of how Paul used sibling language. There is a change in the epistolary and relational context between the times of Paul's letters to the Corinthians, Romans, etc. and the deutero-Pauline writings that demands separate and careful examination of each set of letters. Interestingly Horrell himself directs his comments on the undisputed letters to the entire set as a whole, although he does suggest that the variations in usage within the set call for further study.

Considering, then, *figure 4.b* on page 145, by far the most prevalent variant of ἀδελφός in 1 Corinthians is the vocative plural, ἀδελφοί, which is found no less than 20 times in this letter.[105] Two things should be noted about Paul's use of the vocative. First, although the address was commonly used in Paul's day to refer to compatriots or countrymen,[106] Paul refrained from such usage in his letters and instead reserved ἀδελφοί exclusively for fellow Christian believers. Even in the aforementioned Rom. 9.3, where Paul spoke of the Jews as his brothers, he was quick to add that they were his kindred only "according to the flesh" (τῶν συγγενῶν μου κατὰ σάρκα). Christian brotherhood was grounded not in kinship or common nationality but in the fact that God was Father to all who were "sanctified in Christ Jesus" (1 Cor. 1.2–3).[107] Thus, the ἀδελφός relationship extended beyond the local ἐκκλησία to include all who "call on the name of *our* Lord Jesus Christ, *both their Lord and ours*" (1.2).

Figure 4.b—Occurrences of Ἀδελφός Terms in 1 Corinthians[108]

Vocative, ἀδελφοί (Direct Address)	Specific Persons (Named)	Corinthian Christian(s)	Christian(s) Outside Corinthian Church	"Sister(s)" (ἡ ἀδελφή)
	1.1 - Sosthenes			
1.10				
1.11				
1.26				
2.1				
3.1				
4.6				
		5.11 – One who bears the name of Christian		
		6.5 - Litigants		
		6.6 - Litigants		
		6.8 - Litigants		
		7.12 - Spouse		
		7.14 - Spouse		
		7.15 - Spouse (ἀδελφός, ἀδελφή)		
				7.15
7.24				
7.29				
		8.11 - "Weak"		
		8.12 - "		
		8.13 - "		
			9.5 - "brothers of the Lord"	
10.1				
11.33				
12.1				
14.6				
14.20				
14.26				
14.39				
15.1				
			15.6	
15.31				
15.50				
15.58				
			16.11 - "the brothers"	
	16.12 - Apollos			
16.15				
			16.20 - "all the brothers"	

Second, as seen in *figure 4.b,* in 1 Corinthians ἀδελφοί occurs mostly in the opening (1.10,11,26; 2.1; 3.1; 4.6) and closing chapters (14.6,20,26,39; 15.1,31,50,58) of the body of the letter, while in the other Pauline writings the term is dispersed throughout each letter without any obvious concentration in one area. This may be significant, since it has already been asserted that both the unity and identity of the ἐκκλησία were the most pressing points in 1 Cor. 1–4 and in later chapters focusing on the gathered worshipping assembly. In 1 Thessalonians, where there is also a prolific use of the vocative ἀδελφοί, the Christian siblings were praised for their faith (3.7) and love (4.10), and were urged simply to do "more and more" what they were already doing (4.1,10). In 1 Corinthians, however, ἀδελφοί was linked with words of admonition and reproof to those who appeared still to give priority to the distinctions and values of their other networks.[109] We see this in the first four chapters of the letter, where there is a high correspondence between the direct address and the negatives μή and οὐ: "...that there be no (μή) divisions among you" (1.10); "not many (οὐ πολλοί) of you were wise..." (1.26); "I did not (οὐ) come..." (2.1); "I could not (οὐκ) speak to you..." (3.1); "...so that no one (μὴ εἷς) will be puffed up in favour of one against the other" (4.16).[110] Where he used the imperative μή, Paul was urging the Corinthians to pursue unity and mutual love (1.10; 4.16). Where he used the indicative οὐ, Paul was contrasting the Corinthians' more familiar distinctions κατὰ σάρκα (1.26) with the ways of the true πνευματικοῖς (3.1). This same pattern is found in later sections of the letter, including 14.6 (μὴ παιδία γίνεσθε...), 14.39 (τὸ λαλεῖν μὴ κωλύετε γλώσσαις), and 15.50 (σὰρξ καὶ αἷμα βασιλείαν θεοῦ κληρονομῆσαι οὐ δύναται...).

In fact, the various occurrences of ἀδελφοί in 1 Corinthians are often linked with a series of *contrasts* between the position of the Corinthians as brothers and sisters in Christ and their preference to live according to the standards of other networks in which they found themselves.[111] In 1.10–12, Paul contrasted the unity of mind and purpose that should have marked the interrelationships of Christian ἀδελφοί with the ἔριδες that actually existed, focused on affiliations to the different leaders/teachers. Dio Chrysostom remarked that a great orator entering a city was often greeted with ζῆλος καὶ φιλοτιμία.[112] Paul, in 1 Cor. 3.3, spoke negatively of the ζῆλος καὶ ἔρις existing in the ἐκκλησία, centered on the affiliations of certain members with either Apollos or Paul. Again, Paul's report of such immature behaviour, the actions of mere νηπίοις ἐν Χριστῷ, opened with the address, ἀδελφοί. The same address is found in 1.26, as part of an ongoing contrast between the rhetorical prizes of σοφία and δύναμις, on the one hand, and God's wisdom and power, on the other hand, which appear to many to be μωρός καὶ ἀσθενές. Even among the ἀδελφοί, Paul remarked, "not many" of them could claim to have been among the élite when they first entered the ἐκκλησία. 1 Cor. 2.1 begins a more detailed contrast between worldly σοφία and God's σοφία and, once more, opened with the address to the ἀδελφοί. Finally, in 4.6, Paul contrasted his partnership with Apollos with the "puffed up" attitudes of those ἀδελφοί who "belong" to each of them. Thus, we see in 1 Cor. 1–4 that Paul initiated a pattern of using ἀδελφοί to express again those who were united with one another by virtue of their common lineage ἐν Χριστῷ, but at the same time distinct from others around them.

This pattern, however, does not end with chapter 4. In 7.24 and 7.29, Paul addressed the ἀδελφοί concerning the irrelevance of distinctions from other networks (i.e. slave versus free, married versus unmarried), while in 10.1, he introduced a warning (by way of analogy) to ἀδελφοί who would put their trust in their religious status. In 11.33, Paul confronted those who would not wait for their Christian ἀδελφοί before proceeding to eat the communion meal, while 12.1 introduced the lengthy exposition on interdependence in the worshipping community. Among the several occurrences of ἀδελφοί in chs. 14 and 15 are those which contrast the actions of children (παιδία) and adults over the issue of tongues (14.20), and the concerns of those focusing on the "perishable" with the resurrection faith that focuses on the "imperishable" (15.50).[113] The final occurrence of the vocative, in 16.15–16, is part of Paul's paradoxical plea to the ἀδελφοί to put themselves at the service of those who "worked and toiled" on their behalf.

Plutarch stated that "through the concord of brothers both family and household are sound and flourish."[114] Even so, Paul was advocating an alternative way of viewing one another in the Christian ἐκκλησία which was based on the mutual love and concern of fellow ἀδελφοί. This is evident in his use of ἀδελφός as descriptor (see cols. 2–5 of *4.b*). At the same time, however, it may be said that the apostle utilised the vocative ἀδελφοί when *contrasting* ideal patterns of relationship within the ἐκκλησία with patterns brought in from the Corinthians' other networks.[115] Chrysostom later pointed out: "Although the fault be plain, there was nothing against calling them brethren still."[116] Yet, can it not be argued instead that by calling them ἀδελφοί, Paul was making their fault all the more plain? It was incomprehensible for brothers to take one another to court, yet this is precisely what the Corinthian ἀδελφοί were doing (6.6). Paul called them "brethren," but did they act like brethren? Interestingly, in the Septuagint the familial term often belies the evil or treacherous character of an ἀδελφός.[117] Indeed, Jeremiah's warning against trusting even your brothers, ὅτι πᾶς ἀδελφὸς πτέρνῃ πτερνιεῖ (9.4), seems well-founded in light of the pattern of siblings who in one way or another "supplanted" their brother/sister…or worse.[118] Whether he was consciously aware of this pattern or not, Paul's usage of the vocative address followed a similar path of contrast and challenge: were the Corinthians living as ἀδελφοί, or did their behaviour contradict Paul's address?

Instead of falling into the pattern of those who were differentiating between Apollos and himself (3.1ff.), Paul called him "brother" (16.12). Likewise, Sosthenes, possibly the synagogue official in Acts 18.17, is mentioned simply as ὁ ἀδελφός in the opening greeting (1.1), alongside Paul's self-appellation of ἀπόστολος. As seen in the third column of *4.a*, in the section between Paul's calls to "imitate me" (4.16; 11.1), the use of some other form of ὁ ἀδελφός or ἡ ἀδελφή as *descriptors* of the Corinthian Christians becomes far more prevalent than *the direct address* (which occurs only at 7.24,29 and 10.1). This may be because this section constitutes Paul's address to the Corinthians as his "children" rather than as his "siblings." In the context of something like a household *consilium*, Paul attempted to redirect disputing church members from responding to one another in terms of the patterns of the πολιτεία to responding to one another in terms of their interdependent positions as ἀδελφοί, as mature children and fellow heirs. (Much more will be said about this in the following chapter.) Women in the congregation were mentioned separately as ἀδελφή, a reminder that in this network "sisters" at times were given the same prerogatives as "brothers," at least in the case of marriages to fellow believers (7.4) and even to unbelieving partners (7.15), as well as the ability to pray and prophesy in the worship assembly (albeit with certain conditions for each, 11.2–16). Finally, Paul's reference at the end of the letter to οἱ ἀδελφοί πάντες (16.11,20) hearkens back to the opening assertion that the Corinthians were bound not only to one another but also to all others outside the local community who called on "the name of our Lord Jesus Christ" (1.2). From beginning to end, therefore, Paul's sibling terminology conveyed a new way of ordering relational reality.[119] As in his letter to Philemon, Paul allowed a degree of ambiguity to enter the Corinthians' relational system, so that people formerly understood *only* as slaves, owners, Jews, Greeks, etc., could now be seen *also* as ἀδελφοί ἐν Χριστῷ.[120] They now could choose *how* to define themselves.

While the mutual concern and responsibility of Christian brothers towards each other appears to have been Paul's primary intent when using ἀδελφός language, there were at least two other, related messages being conveyed. The first concerns the connection of sibling to heir. The noun κληρονόμος (heir), found in both Romans and Galatians,[121] does not appear at all in 1 Corinthians. Indeed, the related verb κληρονομέω (inherit) is found only in 6.9–10 (η οὐκ οἴδατε ὅτι ἄδικοι θεοῦ βασιλείαν οὐ κληρονομήσουσιν, cf. Gal 5.21) and in 15.50 (Τοῦτο δέ φημι, ἀδελφοί, ὅτι σὰρξ καὶ αἷμα βασιλείαν θεοῦ κληρονομῆσαι οὐ δύναται οὐδὲ ἡ φθορὰ τὴν ἀφθαρσίαν κληρονομεῖ.) However, while the noun "heir" may be missing, in other ways Paul asserted that inasmuch as the Corinthians were brothers and sisters ἐν Χριστῷ, they were also fellow heirs of the one divine *paterfamilias*. "All things are yours," Paul proclaimed (3.21), but "yours" (ὑμῶν) is plural; hence all things are yours together. Despite the fact that many were "living as kings already" (4.8ff.), Paul reminded his siblings that their inheritance was still to come (cf. 6.9–10; 15.50). Besides questions regarding eschatological beliefs in Corinth, there is an issue here of relational togetherness: those who would one day inherit the imperishable were children of the one Father and, thus, ἀδελφοί to one another. The apostle's interweaving of sibling terminology and "we" language when discussing the kingdom inheritance in 1 Cor. 15, culminating in an appeal to ἀδελφοί μου ἀγαπατοί (15.58), denotes his continued concern for mutuality among the believers. This κοινωνία was based not on a common affiliation with a particular focal individual or shared membership in a *collegium*, but rather on the fact that the Lord

Jesus Christ was *our* (ἡμῶν) Lord Jesus Christ (15.57). To this end, Paul offered several *exempla pietatum* in chapter 16: Timothy (v.10), Stephanas (15), Fortunatus and Achaicus (17), and Aquila and Prisca (19).[122]

The other connection suggested by Paul's sibling language in 1–4 (about which much more will be said in the following chapter) concerns boundary definition and the appropriate context for judgment for those ἐν Χριστῷ. Paul's familial address was not to outsiders but to those inside the Christian network who resisted the relational implications of the cross. Indeed, it is crucial to note that Paul did not appear to use his language of differentiation to exclude the outsider, but rather *to reshape the thinking of those inside*. In his later discussions on marriage and sexual ethics, civil litigation, the idol meat controversy, and orderly worship, Paul's focus remained on the behaviour of ἀδελφῶν, and not the mores of the larger society.[123] Even when he displayed a concern for the ἄπιστος who would enter their midst (14.24), his words of instruction concerning proper behaviour in worship were directed to believers (12.22), to his brothers and sisters ἐν Χριστῷ. Throughout the letter, it would be "the Christian ἐκκλησία, not the secular ἐκκλησία, [which was] the forum for hearing and heeding his discourse."[124]

Similarly, Paul was quick to point out that judgment for Christians was to be rendered not through disinterested civil judges in the πολιτεία but within the boundaries of the church itself, where ἀδελφοί could show true σοφία in working through issues together, as in a household *consilium* or Jewish πολίτευμα.[125] Indeed, judgment language (ἀνακρίνω) is quite prevalent in 1 Corinthians, but always within the confines of the community of Christian brothers and sisters.[126] Judging the behaviour of those outside the Christian network appears to have been almost an irrelevant issue for Paul, "for what have I to do with judging outsiders" (5.12)? He was certainly "not a sociologist before his time."[127] Neither was he a group counsellor or social ethicist as we understand those terms today. Paul's chief concern was the gospel and its promulgation. Paul the pastor cannot be disassociated from Paul the evangelist/missionary. Christian community was to be found "in Christ" together. The corollary, of course, is that there were also many who were *not yet* "in Christ." Indeed, Paul's desire was that the unbeliever (ἄπιστος) and the uninitiated (ἰδιώτης) might be convicted of sin and declare to the assembly, "God is really among you" (14.23–25). A clear identity for the church was needed to communicate to those looking in both its distinctiveness and its attractiveness.

With such a simple address—ἀδελφοί—used over and over again (not only in the first four chapters but, as seen in *figure 4.b*, throughout the letter), Paul was slowly and subtly introducing a different paradigm of Christian community than the one espoused by at least some Corinthians. To those who would introduce into the ἐκκλησία the standards and differentiations of the outside world, Paul's appeals to brothers and sisters ἐν Χριστῷ presupposed that their "ties to their fellow ἀδελφοί and ἀδελφαί [were] to be more significant than any others."[128] The address expressed intimacy, for to Paul these fellow believers were ἀδελφοί μου (1.11; 15.58).[129] This language also placed Paul's own relationship with the Corinthians in the context of their common position before Christ as fellow siblings and fellow heirs. Yes, he was their apostle and "father," but this was only true inasmuch as he and they were together children of the one heavenly Father. However, it should be reiterated that by speaking to his ἀδελφοί ("us"), Paul was also increasing a sense of relational distance between members of the Christian network and those outside it ("them").[130] In providing a new set of systemic dichotomies, the apostle implicitly raised the question which would be made explicit in 1 Cor. 5–6: why should conflict resolution or judgment for those inside be handled by those outside, and vice versa? If he and his fellow Christians were truly ἀδελφοί, then their problems could, and should, be settled "in-house." Thus, by addressing his fellow believers as his ἀδελφοί, Paul challenged them once more to think of themselves as something far more intimate than simply one more subset of the surrounding Corinthian πολιτεία.

Paul and Apollos as συνεργοί

Paul's household imagery, however, was not limited to the various forms of ἀδελφός, particularly when it involved his own position in the network. We have already seen that part of the Corinthian problem was confusion regarding Paul's role in the church *vis-à-vis* other leaders/focal individuals. In Acts, Apollos is presented as having an inadequate theology, knowing "only the baptism of John" (18.24ff.), and while in

Galatians Cephas was disparaged by Paul for preaching "another gospel" (2.11ff.). Paul's concern in 1 Corinthians, however, was simply to show those persons who "found Apollos [or Cephas] the more impressive figure"[131] that these leaders were his co-workers. Through his sibling terminology, Paul set a context of mutuality and shared calling for all Christians. However, he did not refer to himself as ὁ ἀδελφός. Rather, in regards to his own position in the system, Paul utilised two seemingly paradoxical images. On the one hand, he emphasised the common and complementary mission of Apollos and himself as household servants under God. On the other hand, he pointed to his unique and primary position of "father" of that particular congregation. This subsection focuses on Paul's servant and co-worker language, particularly in terms of the way Paul used such terminology to move the focus of the congregation away from himself and other human leaders and towards God.

Concerning the image of servant in 1 Cor. 1–4, three points may be made. First, Paul used not one, but several related "servant" terms to redefine his and Apollos' position in the overall system in relation to God instead of in relation to one another. Having wrestled with the issue of human wisdom versus the message of the cross in chapters 1 and 2, Paul would return in 3.1 to the theme of "who belongs to whom." To his ἀδελφοί who considered themselves wise and mature, based on standards of σοφία and eloquence familiar to them in their other networks, Paul instead pointed out that their partisanship revealed how immature and "fleshly" they really were (3.1–4). Different members were placing Paul and Apollos in positions which they (or at least Paul) clearly did not want. In response, Paul described both himself and Apollos as διάκονοι (3.5), those who ministered to the needs of another and usually with some sense of devotion or εὐσεβεία (Lat. *pietas*).[132] Though the term later came to be used in the more narrow sense of a church official (Phil. 1.1; 1 Tim. 3.8), in Paul's time it often referred to household servants.[133] The motivation of the person serving, and the relationship of the servant to the one being served, contrast this term with δοῦλος, or one who is under subjection, i.e. a slave. When Paul went on to use the related term ὑπηρέτης (4.1), this also pointed to the close relation between the one serving and the one being served. As with Jesus in Matt. 20.26, Paul's usage of διάκονος here reflects a reversal of the norms familiar to his readers, i.e. to be "great" (μέγας) one must first become a διάκονος. "How can a man be happy when he has to serve someone?"—so the proverbial formula stated.[134]

Paul and Apollos, whom different members of the ἐκκλησία looked to with such high regard, were themselves simply servants of one far greater than themselves.[135] Inasmuch as his language of service was relational language, i.e. service to God on behalf of the Corinthians, then Paul was pointing beyond himself and Apollos to the Lord. Thus, although the Corinthians might have come to believe through them and their respective ministries, this was only inasmuch as ἑκάστῳ ὡς ὁ κύριος ἔδωκεν (3.5).[136] Likewise, interweaving terminology from agricultural and building work, Paul points to the God as the one who gives growth and the grace to build (3.7,10). Not unlike Jesus who came not διακονηθῆναι but διακονῆσαι (Mk. 10.45), Paul and his so-called rivals were engaged in κόπος, hard and exhaustive labour or toil (3.8; cf. Matt. 26.10; Jn. 4.38). As such, they lacked the luxury of quarreling over who was the greater servant. By focusing on the One whom they served, Paul and Apollos became to one another not rivals but συνεργοί ("fellow workers," 3.9) and οἰκονόμοι (stewards together in charge of the household, 4.1).[137]

All these terms, used together and in largely complementary fashion, emphasise the absurdity of placing too much importance on either Paul or Apollos, especially within the context of disputes surrounding baptism (1.13). That which is truly important, said Paul, was not "who baptised whom" but, rather, "who died for whom" and thereby exhibited the ultimate act of personal service (Mk. 10.45). Some have asserted that Paul's disclaimer about not having baptised many is evidence that baptism was not terribly important to Paul. However, the apostle "did not place a low value on baptism," but viewed it in light of ὁ σταυρός.[138] Inasmuch as Christian baptism, like Paul's or Apollos' ministry, pointed beyond itself to the salvific events of Christ's death and resurrection, then it was something of great value. However, too much focus on the one who baptised—who was simply a servant in the οἶκος—could only lead to further divisions within the one ἐκκλησία, as indeed was the case.

This is why Paul the διάκονος responded to the baptism issue with a *reductio ad absurdum,* asking the Corinthians if it was he who had been crucified for them or whether they had been baptised εἰς τὸ ὄνομα Παύλου (1.13).[139] The latter phrase was most likely familiar to many

Christians in a commercial centre such as Corinth. A technical term from the world of commerce, the phrase referred to an account which "bears the name of the one who owns it."[140] Thus, the phrase was a way of expressing possession, not unlike the phrase "I belong to" (see *3.5.2*). Paul reminded the Corinthians that even those who claimed to "belong to Paul" were no more Paul's possession than they were their own (6.19). Indeed, since he and Apollos were διάκονοι under God for the benefit of the church's members, they (and other Christian leaders) actually "belonged" to the Corinthians although, ultimately, all belonged to Christ (3.21–23). This is also why Paul clearly refused to accept the role of Apollos' rival...and a less eloquent one at that! While he concurred that "*my* message and *my* preaching were not with plausible words of wisdom" (2.4, NRSV), Paul then shifted once more to "we" statements from 2.6 onwards, suggesting that as συνεργοί, he and Apollos were together speaking God's wisdom (2.7).[141] In terms of position in the system, Paul effectively turned from facing Apollos as rival—which would have signalled acceptance of the familiar categories of the secular ἐκκλησία which had infiltrated the Christian ἐκκλησία—to facing God, under whom both were fellow servants. He essentially "de-triangled" himself from what he deemed unacceptable roles (i.e. hero or unimpressive leader) and placed the attention and the responsibility back on God. Inasmuch as he found himself in his particular position in the system only διὰ θελήματος θεοῦ (1.1; cf. also 15.10), Paul would not be baited into a contest which was "merely human" (3.4) in its approach. After all, as a servant, he was under obligation to God and entrusted with an οἰκονομία (9.17).[142]

Thus, Paul had little problem, at least on the surface, in agreeing with those who attacked him as weak. Indeed, by admitting that ἐν ἀσθενείᾳ καὶ ἐν φόβῳ καὶ ἐν τρόμῳ πολλῷ ἐγενόμην πρὸς ὑμᾶς (2.3), the apostle essentially disarmed his detractors' arguments. This is why he counted it a "very small thing" (4.3) to be judged by members of the congregation, assumedly concerning his apostolic "performance" in comparison with Apollos or other leaders.[143] Paul's "boasting" was not grounded in the existence of a smaller subset of persons who affiliated themselves with him, but in God, ἐξ αὐτοῦ δὲ ὑμεῖς ἐστε ἐν Χριστῷ Ἰησοῦ (1.30). It made little sense for others in the ἐκκλησία to boast (καυχάσθω) about their affiliations with Paul or his "rivals," who were not rivals at all, but simply fellow servants. His abilities or weaknesses, and theirs, had to be considered in light of the cross of Christ which, paradoxically, was a sign of weakness that actually conveyed the δύναμις θεοῦ (1.18). Similarly, as long as the message he proclaimed was interpreted simply as "Paul's words," the message was in danger of being ignored. Here again, the issue was one of "belonging," i.e. to whom did his spoken message or doctrine belong? If Paul had remained on the level of argument that his words were indeed eloquent and wise, he would have proven himself not wise but "merely human" (3.4). Instead, he and Apollos were stewards of μυστηρία θεοῦ (4.1).

Later in the letter, Paul would further overturn the arguments of his detractors by asserting that two major identity-marking doctrines or practices of the Christian faith—the Lord's Supper and the Resurrection —were ones he himself had "received" (παρέλαβον) and "passed on" (παρέδωκα) to the Corinthians (11.23; 15.3; cf. Gal. 1.12). His work, Apollos' work, indeed the Corinthians' work all would one day be tested, and the one standard was not the σοφία so prized by the church's members and so familiar to them in their other networks, but rather the foundation of a crucified Christ (3.11–15). Thus, by asserting that he himself was simply a servant of the one divine Householder, Paul was able to step out of a scenario created for him and Apollos by others.

There is a second point to be made, however, and this concerns the *absence* of the term δοῦλος (slave) from Paul's self-descriptors in 1–4, despite his use of the several other terms for service. Indeed, the few times the language of slavery is found in 1 Corinthians are usually in the context of the *irrelevance* of the social or societal condition of persons when they were "called" into the κοινωνία of Christ and the church (7.21–24; 12.13; cf. Gal. 3.28). Elsewhere in the Pauline writings the term δοῦλος is quite prevalent, nowhere more so than in Romans. Indeed, that epistle even begins with the self-description of Paul as δοῦλος Χριστοῦ Ἰησοῦ (1.1), and Rom. 6–7 contrasts being a δοῦλος of sin with being a δοῦλος of righteousness (6.18).[144] We can see similar language in Gal. 1.10 (Χριστοῦ δοῦλος) and even in 2 Cor. 4.5 (δούλους ὑμῶν διὰ Ἰησοῦ). However, when Paul wrote concerning his and Apollos' roles in the system in 1 Cor. 1–4, he did not use the term. One reason for this might be that, in redefining the Corinthians' systemic paradigm, Paul precisely wanted to contrast the immaturity and "slavishness" of members of the ἐκκλησία who "belonged to" human leaders with the wisdom and spiritual maturity expected of adult ἀδελφοί.[145]

Another reason for using terms like διάκονος and ὑπηρέτης, as opposed to δοῦλος, to describe his and Apollos' positions in the system might have been that Paul wanted to express not servitude as much as *willing* service. In this way, even when he did speak of himself later as one who, though free, enslaved himself to all for the sake of winning more to Christ ('Ελεύθερος γὰρ ων ἐκ πάντων πᾶσιν ἐμαυτὸν ἐδούλωσα, ἵνα τοὺς πλείονας κερδήσω, 9.19), the stress was on his voluntary submission.[146] For Paul, the relational paradigm in *this* ἐκκλησία was not centred on one's rights or ἐξουσία, as in the Corinthian secular ἐκκλησία, but rather on the relinquishment of such rights for the sake of something far more important. The importance of Paul's *apologia* in 1 Cor. 9 in terms of the surrounding controversy regarding idol meat will be discussed more in chapter 5, but for now, it is important to note that here and in 1 Cor. 1–4, "Paul's example is of one who has deliberately given up status and freedom," precisely because in the Christian ἐκκλησία those things which were so highly prized in the πολιτεία were irrelevant.[147]

A final point to be made concerns the contrast of images Paul used to describe his own role in the system. Although in relation to Apollos and other leaders he was ὁ συνεργός, a fellow household servant, yet *in relation to the Corinthians themselves* Paul held a unique and primary position in the system. Even more than the role of οἰκονόμος, which he claimed to share with Apollos, it was Paul alone who first planted the field (3.6) and laid the foundation of the building (3.10). Yet, while such "worker" analogies pointed to the uniqueness of Paul's position, they did not necessarily show why the ἀδελφοί should hear and heed him on matters of internal disputes. Before turning to that intra-church conflict, Paul pronounced that he was not only the planter and master builder, but also the *paterfamilias* who would call his beloved children to order.

Father of the Family

Having discussed Paul's attempts to reconfigure the interrelationships of the Corinthian ἐκκλησία as fellow siblings and fellow heirs and his own position in relation to Apollos and other leaders as fellow servants of one

Lord, we turn at last to 4.14–21, where Paul introduced what was to become the most provocative of his familial terms,[148] describing himself as the Corinthians' earthly father. As we shall see, although this is the only occurrence of his πατήρ imagery in 1 Corinthians, its significance lies in its placement. Indeed, it will be argued that the deeper significance of this final part of 1 Cor. 1–4 lies in its ability to serve as a bridge between the opening discussion on unity and identity in the Christian network to subsequent chapters' engagement with specific internal disputes. We now turn, therefore, to 1 Cor. 4.14–21:

Οὐκ ἐντρέπων ὑμᾶς γράφω ταῦτα ἀλλ' ὡς τέκνα μου ἀγαπητὰ νουθετῶ[ν]. 15 ἐὰν γὰρ μυρίους παιδαγωγοὺς ἔχητε ἐν Χριστῷ ἀλλ' οὐ πολλοὺς πατέρας. ἐν γὰρ Χριστῷ Ἰησοῦ διὰ τοῦ εὐαγγελίου ἐγὼ ὑμᾶς ἐγέννησα. 16 παρακαλῶ οὖν ὑμᾶς, μιμηταί μου γίνεσθε. 17 διὰ τοῦτο ἔπεμψα ὑμῖν Τιμόθεον, ὅς ἐστίν μου τέκνον ἀγαπητὸν καὶ πιστὸν ἐν κυρίῳ, ὃς ὑμᾶς ἀναμνήσει τὰς ὁδούς μου τὰς ἐν Χριστῷ [Ἰησοῦ], καθὼς πανταχοῦ ἐν πάσῃ ἐκκλησίᾳ διδάσκω. 18 ὡς μὴ ἐρχομένου δέ μου πρὸς ὑμᾶς ἐφυσιώθησάν τινες· 19 ἐλεύσομαι δὲ ταχέως πρὸς ὑμᾶς, ἐὰν ὁ κύριος θελήσῃ, καὶ γνώσομαι οὐ τὸν λόγον τῶν πεφυσιωμένων ἀλλὰ τὴν δύναμιν· 20 οὐ γὰρ ἐν λόγῳ ἡ βασιλεία τοῦ θεοῦ ἀλλ' ἐν δυνάμει. 21 τί θέλετε; ἐν ῥάβδῳ ἔλθω πρὸς ὑμᾶς η ἐν ἀγάπῃ πνεύματί τε πραΰτητος;

Having established in 1 Cor. 3 and 4 that he and Apollos were actually fellow-servants of God for the sake of the church's members, Paul proceeded to contrast his "weak" and "foolish" position not with that of Apollos, but with the Corinthians themselves (4.10ff.; cf. 1.25). They enjoyed the very privileges and rights which he and other apostles were denied. Yet in the midst of becoming the περικάθαρμα τοῦ κόσμου, Paul and those included in his apostolic "we" continued to work, bless, endure, and conciliate. Could the rich, regal, wise and distinguished Corinthian Christians say the same? Yet even though he had in 1.27 proclaimed that God had chosen the foolish and weak things of the world (Paul himself?) "to bring to shame" (καταισχύνω) the wise and powerful, i.e. eloquent, Paul assured the believers that it was not his desire to shame (ἐντρέπω) them,[149] but rather to "admonish" (νουθεσία) them. With verse 14, Paul changed his tone and quickly stated the reasons for the harsh nature of his preceding words. The term νουθεσία, found also in 10.11, refers to instruction in regard to belief or behaviour. It can, therefore, be translated in various instances as "warn," "instruct" or "admonish." While elsewhere Paul acknowledged the special role of those who "had charge" over the believers (προΐστημι) to admonish them (1 Thes. 5.12), he also made it clear that godly admonition was the common responsibility of all members of the local ἐκκλησία (1 Thes. 5.14; Rom. 15.14; cf. Col. 3.16). Thus, the thing to note in 4.14 is not simply that Paul was admonishing the believers, but rather that his admonitions were from a father to *his beloved children* (τέκνα μου ἀγαπητά).

In expressing his relationship with the Corinthians in terms of a father-children relationship, Paul was in no way making an outrageous or arrogant claim.[150] After all, it was only "through the gospel" (διὰ τοῦ εὐαγγελίου) that this parturition had taken place. Paul actually made sparing use of πατήρ in 1 Corinthians, especially when compared with his prolific use of ἀδελφός terminology.[151] Out of the over three-hundred occurrences of "father" language in the New Testament, only a handful are found in this letter…and mostly in reference to God (e.g. 8.6; 15.24).[152] Indeed, in 8.5-6, Paul would argue that although there may be many "so-called gods" (λεγόμενοι θεοί) in heaven and on earth, "yet *for us* there is but one God, the Father (ὁ πατήρ), from whom are all things." Even so, in 4.14–15, Paul asserted that although the Corinthians may have had many guardians (παιδαγωγοί) in Christ, they did not have many fathers (πατέρας). Rather, he proclaimed, ἐγὼ ὑμᾶς ἐγέννησα. Unlike the related passage in Gal. 4.19, where the apostle spoke of still being in the pains of childbirth "until Christ is formed in you" (μέχρις οὗ μορφωθῇ Χριστὸς ἐν ὑμῖν),[153] in 1 Cor. 4.15, the reference is to a past event (ἐγέννησα, first aorist active indicative).[154] The Corinthians' very existence ἐν Χριστῷ was due to Paul's "engendering" role. Here, it is possible to see strong similarities with the apostolic *apologia* in 1 Cor. 9. Indeed, in 9.2, Paul argued that if to no one else he could claim the title, to the Corinthians, at least, he was ἀπόστολος.[155] They were, after all, his "work" (ἔργον, 9.1;cf. 3.13–15) and the "seal" (σφραγίς, 9.2) of his apostleship. This unique relationship between Paul and the Corinthians was the basis for his defense to those who would examine him (τοῖς ἐμὲ ἀνακρίνουσίν, 9.3; cf. 4.3ff.). Paul was emphasising the unique and, as we shall see, primary role he held in that relational system as progenitor.

Apollos and others who had laboured among the Corinthians since Paul left were no more than the slaves who took the children/heirs to their teacher...not even the teacher himself! Although there was nothing necessarily "derogatory" in the term παιδαγωγός, it still conveyed a servile role.[156] Although the word is rare in the New Testament, found only here and in Gal. 3.24–25, it was a common term in the ancient world. Literally meaning "boy leader," the παιδαγωγός was a slave employed by a family to watch over a child somewhere between the ages of six and sixteen, supervising the child's behaviour at home and also taking him to the teacher/schoolmaster for instruction outside the home. As seen in *figure 3.a* above, this "guardian" often had unofficial influence over the child, even wielding the rod of discipline (ῥάβδος). It is interesting to note that παιδαγωγοί were only needed during the child's "in-between" stage. When the child was very young, he would be taught basic principles at home and "exposed to few, I would rather say to no, temptations."[157] Then, after a certain age, the guardian was no longer needed, for the child had reached maturity. While the Galatians passage focuses on the temporary nature of the position (ἐλθούσης δὲ τῆς πίστεως οὐκέτι ὑπὸ παιδαγωγόν ἐσμεν, 3.25)—with הרה leading the child-student to Christ (3.24) only then to be needed no longer—in 1 Cor. 4.15 the emphasis is instead on the primacy of the father's role in contrast with that of the guardian. Indeed, it was usually the father's prerogative to seek out a παιδαγωγός and thereby ensure that the child would be supervised in the proper way of life and not in eloquence alone.[158] In the Corinthian situation, however, it appears that the "children" themselves chose their παιδαγωγοί, displaying a loyalty toward them that was infantile and "merely human" (3.3–4), thereby contradicting their claims to spiritual maturity. These νήπιοι also mistook the "wisdom" and eloquence which they saw displayed in some of their teachers for the true wisdom and power (δύναμις) which belongs to those who belong to Christ (2.16; 4.20). More than this, they mistook Paul their πατήρ for just another παιδαγωγός. For his part, Paul in no way decried the work of Apollos and others as invalid, an argument he could hardly have won. Rather, he avoided the position of "rival," which would have placed him firmly in the "merely human" paradigm of his children, and instead acknowledged the work of all such guardians, even if they numbered in the thousands (μυρίος)! For this did not change the indisputable fact that he alone had "fathered" the Christian community.[159]

Even as God, the Father, exhibited a devotion and *pietas* towards his children, bestowing upon them a wealth of spiritual gifts and blessings (1.5),[160] so did Paul do all that he did for the sake of his τέκνα ἀγαπητά.[161] What did he desire from them in return? Paul answered this query in 4.16 by calling his beloved children to imitate him, presumably in the ways already listed in 4.12–13 and again later in ch.9.[162] To this end, he set Timothy before them as an example of a child who was not only ἀγαπητός (like the Corinthians), but also faithful (πιστός, 4.17). Timothy had been sent to remind the Corinthians not only of Paul's words but also "his ways" in Christ.[163] Indeed, in 16.10, Paul expressly stated that his "son" was doing "the Lord's work," (ἔργον κυρίου), even as Paul himself was. Thus, Paul's fatherly desire for his children was that they would grow up and by their life and example prove themselves worthy of their parentage.[164]

Interestingly, patristic writers gave little attention to verses 15–16 as such, and instead focused on those parts of the passage which concern discipline and the "rod."[165] Clement spoke not at all of Paul as the "father" of the Corinthian community, but rather as its "blessed apostle," although the author did echo Paul in using the familiar ἀδελφοί when addressing the Corinthians (ch. 1), and later called them to unity and φιλαδελφία (48). Only one verse of Paul's "father" passage is cited by Ignatius, and that is only in the long version of his letter to the Ephesians.[166] There appeared to be a greater concern among many of the Fathers for the authoritative, rather than the "procreative," dimension of spiritual fatherhood.[167]

Augustine, however, caught a glimpse of the dynamic qualities of Paul's familial language, noting that although Paul "begat by the gospel" the Corinthian Christians, it was the apostle's desire that they not remain as little children but grow and extend the family themselves by doing the Lord's work, like Timothy (16.10).[168] Likewise Methodius, in his *Banquet of the Ten Virgins,* spoke of Paul as being "first born and suckled," then growing in spiritual maturity until he could give birth to other believers, who themselves could "assist in labouring for the birth and nurture of other children."[169] The father's unique calling, then, was to issue forth children and lead them by teaching, example and discipline, with the expectation that one day they would become mature adults. Yet, at the same time, no matter how mature these children become, they would never cease to be the *paterfamilias'* "beloved children." Timothy, as seen in 4.17, remained Paul's τέκνον ἀγαπητόν even though he was clearly mature in the faith himself. From earliest days, then, there were some commentators who perceived a more dynamic and complex reasoning behind Paul's paternal imagery than an overly simplistic authoritarianism: "I am your father, so you had better listen to me."[170]

In this sense, the authority of the father was quite distinct from the authority of the master, as mentioned above. Any who immediately argue that Paul's "father" language, especially his statements about coming to the Corinthians either in love or with a rod, was simply patriarchal and oppressive are focusing on stereotypes of ancient fatherhood. It was argued above that the social reality of the father's power in an οἶκος was quite different from what has often been assumed from ancient legal treatises. As noted in that section, devotion more than obedience was ideally at the heart of the father-child relationship, especially as contrasted with the master-slave relationship. Indeed, beginning with Julius Caesar, the Roman emperors promoted usage of the appellation *pater* for themselves while avoiding the designation of *dominus.*[171] Despite some individual cases where a master chose to give freedom to a slave, generally the master's role did *not* include helping a slave become a slave owner himself. Chrysostom acknowledged this important difference when he spoke of the distinction Paul was making: "[Not] as a master, nor yet as an apostle, nor yet as having you for my disciples" (which had well suited his claims on them), but "as my beloved children I admonish you."[172]

It is intriguing that distinctions between father and master, or even between the absolute legal powers of the *paterfamilias* and the daily realities of differentiated household relationships, have often been lost on modern interpreters of Paul. Like some of the patristic writers, such modern interpreters have chosen to focus almost solely on the authoritative aspects of Paul's "father" language,[173] while failing to see that 4.14–21 is as much about the identity and position of the Corinthians in the system as it is about Paul's unique place in that network. The apostle's "language of incorporation," typified by family relationships with primary mutual responsibilities, is not as much declaratory as it is challenging.[174] Into which identity, which set of relationships, would the Corinthians choose to live? Paul made it clear throughout the first four chapters that certain options were not open to them: they could not perceive themselves as simply another *collegium,* and they could not perceive Paul as simply another charismatic teacher/leader like Apollos. Paul argued that these options were no longer open to them.[175] Though he admitted gladly that he was *God's* servant, yet he was *their* father. In saying this, Paul effectively cut off any arguments that he was not eloquent enough or wise enough, or anything else a child might say of his/her parent; he was still the one who had brought them into life. But he also gave them, in the final verses of chapter four, the very real option of relating to him "by the book"—as a stern *paterfamilias* who had the power and right to wield the rod as he might with a slave—or ἐν ἀγάπῃ πνεύματί τε πραΰτητος, as towards one's mature children (4.21). The choice was theirs: the Corinthians could continue to live as νήπιοι who as yet lacked true wisdom (3.1) and who "belonged" to various παιδαγωγοί. Or, rather, they could choose to exhibit the maturity of adult children who recognised that they belonged ultimately to God (3.23). Paul's greatest pleasure would be that the ἀδελφοί live together in love and work through their differences in a way that honoured their common "familial" bond ἐν Χριστῷ.[176]

In this sense, it should be noted that the passage (4.14–21) serves as a bridge to the next several chapters. The "sudden shift" in topic that comes with chapter five has led many through the years to question the unity of 1 Corinthians, a point contested by M. Mitchell and others.[177] Calvin noticed the seemingly drastic change from chapters four to five, although he proposed in the end that 4.21 (and not 5.1) should mark the beginning of chapter five, as it seems to belong more to that which follows it than to that which precedes it.[178] Following K. Bailey, B. Dodd has recently offered several reasons for viewing 4.14–21 (as a unit) as an introductory section to the chapters which follow.[179] Among these reasons are the change in tone with 4.14 and the emphasis on self-presentation and imitation in the *inclusio* formed by 4.16 and 11.1 (both read μιμηταί μου γίνεσθε). Dodd also notes the shift in Paul's language from "we/us" before 4.14 to "I/me" in 4.14ff. Most significant, however, is the fact that "the father metaphor begun in 4.14 continues through 4.21 and prepares for Paul's assertion of disciplinary authority in ch.5."[180] To those in the church who were arrogant or "puffed-up" (φυσιόω) as a result of his absence (4.18) and lack of eloquence (4.19),[181] Paul responded with a challenge concerning the power (δύναμις) of his unruly children, not simply their eloquence. It has already been noted that, legal treatises aside, the πατήρ in actuality did not wield unilateral and indiscriminate power over all in the οἶκος. His authority was tempered by the family council that acted as an informal, *ad hoc* body deliberative and judicial functions.[182] What is noteworthy about 4.14–21 is that, immediately after claiming the primacy of the *paterfamilias*, Paul went on to discuss the very topics one would expect to see in a family *consilium:* namely, issues of scandal and discipline (1 Cor. 5),[183] sibling conflict (6), marriage and divorce (7),[184] and business or collegial dealings (typified by the formal feasts which accompanied them, 8–10). It could be argued, therefore, that Paul's own δύναμις was not that of a despot, but the power and authority to call adult children together for deliberation and judgment in something like a family *consilium.*[185] In both 1 Cor. 4.18–20 and 5.3–5, Paul admitted to his absence from the very assembly which he appears to have called (συναχθέντων ὑμῶν, 5.4), yet still claimed the presidency, as it were, of the "family meeting," even if only through his correspondence (5.3) or appointed representative (4.17). The purpose of this *consilium* will be the subject of the following chapter.

Thus, utilising the various terms found in the οἶκος, Paul asserted that he who was a brother *through Christ* to the Corinthians, and a servant *of Christ* for their sake, was also a father *in Christ* to them. Furthermore, just as several of the ἀδελφοί passages were positioned at points of transition in the letter, so did the πατήρ passage in 4.14–21 initiate a series of "family issues" which were best introduced by the father of that family. Much more will be said next chapter about the nature of these "family issues"—and the type of intra-church conflict management Paul advocated in different situations—but for now it is enough to see that, as the father called together an "in-house" family *consilium,* so Paul affirmed his own role as the progenitor, the *paterfamilias,* before opening his own "family meeting."

Conclusion

It has been argued here that the key issue in 1 Cor. 1–4 was not a tension between those of different social status (1.26) or between this subgroup and that subgroup (1.11ff.) as much as it was a confusion surrounding the identity and operative boundaries of the ἐκκλησία in the midst of its environment.[186] It was further suggested that Paul utilised his unique position in the system as founding apostle and *paterfamilias* to set in place for those "inside" a tension between the familiar and the challenging. The cross of Christ represented nothing less than death to the old and the familiar, and for those in the Christian ἐκκλησία it resulted in "a sharpening of critical issues"[187] and "a strengthening of group consciousness."[188] Likewise, the need for reconfigured relationships drew Paul into a different kind of boundary language, not for the primary purpose of excluding those outside (i.e. potential insiders), but to promote greater unity for those within the network. By addressing the Corinthian Christians in familial rather than collegial terms, the apostle suggested that the Corinthians belonged to one another as ἀδελφοί, inasmuch as they were united in Christ.[189] At the same time, they were Paul's beloved children who honoured him best when they chose to imitate him (4.16). Indeed, Paul admonished his "beloved children" in 1 Cor. 4 precisely because they were *not* experiencing the trials and struggles which he endured. While he worked "with his own hands" they had "already become rich" (4.8). Yet, in a paradoxical twist, the very things about the apostle's ministry which caused his critics to cry out against him (i.e. being poorly clothed, beaten, reviled, persecuted) were instead evidence that Paul (and those like him) belonged to God, though visibly περικαθάρματα τοῦ κόσμου.[190] As he later made clear in 1 Cor. 9, Paul's choice to earn his own living rather than be a client to some patron led to accusations against his leadership, yet it also echoes his admonition to the Thessalonians to "mind your own affairs and work with your [own] hands" (πράσσειν τὰ ἴδια καὶ ἐργάζεσθαι ταῖς [ἰδίαις] χερσὶν ὑμῶν, 1 Th. 4.11).[191] It is interesting that this Pauline principle, which effectively allowed for the Christian life to be lived as parallel to, but not dependent on, the rest of society (cf. Gal. 6.5) evolved, by the time of the Pastorals and 1 Peter, into a reinforcement of the societal status quo.[192] Paul himself, however, would have none of that![193] Rather, as we have seen, in

1 Cor. 1–4 Paul the πατήρ attempted to effect a paradigm shift for his "beloved children" in the ἐκκλησία, challenging the familiar roles and patterns of outside networks through a focus on the cross of Christ (1.17), the δύναμις θεοῦ for those who would be transformed by it.

NOTES

[1] Cf. Malina and Neyrey 1996, 158ff., where the authors list several different relational systems or "in-groups" in which social "embeddedness" occurred. Unfortunately, they say little about a person belonging to more than one "in-group", and the possible effects of multiple social roles as a result of such multiple "belonging."

[2] As Grosheide has remarked, "no other difference [between the cliques] is noted except the slogans" (1953, 37). Pickett has asserted that a theological explanation for the conflict "can explain neither the party strife nor the criticisms of Paul" (1997, 55–56). While most scholars have now dismissed Baur's earlier arguments regarding divisions between Petrine and Pauline subgroups in the church, there continue to be some who attempt to piece together the theological positions underlying the slogans of 1.12 (cf. Goulder 1994; earlier, see Héring 1962, 5–6). See Conzelmann 1975, 33–34 for more.

[3] In commenting on Munck's description of Corinth as *"Die Gemeinde ohne Partien,"* Barrett admits that Paul "could expect that all would read or hear what he had to say" (1982, 3).

[4] Cf. 1.10; 2.1; 3.1; cf. also the numerous instances of the plural "you" throughout 1–4.

[5] Cf. Plutarch, *Praec. Ger. Reip.* 10.

[6] Ruef points this out emphatically (1971, 9). Bruce concurs, but adds that "if the quarreling and party-spirit…were allowed to develop unchecked, outright division might be the result" (1971, 32). The ἵνα μή of 12.25 displays a similar stress on the potential for σχίσμα.

[7] Murphy-O'Connor 1979, 10. Grosheide's assertion that Paul did not consider the ἔριδες "of very great importance," but instead was more concerned with issues of baptism and the cross, makes little sense unless one partitions Paul's own thought patterns in very non-systemic ways (1953, 41).

[8] Cf. Barrett 1982, 4.

[9] Combined with ζῆλος both in 3.3 and in Rom. 13.13, the term was often used to describe political strife or factionalism, and when used by Paul refers to both "the discord itself and the contentions which give rise to it" (Mitchell 1991, 82, n. 96).

[10] Plin. *Letters* X.34: "Quodcunque nomen ex quacunque causa dederimus iis qui in idem contracti fuerint…hetaeriae aeque brevi fient." As we will see, while later Christians would freely use collegial imagery for the church, Paul had good reason in his time to avoid it.

[11] Epstein 1987, 80.

[12] Besides Welborn (1987, 90–91) and Mitchell (1991,82), cf. Clarke 1993, 112: "Paul's disapproval of their quarrels…is played a partisanship characteristic of the surrounding society." Cf. Barclay 1991; Chow 1992; Eisenstadt 1984; Gill 1994 (though focusing on Acts, this offers much concerning the role of the social elite); Saller 1982; Stambaugh and Balch 1986.

[13] "Concerning the slogans in 1.12—Ἐγὼ μέν εἰμι Παύλου (ἀπολλῶ, Κηφᾶ, Χριστοῦ)—most modern scholars have dismissed Chrysostom's early argument that they represent a 'rhetorical invention' on Paul's part, making his argument 'less severe' by concealing the names of the true instigators of the dissensions 'as behind a sort of masks' of known and respected apostles/leaders" (Héring 1962, 4–5, referring to *Hom. on I Cor.* III, 4). Mitchell does make the point that these slogans may indeed have been rhetorical caricatures used by Paul in his deliberative argumentation and not actual statements made by the Corinthians themselves (1991, 82–86). In any case, whether these slogans were "actual party cries" or "Paul's impersonation" of the Corinthians' position, it is highly unlikely that Paul was using fictional names, especially his own, to protect others, particularly in light of the fact that elsewhere he showed no such compunctions (i.e. Phil. 4.2–3).

[14] Cf. Balz' article on *eimi* in *EDNT (I)* 392–393.

[15] Paul's strategy in offering Philemon the opportunity to welcome back his former slave as a Christian brother is not unlike that of Pliny in his letter to Priscus (2.13).

[16] Cf. Mitchell 1991, 83–86, esp. 85. The phraseology is usually used in the third-person, not personally as a slogan but as a description by another. Cf. Dem., Or. 9.56. See also Acts 27.23 (τοῦ θεοῦ, οὗ εἰμι ἐγώ), which clearly speaks of possession. For a detailed look at the rhetorical background to the slogans, see Winter 1997, 170–176.

[17] Van Stempvoort 1950, 217.

[18] D. Martin 1995, 132. See also Dunn 1999, 193, who notes that both Paul and early Christianity experienced an "identity in transition."

[19] Morgan, et al., 1981, 137; also Klein and White 1996, 158; Meeks 1983, 105–108.

[20] As children we have fairly obvious boundaries, such as playpens or cots, but our adult boundaries, though more subtle in nature (such as personal space) are no less real.

[21] Crafton 1991, 31. Cf. DeMaris's "integration into a new condition" (1995, 677).

[22] Cf. Hartman 1996, 588.

[23] Douglas 1966, 4. Schürer concurs: "In continuous contact with a Gentile environment, the Jewish communities could only preserve themselves by constantly and carefully eliminating alien elements" (1973, 431).

[24] DeMaris 1995, 672.

[25] Winter asks whether a previously established policy of access on the part of Jews (and Jewish Christians) to meat not offered to idols (as in Rome, where such a policy existed had been overturned as a result of anti-semitism in Rome. If this was the case, Winter continues, it might explain more clearly the motivation behind the beating of Sosthenes as "the local expression" of the anti-semitic programme in the capital city, and certainly makes greater sense of the timing of the idol meat issue in 1 Corinthians (1999, 8–9).

[26] It would appear from his lengthy explication in Romans that Paul did not wish to dispense with the Law but, rather, to determine its role within a Christian paradigm. Volumes have been written on Paul's treatment of the Law. A thorough introduction to the place of Torah in Paul's theology may be found in Dunn 1998, 128–161. Cf. also Barton 1996; Craffert 1993; Kee 1993; Segal 1990; Thielman 1994; and Ziesler 1990.

[27] Dunn 1991, 324, n. 40.

[28] *ABD (I)* 587. For more on the role of baptism in Paul's thought, see Carlson 1993.

[29] From Herman 1987, 155.

[30] Cf. Horrell 1996, 116–117.

[31] Contra Best 1980, 11, whose argument that Paul's "group" would have been small indeed if it only included those he personally baptised fails to account for the influential network of family, clients and friends. As Herman remarks, "a ξένος, a friend's friend, was almost as valuable an asset as the friend himself" (1987, 152).

[32] Cf. Pitt-Rivers 1977, as well as Douglas 1982.

[33] DeMaris 1995, 662: "From the standpoint of the Christian community, baptism for the dead was an expression of confidence that death posed no threat to the Christian, living or deceased" (676–677). In *Ep.* 3.9, Pliny spoke of a legal case that was noteworthy precisely because it was so rare, in which the defendant was a man recently deceased (*in defuncti*).

[34] Cf. Winter 1999.

[35] In the LXX and Pseudepigrapha, the focus is often on issues of final judgment, as opposed to resuscitation from the dead. Cf. *1 Enoch* 22.1–7 and chs. 92–105; Dan. 12.1–3; *Jub.* 23.11–31; 4 Ezra 7.31–39; Wis. of Sol. 1–6; *Ps. Sol.* 3, 13–15; *2 Bar.* 49–51; *Avoth de-Rabbi Nathan* 28.

[36] D Martin reiterates that "existence in the body of Christ [was] not the only reality" for the Corinthians, as they continued to move in and about their multiple networks (1995, 132).

[37] We can hear echoes here of Paul's earlier wording concerning those who were "merely human" (3.4) and those with "the mind of Christ" (2.16). Indeed, several points of correspondence appear to exist between 1 Cor.1–4 and 15 (e.g. 15.30–32 and 4.9ff.).

[38] Fee 1987, 61 suggests that various church members had a "magical view" of baptism, resulting in an elevated view of those who performed the baptisms.

[39] While it might be too much to describe Jesus' words here as paradigmatic, it is interesting to note that when he called his first disciples *out of* their primary relational systems to follow him, he at the same time called them *into* a relational system that was both new and familiar, by taking their former life, as it were, to a new level. It should be noted in Matthew's narrative that while Jesus clearly accepted the man behind the occupation as one of his core followers, he did not speak to the tax collector as he did to the fishermen; there is no mention of becoming a "tax collector for God." Cf. Luke 19.1ff.

[40] Cf. 2 Cor. 1.1: τοῖς ἁγίοις πᾶσιν τοῖς οὖσιν ἐν ὅλῃ τῇ ᾿Αχαΐᾳ. Kraybill notes that the apostle's terminology in 2 Cor. 6.14–17, e.g. μετοχή and κοινωνός, is probably influenced by the ceremonies of city trade associations and guilds (1992, 35).

[41] Curiously, ἐκκλησία is not found in the opening of his letters to the Romans (instead ἀγαπητοῖς θεοῦ, κλητοῖς ἁγίοις, 1.7) or Philippians (τοῖς ἁγίοις ἐν Χριστοῦ ᾿Ιησοῦ, 1.1), two Christian communities which were praised by Paul for their distinctive faith (Rom. 1.8) and evangelism (Phil. 1.5). I do not wish to press this point too far, particularly as my larger argument concerning Paul's use of ἐκκλησία in 1 Corinthians does not depend on it. However, it is an intriguing phenomenon which may deserve further study elsewhere.

[42] A similar point may be made about Philemon, where the master-slave relationship so prevalent in other outside networks was threatening the κοινωνία of the ἐκκλησία.

[43] Witherington 1995, 47: "It was not a technical term for a religious gathering, much less a Christian one." Kee notes that "surprisingly, the term [in the LXX] for the whole assembly of Israel in 1 Sam. 17.47 is ἐκκλησία" (1995, 485).

[44] Cf. Deut. 23.2; 1 Chr. 28.8; Neh. 13.1. Schmidt remarks that while there is at times "room for doubt," usually the addition of τοῦ θεοῦ is "either explicit or implicit" (*TDNT* III, 527).

[45] In Deuteronomy, the phrase "the day of the assembly" (τῇ ἡμέρᾳ τῆς ἐκκλησίας) is also used several times (4.10; 9.10; 18.16).

[46] Although Webb remarks that the "ad hoc meeting of representatives of the various tribes" was an "important institution" in the days before the monarchy, he admits that in this particular case—where a man of dubious moral character instigates civil war among the tribes—the behaviour of the assembly…shows how morally and spiritually bankrupt Israel had become" (1994, 283–286).

[47] Here, then, we can see that concern with "correct definition, discrimination and order" mentioned in brief at the end of the last chapter (Douglas 1966, 53).

[48] Note here Douglas' idea of "dirt out of place." For more, see Barton 1986.

[49] It is interesting to note that within the one structure there existed "zones of differential access" (cf. Broderick 1993, 124ff.), so that the most sacred section, known simply as ὁ ἅγιος τῶν ἁγίων (Ex. 26.33), was cut off from the rest of the Tabernacle/Temple by a curtain, thereby limiting access both in terms of number of persons (only one, the High Priest, may enter) and time (only one day a year). See Lk. 1.8–9; Mk. 15.38.

[50] Schütz 1975 remains an excellent study on the legitimation of authority. Cf. also Friedman 1985, 223–249, who notes that successful leadership relies as much on the consensus of those who follow as on the charisma of the leader (see esp. 224–225).

[51] For a summary of the various arguments concerning 1 Cor. 2.9, see Barrett 1968, 72–73; Conzelmann 1975, 63–64; Fee 1987, 108–109; Hays 1997, 44–45.

[52] Fee 1993, 55. For this reason, the author asserts, Paul often speaks in 1 Corinthians about Christian ethics *in light of the church's identity*, for the overriding issue "is not simply a low vein of sin; rather, it is the church itself."

[53] I do not wish to imply that such language is unique to 1 Corinthians, as it also may be found in other Pauline letters, applied at times to Christ (1 Cor.1.30 — cf. Vulgate: sapientia nobis a Deo et iustitia et sanctificatio (ἁγιασμὸς) et redemptio — see also 1 Th. 1.3), to the Spirit (1 Cor.12.3, πνεύματι ἁγίῳ; see also Rom. 9.1; 14.17; 15.16; Eph. 1.13; 1 Th. 1.5), to the kiss of greeting between fellow believers

(16:20, φιλήματι ἁγίῳ; see also 2 Cor. 13.12; Rom. 16.16; 1 Th. 5.26), to "the saints in Jerusalem" (1 Cor.16.1; see also 2 Cor. 8.4; 9.1; Rom. 16.15) or, more generally, to "the saints" (1 Cor.16.15; see also Phlm. 1.5; Eph. 1.15; Col. 1.4). It is not the uniqueness of ἅγιος language which is notable in 1 Corinthians, but the high correspondence between holiness language and the identity of the ἐκκλησία. As for the church being "called out" ones, ἐκ καλέω, Dunn notes that "it is very noticeable that Paul refrains from just such an interplay of ideas" (1998,537).

[54] Acts 26.18 says explicitly that sanctification occurs "by faith in [Christ]." It is not something that occurs as a result of one's own efforts, hence the passive form which is found herein.

[55] See Stanley 1996 for more on this terminology.

[56] Cf. Hays 1997, 34.

[57] Cf. Acts 7.48 and 17.24 for the assertion that God does not dwell (οἰκεῖ) in temples "made by human hands." In 1 Cor. 7.12–13, Paul used the same verb to explain how an unbelieving spouse might choose "to dwell" or "to live with" (οἰκεῖν) the Christian believer.

[58] Hays 1997, 34. Murphy-O'Connor asserts that unlike the Essenes, Paul associated the spiritual temple with the Spirit's presence (1979, 28; cf. 1QS 9.3–6). Concerning the apostle's use of this kind of imagery in a letter to a predominantly Gentile congregation, see Origen's words in *Hom. on Ex. 5.1:* "Paul, teacher of the Gentiles, taught Gentile Christians how to understand books of the Law."

[59] A variation of this theme is found in 7.2, 4, where ἴδιον and ἰδίου respectively are utilised to indicate that each married believer's body *belongs* to his or her spouse.

[60] Hays notes: "the right action must be *discerned* on the basis of a christological paradigm, with a view to the need of the community" (1997, 43).

[61] Fee 1987, 263, n. 65 (following Turner's *Syntax*). Cf. Witherington 1995, 169, who follows Fee's reading of the text, and Horrell 1996, 118. Earlier, Conzelmann admitted that "the facts [concerning an individualistic reading of the temple imagery] are not adequately grasped" and that there are questions as to "how this transfer from the collective body to the individual is rendered possible" (1975, 112, n. 37).

[62] Mus. Ruf., *On Sexual Indulgence;* the author goes on to say that the one consequence is to the transgressor himself, who "immediately reveals himself as a worse and a less honourable person," emphasising this loss of honour over "the injustice of the thing."

[63] We can see here some consonance between the church and the Diaspora συναγωγή. Cf. Meyers 1992, 253; Schürer 1973, 431. Also see Forbes 1995.

[64] There is continued discussion concerning whether the ἰδιώτης was an "outsider" who happened to be present in the Christian worship (Fee 1987, 685 suggests that the ἰδιώτης might have been an unbelieving spouse) or an "insider" who was uninitiated in tongues and, thus, found him/herself outside the inner circle "in the position of an outsider or untrained one." Cf. Schlier's article in *TDNT*, III, 215–217, who notes that among other ancient writers, Pausanius in particular speaks of the distinction between "the man without charismatic gifts" (the ἰδιώτης) and the so-called "diviners" (the μάντεις, cf. II, *Korinthiaca,*13, 7). See also Conzelmann

1975, 243, and Barrett 1968, 324, who both see ἰδιώτης in some way synonymous with "unbeliever," with which the term is linked in verses 23 and 24. Since it is assumed that the ἰδιώτης would indeed say the "Amen" if s/he understood the speaker's words, it could be argued that this person was a fellow believer who simply was uninitiated in tongues, and not a true outsider or unbeliever. However, Paul clearly made a distinction between ἐκκλησία ὅλη and those who εἰσέρχομαι, suggesting actual "outsiders."

[65] As Winter has recently pointed out, ancient religion was about controlling your own fate, not about "building up" the rest of the community (cf. Winter 1999).

[66] There is a possible echo here of Sir. 21.17, in which στόμα φρονίμου ζητηθήσεται ἐν ἐκκλησίᾳ.

[67] Cf. 1 Tim. 5.8 (οἰκείων); 5.14 (οἰκοδεσπότειν); Titus 2.5 (οἰκουργούς).

[68] Thielman asserts that despite the lack of many explicit citations in the Corinthian letters, Paul indeed relied on "concepts whose full significance becomes clear only against the background of the Mosaic Law" (1994, 86). Consider Hays' comments concerning resonances of an earlier text *"beyond those explictly cited"* (1999, 392).

[69] This does not imply that Paul never spoke of church*es* in the plural, for he most certainly did (7.17; 11.16; 14.33,34; 16.1,19), and at one point he acknowledged a specific "house church" hosted by Aquila and Priscilla (τῇ κατ' οἰκον αὐτῶν ἐκκλησίᾳ, 16.19). However, when he used ἐκκλησία to define the entire Corinthian church, it was for the purpose of delineating a group set apart from other networks which was to be unified in itself.

[70] Theissen 1992, 214; he adds that this "diastratic structure...was bound to encourage the relativisation of status differences." Cf. Hays 1998, 32.

[71] For more on the difference between temporary change and lasting systemic change, cf. Morgan, et. al., 1981, 137–138; also Watzlawick, et. al., pp. 10–11.

[72] Osiek and Balch 1997, 192.

[73] Strauss 1993, 215.

[74] Cf. Conzelmann 1975, 39.

[75] Horrell chooses to view the text largely through the lens of 1.26, arguing that social status is the key to understanding Paul's comments on the cross and worldly wisdom (1996, 131–137).

[76] A similar overarching relational dichotomy is seen in Aelius Aristides' observance of conditions during the reign of Antoninus Pius: "For you have divided all the people of the Empire...in two classes: the more cultured, better born, and more influential everywhere you have declared Roman citizens and even of the same stock; the rest vassals and subjects" (*To Rome* 59–60, cited in Gill 1994, 107).

[77] Συνεσταύρωμαι is found in both Gal. 2.19–20 and Rom. 6.6.

[78] Conzelmann 1975, 46.

[79] See Barrett 1968, 54. For more on reading "Jew and Greek" rather than "Jew and Gentile" see Stanley 1996 (see p. 89, n.190 above).

[80] Cf. Conzelmann 1975, 47. See also Hays 1999, 406, who speaks of Paul's attempt to "reconfigure their self-understanding and conduct in light of Christ crucified."

[81] Meeks 1983, 79.

[82] Douglas 1966, 114: "thresholds symbolise beginnings of new statuses."

[83] Cf. Van Stempvoort 1950, 163 (217), who describes the cross as "the source of unity."

[84] The Corinthian Christians "failed to realise what fellowship with the Lord and with one another implied" (Moffatt 1938, 9). The author likened this situation to the competing alliances that emerged in the days of the Oxford Movement, and quoted Newman: "Such persons attach themselves to particular persons...and say things merely because others do."

[85] Compare with *1 Clement* 46.7: There is one Christ who has been crucified for us; how then can Christ's body, the church, be divided into factions and subgroups?

[86] Pickett 1997, 125. In a similar way, Paul later points to the shadow of the cross in the Lord's Supper: "For as often as you eat this bread and drink this cup, you proclaim the Lord's death until he comes" (11.26). The cross results in true communion.

[87] Friedman 1985, 131.

[88] Van Stempvoort points out the various occurrences of the names of key figures in the Corinthian church, in 1.12; 1.13; 3.4–5; 3.22; 4.6. (1950, 173).

[89] Cf. Oropeza 1999, on Paul's comparison of the Israelites' complaints to the attitude and faithlessness of the Corinthians in 1 Cor. 10.10. Cf. also Horrell 1997.

[90] Friedman 1985, 132.

[91] Cf. Kee 1993, 96, who asserts that, in contrast to the ethical and religious distinctions presented by the Judaism of its day, the church offered the way "through Jesus and his teachings, his death and his resurrection...to share in the new covenant without respect to ethical or ritual requirements."

[92] Furnish 1993, 67–68.

[93] D. Martin 1995, 268, n. 13. Martin notes that body imagery was often used in antiquity to support the existing hierarchical social structures (pp. 29–37, 92–94).

[94] There are a few notable exceptions, such as Gal. 6.17, where the apostle spoke of bearing the marks of Christ "on my body," or Phil. 1.20 and 3.21, where he spoke respectively of the exaltation of Christ "in my body" and "this body of humiliation." Otherwise, it is only in 2 Corinthians that we find any more of Paul's "body language," and even there it is not in terms of the church as Christ's body (5.8 and 10; 12.2 and 3). Examples of σῶμα Χριστοῦ outside Romans and 1 Corinthians can be found in the deutero-Paulines (Eph.1.23; 2.16; 4.4, 12, 16; 5.23, 30; Col. 1.18, 24; 2.17, 19; 3.15).

[95] This absence of σῶμα in chs. 1–4, noted in 1950 by Van Stempvoort (pp. 163, 217), has often been ignored by those who argue for a place of primacy for the body motif.

[96] Hays 1997, 36.

[97] Meeks 1983, 86–87. Banks thereby seems justified in asserting that "the comparison of the Christian community with a 'family' must be regarded as the most significant metaphorical usage of all" (1994, 49).

[98] Again, see Banks 1994, 49: "The inadequacy of the organic unity of the 'body' metaphor leads Paul to utilise the language of...family relationships."

[99] Consider in 1 Timothy, for example, the challenge to ἐπίσκοποι (3.4) and διάκονοι (3.12) to "manage their households (and children) well" (προϊστάμενοι τῶν ἰδίων οἴκων). Even young widows are urged to οἰκοδεσποτεῖν (5.14). Titus 2.5 likewise

speaks of οἰκουργούς ἀγαθάς, and in 1.11 silence is demanded of those "upsetting whole households." 1 Peter makes fairly extensive and explicit use of household language, even describing the community of Christian believers as τοῦ οἴκου τοῦ θεοῦ (4.17). Cf. Osiek 1992, 84–86.

[100] Malina and Neyrey argue, in fact, that inasmuch as either a *collegium* or the Christian ἐκκλησία utilised the language and displayed characteristics of a "fictive family," that group had "the structure and...values of a patriarchal family" (1996, 160).

[101] Plato, *Menex.* 239a, where ἀδελφός is used for a compatriot; Xenophon *An.* 7.2.25, where it is used for a friend; Plotinus, *Enn.* 2.9.18, where all things in the world are ἀδελφοί.

[102] Among the many examples are: Jer 31.34; 2 Chr. 35.14; 1 Macc. 12.10, 17.

[103] Mt. 5.22, 47; 7.33; 18.15ff.; Acts 2.29; 3.17; 7.2; 13.15; 22.1; 23.1; 26.38; Heb. 7.5.

[104] In the undisputed letters of Paul, there are 113 occurrences of ἀδελφός (in some form), a fairly high figure when compared with the 97 occurrences in the Gospels and 57 in Acts. Also, as pointed out by Beutler (*EDNT* I, 28), while in the Gospels the term most often refers to physical brothers, in Paul's case the meaning is usually figurative and linked with fellow Christian believers. Forbes adds that Paul's usage is not reserved for "missionary associates," instead known as "fellow workers" (συνεργοί) but instead referred to "any or all Christian believers" (1995, 257; cf. Dunn 1975, 288).

[105] Only 1 Thessalonians has a higher proportion of ἀδελφοί usage than 1 Corinthians.

[106] Cf. Aem. 5.9.1, where similar terms are used together: οἱ δὲ νῦν ἀδελφοὶ καὶ συγγενεῖς ("but now brothers and countrymen").

[107] For this reason, God is not simply "Father," but "*our* Father" (πατρός ἡμῶν, 1.3). Cf. also Rom. 1.7; 2 Cor. 1.2; Gal. 1.3; Phil. 1.2; 1 Thes. 1.3; Phlm. 3. The theme of commonality is stressed from the start of 1 Corinthians through the prolific use of the plural genitive. Indeed, out of the 21 occurrences of ἡμῶν in the letter, almost one-third are in 1.1–10.

[108] It should be noted that among the various occurrences of the vocative, there are numerous repetitive patterns. For example, in 1.26, 2.1 and 3.1, a form of the negative οὐ is linked with ἀδελφοί. Likewise, the negative imperative μή is connected with the direct address in 1.10, 14.20 and 14.39. There is also great similarity between 10.1 ("I do not want you to be unaware"), 12.1 ("I do not want you to be uninformed"), and 15.1 ("I would remind you"). The same is true of 11.33 and 14.26 ("when you come together"). In chs. 5, 6 and 8, ἀδελφός is most often used as part of a reproof, while in ch. 7 it is part of Paul's recommendations.

[109] As Barrett has noted, other influences besides Paul's were present in the ἐκκλησία, and "some fell back on the old and familiar" (1982, 4).

[110] A similar pattern of joining the vocative with the negative imperative—ἀδελφοί μή— is found in the LXX. Cf. Gen 19.7 (μὴ πονηρεύσησθε); Judg. 19.23 (μὴ κακοποιήσητε); Jdth. 8.14 (μὴ παροργίζετε κύριον τὸν θεὸν ἡμῶν).

[111] This usage of sibling terminology as the language of an alternative relational network is reflected later in Paul's letter to Philemon, where he addressed the latter as ἀδελφέ (v.7), and then suggested that Philemon view his runaway slave, Onesimus,

in similar terms, as a "beloved brother" (16). It is the subtle nature of this kind of address, in Philemon and 1 Corinthians, that allowed a degree of "ambiguity" to enter the relational system: a person formerly understood *only* as slave or owner could now be seen also as an ἀδελφός.

[112] *Or.* 47.22. As Winter notes: "Such loyalty often resulted in strong competition between the disciples of different sophists in the cities of the East" (1997, 170). Cf. Aristides, *Or.51.29.*

[113] It is perhaps worth noting that the imperative γίνεσθε, linked with the direct address in 7.23–24, 14.20 and 15.58, appears far more in 1 Corinthians (see also 4.16; 10.7; 10.32; 11.1) than in all the other Pauline letters combined (Rom. 12.16; 2 Cor. 6.14; Gal. 4.12; Phil 3.17). The word denotes "becoming" and Paul uses it both in a negative sense, i.e. "do not become slaves [children, offensive ones]," and in a positive plea, i.e. become imitators of me, be steadfast. The Christian ἀδελφοί were to move from one way of thinking and acting to another.

[114] Cf. Plutarch, *De Frat. Amor.* 479A.

[115] The closest parallels to many of the uses in 1 Corinthians may be found in Galatians, where Paul offered strong words of admonition to the "brothers." His plea in Gal. 4.12 that κἀγὼ ὡς ὑμεῖς, ἀδελφοί, δέομαι ὑμῶν, and his call to imitation of himself (6.1) together seem to be very similar indeed to 1 Cor. 4.16 and 11.1. More relevant to intra-church conflict is the challenge to the ἀδελφοί in Gal. 5.13 to put aside the freedom and ἐξουσία that was theirs and instead διὰ τῆς ἀγάπης δουλεύετε ἀλλήλοις, as well as the specific injunction concerning the restoration of a member detected ἐν τινι παραπτώματι. Yet even in Galatians, there is but a fraction of ἀδελφοί usage as there is in 1 Corinthians.

[116] Chrysostom, *Hom. On 1 Cor.* 3.3.4.

[117] For example, in 2 Sam. 13.12, Tamar addressed her half-brother Amnon as ἀδελφέ, but in the context of pleading with him, μὴ ταπεινώσης με. Later, in 2 Sam. 20.9, Joab greeted his fellow commander and rival Amasa as ἀδελφέ, only then to murder him. Hiram, in 1 Kings 9.13, addressed Solomon as ἀδελφέ, yet in the context of asking why such a comrade would give him such poor lands. Even David's mournful lament over ἀδελφέ μου Ιωναθαν (2 Sam. 1.26) should be read in the context of David's now-unchallenged claim to Saul's throne (cf. 1.10), though such a reading is admittedly more cynical than some scholars would prefer. It is only in later texts that we find unambiguously positive references to ἀδελφοί (cf. 4 Macc. 13.9–10; Tob. 5.11–14; 6.7–16; 7.9; 11.2; Jdth. 7.30; 8.14,24; 14.1).

[118] The reference here is, of course, Gen. 33.9, where Esau addresses Jacob as "brother," the very one who cheated Esau out of his birthright and inheritance. Ironically, though the context in Gen. 33 is that of the reconciliation between brothers, Jacob's reluctance to join Esau on the subsequent journey suggests that he was not fully convinced of his brother's unqualified forgiveness. In ways that cannot be explored in detail at this time, this story is paradigmatic of future occurrences of sibling strife and suspicion, cited in n. 108 above.

[119] In this sense, there is far more in common between Paul's family talk and that of Jesus in the Synoptics, who linked family ties with a shared obedience to God (Mk.

3.31–35; Mt. 12.46–50; Lk. 8.19–21). Cf. Wenham 1995, 35 and 259, in which the author suggests that Paul was "familiar with Jesus' teaching about brotherly love."

[120]Cf. Petersen 1985, esp. p. 98. Another parallel may be found in James 2.1–9.

[121] Cf. Rom. 4.13–14; 8.17 ("heirs of God, joint-heirs of Christ"); Gal. 3.18, 29 ("heirs according to the promise"); 4.1,7 ("if a child, then also an heir"); 5.21. See also Eph. 1.14, 18; 5.5; Col. 3.24; Tit. 3.7; 1 Pet. 1.4; 3.9; Heb. 1.10,14; 6.12,17; 9.15; 11.7,8; 12.17; Acts 7.5; 20.32; Rev. 21.7.

[122] Skidmore offers several examples in ancient writings of the importance of human examples in moral instruction (1996, 14–15; cf. Livy 1.10; Tacitus, *Hist.*1.3).

[123] It should be emphasised that such language was not utilised by Paul in order to exclude those already outside the community (cf. 5.10; 14.23–25). Rather, as will be seen here, his concern was with the divisiveness among those *already in Christ*.

[124] Witherington 1995, 75. Indeed, Barclay notes that Paul showed "little concern with social questions beyond the boundaries of the church" (1991, 183).

[125] For more on the *concilium*, see esp. Dixon 1992, 72 (as well as pp. 39, 47, 62–64, 77–78) and next chapter.

[126] Cf. 2.14; 4.1–5; 5.3–5, 9–13; 6.1–11; 9.3ff.; 10.14–15. Paul's language here was not wholly unique in his time. However, while Aurelius subsequently questioned why a person often placed "less value on his own opinion of himself than on the opinions of others" (12.4), Paul went further in devaluing even his own opinion of himself in light of the only judgment that mattered to him...that of God (1 Cor. 4.1–5). See Derrett 1991; Kuck 1992.

[127] Barton 1997, 15.

[128] Barclay 1992, 60. Cf. Longenecker 1997, 40, who speaks of "new redemptive categories."

[129] Cf. Banks 1994, 51, who points to 1 Cor. 8.11,13 for a specific example of the personal nature of this kind of interdependence in the Christian community.

[130] Cf. Coser 1956, 35, as well as section 1.1 of this thesis.

[131] Hays 1997. 22.

[132] As seen above, the kind of εὐσεβεία exhibited by children or even trusted servants in the οἶκος is to be contrasted with the fear of reprisal which often motivated ὁ δοῦλος.

[133] While Greeks in general found service somewhat demeaning, when rendered to the πόλις it was lifted to a higher, more respected level; cf. Demosthenes 50.2.

[134] Plato, *Gorg.* 491e. The only truly dignified διακονία in the eyes of many Corinthians would have been that performed for the benefit of the πολιτεία, i.e. the statesman in the secular ἐκκλησία was the respected διάκονος τῆς πόλεως. It should be noted that the Judaism into which Paul was born did not have the same prejudices against service; cf. R. Jehoshua's comment regarding R. Gamaliel's service at table (b.Qid. 32b).

[135] Concerning 3.5, Ellingworth and Hatton note that although "the Greek word for servants refers to people who had a higher status than slaves' it does not mean therefore that such servants had any special importance" (1985, 61).

[136] *Ibid.*, 17. Paul, as an apostle, was a messenger who spoke and acted *in nomine Christi*. Such a messenger "must be heard and obeyed as if the one who sent him were there in person." Cf. also Van Stempvoort 1950, 72–73.

[137] Although an οἰκονόμος was *under* the authority of the master of the house (cf. Lk. 12.42), he was simultaneously *over* the other slaves in the οἶκος (cf. Lk. 16.1).

[138] Cf. Bieder's article in *EDNT (1)*, 196. See Hays 1997, 23–24 for more on this point.

[139] It is interesting to note that these questions-as-response echo the Jesus tradition, in which Jesus would often respond to his challengers with a question of his own, thus stepping out of the various "traps" into which they might have placed him. While it is not possible in this study to pursue the implications of such a potential "echo," it does suggest either that Paul was aware of Jesus' style of disputation or that the rhetorical method of question-as-response served both Jesus and Paul in similar confrontations.

[140] *TDNT (I)* 539–540. While Hartman considers as "odd" the image of money in an account, he does not take into account the fact that Paul might well have had more than one meaning in his mind as he thought of his readership in commercial Corinth (cf. Hartman 199, 586–588). For a view of Corinth as a commercial center, see Williams 1994.

[141] Crafton has argued that Paul's consistent use of "we" rather than "I" directs attention "away from Paul the apostle toward Paul and his colleagues, toward apostles in general, and toward the apostolic office" (1990, 67).

[142] Cf. Crafton 1990, 69: "Practically every statement concerning Paul's work is qualified by a phrase which sets it in the context of God's activity."

[143] Like so much of Paul's language in 1 Cor. 1–4 and, indeed, throughout the letter, the idiom used here (ἐλάχιστον) was a relational or systemic one, i.e. "it is a small thing in relation to something else far greater." Cf. Lk. 12.26; Jas. 3.4; also Fee 1987, 161 and *EDNT* I, 427. Paul turned "upside-down" the Corinthians' concept of leadership: "The leaders whom they are exalting should be perceived as household servants of God" (Clarke 1993, 121).

[144] Even this bold statement is qualified in the next verse by Paul's admission that he spoke in this way only διὰ τὴν ἀσθένειαν τῆς σαρκὸς ὑμῶν.

[145] It should be remembered that many of Roman Corinth's earliest inhabitants were freedmen, for whom talk of slavery might well have left a distinctly poor taste in the mouth. Cf. Bradley 1994; Murphy-O'Connor 1992; Romano 1994; Horrell 1996, 209.

[146] On Paul's slave terminology, see Martin 1990, 74–76; Horrell 1996, 206–210.

[147] It is also worth noting that a term like δοῦλος Χριστοῦ (7.22) could "have been heard as a metaphor of power by affiliation with the most important person in the cosmos, much as a member of the *familia Caesaris* might claim his or her unique social status as Caesar's slave" (Dodd 1996, 97). For more on this, see D. Martin 1990, 1–49.

[148] Cf. Gaventa 1993, 182–199; also Schüssler-Fiorenza 1984, 1987 (esp. p. 398).

[149] The term used here, the present active participle of ἐντρέπω, literally meaning "to shame," is quite rare in the New Testament (especially when contrasted with καταισχύνω, which is found in 1 Cor 1.27; 11.4,5,22; Rom. 5.5; 9.33; 10.11). Only

2 Thes. 3.14 and Tit. 2.8 use ἐντρέπω in the same sense as in 1 Cor. 4.14. When used in the passive/middle voice, in terms of one's position in relation to another, it can signify "reverence" or "respect" (Mat. 21.37; Mk. 12.6; Lk. 20.13; also Lk. 18.2,4). Perhaps it was because of the relational nature of the term, i.e. shame in contrast with something or someone else, that commended its usage in 4.14. in any case, it is important to recognise that honour was "the greatest social value, to be preferred over wealth and even life itself" (Osiek 1992, 27). For more on honour and shame in the ancient world, cf. Chance 1994; Malina 1993; Malina and Neyrey 1996. Concerning 1 Cor. 1–4 as an extended admonition, see Fitzgerald 1988, 117–128. On the ironic nature of Paul's admonition in relation to the previous list of social dichotomies, see Winter 1997a, 196–200.

[150] See, for example, 4 Macc. 7.1, 5, 9, in which Eleazar the martyr is referred to as "father." Later, in Jewish circles, rabbis and teachers were often called "fathers," as the teacher of Torah was said to have "begotten" his pupil (b.Sanh. 19b).

[151] Paul did, however, make three more references to his role as πατήρ in 2 Corinthians: 6.13 (ὡς τέκνοις λέγω), 11.2–3 (ἡρμοσάμην γὰρ ὑμᾶς ἑνὶ ἀνδρὶ παρθένον ἁγνὴν παραστῆσαι τῷ Χριστῷ, the work of a Jewish father on behalf of his betrothed daughter), and 12.14 (οὐ γὰρ ὀφείλει τὰ τέκνα τοῖς γονεῦσιν θησαυρίζειν ἀλλὰ οἱ γονεῖς τοῖς τέκνοις).

[152] For examples of "father" imagery for a deity, cf. Aesch. *Choeph.* 984f.; Arist. *De Plantis* 1, 2, 817a, 23; Homer *Od.*1.28; *Iliad* 1.544. Philo gave special precedence to πατήρ imagery (cf. *de Fuga 62*). Paul's language, however, more closely resembled that of Jesus who designated a more intimate relationship between deity and worshipper by use of the infant's cry of *abba* (Matt. 7.21–23; 18.23–25).

[153] This use of the first aorist passive subjunctive of μορφόω is found only here in the New Testament and not at all in the LXX or papyri. Compare with 1 Thes. 2.7.

[154] The same term is used in Phlm. 10, where reference is made to Onesimus as Paul's dear child, one whom he had begotten (ὃν ἐγέννησα).

[155] Dunn 1995, 92: "As their founding apostle, Paul claims a 'primacy of authority' (12.28) which [the Corinthians] above all ought to acknowledge." Gaventa notes the connection between Paul's πατήρ language and his own sense of "fatherly" responsibility (1993, 195).

[156] Cf. TDNT, v, 620; also Lightfoot 1957 148–149; Fee 1987, 185; Saller 1994.

[157] See Pliny, *Ep.* 3.3. Paul referred to the first stage in the Corinthians' lives as the period of infancy (νηπίοι ἐν Χριστῷ), when he had to feed them with milk, not solid food (3.1–2).

[158] Pliny, *Ep.* 3.3–*Proinde faventibus diis trade eum praeceptori, a quo mores primum, mox eloquentiam discat, quae male sine moribus discitur.* Winter notes the disappointing tendency of many pupils to focus on φιλαυτία rather than φιλοθεῖα (1997a, 85).

[159] Indeed, the work of those who came after Paul initiated the church would be built upon and tested against the foundation which Paul the "master builder" had already laid (3.10).

[160] The term ἐπλουτίσθητε (to make someone rich), the first aorist passive indicative of πλουτίζω, is unique to Paul in the New Testament, appearing only in 1 Cor. 1.5

and 2 Cor. 6.10,11. It is a word that was common in Attic writings, and then disappeared for several centuries, before it found its way into the Septuagint. Interestingly, while Prov. 10.22 asserts that "the blessing of the Lord enriches, *and he adds no sorrow with it*" (NRSV; Gk. καὶ οὐ μὴ προστεθῇ αὐτῇ λύπη ἐν καρδίᾳ), 1 Sam. 2.7 states that "the Lord makes poor and makes rich" (πτωχίζει καὶ πλουτίζει; Heb. יְהוָה מוֹרִישׁ וּמַעֲשִׁיר).

[161] Here, there is a parallel in Philo, who notes that a parent gave to his/her children (τέκνα) much more than simply existence, enabling them "not only to live, but also to live well" (*Spec. Leg. II*, 229–230).

[162] Malina and Neyrey add: "It was the duty of children to treat a father honourably – in the specific ways in which that culture defined respect and honour" (1996, 166). Cf. Cicero, *Inv.* 1.13.18–14.19; *Rh. Her.* 1.10.17. See also Hays 1997, 74, who argues against those who might see Paul's call to imitation as "manipulative and arrogant" by saying that the appeal "is based upon his claim to have fathered them." Paul's unique role allowed him to be a role model, but only insofar as in his own life he imitated Christ (11.1).

[163] Presumably, Timothy had already visited and left Corinth by the time of this writing, since in 16.10–11, Paul explicitly spoke of a possible future visit by his colleague.

[164] Consider Pliny's comments to his friend Mauricus concerning the latter's nephews: *nam quid magis interest vestra, quam ut liberi...digni illo patre, te patruo reperiantur* (2,18).

[165] Cf. Clem. of Alex., *Instr.* 7–8.

[166] Cf. Ign. *Eph.* 15, citing 1 Cor. 4.17 in a call to less talk and more action. On the other hand, the second century Clement of Alexandria, in his discussion on spiritual regeneration, brought together citations from Plato's *Theætetus* and 1 Cor. 4.15 (cf. *Stromata*, 5, 2: "'I have begotten you in Christ,' says the good apostle somewhere").

[167] Cf. Tert., *Against Marcion*, 5, 8, in which 1 Cor. 4.15 is used in a passage in authority.

[168] *Conf.*, 13, 22; cf. also *Epis.* 208, 5 (to Felicia, C.E. 423). A contemporary example for Augustine was Ambrose, who claimed Bishop Simplicianus as his spiritual *pater*, only then to "father" others himself, one being Augustine (*Conf.* 8.2).

[169] Chaps. 8 and 9: Methodius does speak of Paul's role as that of a mother, and not a father, while citing the "begetting" passage of 1 Cor. 4.15.

[170] Cf. Chrys., *Hom. on 1 Cor.* 13.4: "The superiority in love...is the force of the word *father*"

[171] Cf. Saller 1994, 73: "Roman culture drew a clear distinction between the father's relationship with his children...and the master's exploitative relationship over his slaves". Strauss notes that in an earlier era, πατήρ derivatives "played an important role in Athenian politics, society and economics" (1993, 24). Cf. Herman 1987, 18.

[172] *Hom. 1 Cor.*, 13, 3–4. Later, Chrysostom again shows how Paul chose not to say "not many masters," but rather "not many fathers," thus differentiating between the two roles.

[173] Callan's suggestion, for example, that Paul's figurative use of language about parents and children is "rather negative," pointing perhaps to "negative feelings about his

own childhood and his relationship with his parents," owes more to the author's own psychological theorising than to actual exegesis. The author's claim that Paul's silence concerning the binding of Isaac in his references to Abraham are "the result of repression" appears to rest on conjecture rather than critical examination. Cf. Callan 1990, 82–83. See Castelli 1991, 98–111, as well as Pickett 1997, 206, who speaks of an "authoritarianism" on Paul's part which was "masked by his role as father." As will be shown in the following chapter, the seemingly "unilateral" authority which Paul wielded in the case of the incestuous man was still in the context of the "family meeting," and it was Paul's desire that the ἀδελφοί would be the ones to exercise such discipline.

[174] Cf. Beker 1980, 272ff.

[175] In saying this, Paul essentially "changed the playing field" and exchanged one paradigm of the system for another.

[176] See Plutarch's *De Frat. Amor.* 485a. Cf. also Fitzgerald 1988, 139, who notes Paul's contrastings images of those Corinthian Christians "who powerfully assert their rights 6.7)." Cf. also Elliger 1987, 250, who remarks: "Die Verbindung des Begriffs τέκνη mit Korinth hat symptomatische Bedeutung."

[177] See above; also cf. M. Mitchell 1992, 296ff.; Hurd 1983, 43–47; Fee 1987, 15–16.

[178] Cf. Moffatt's commentary (1938), pp. 53–54, for a response to Calvin's proposal.

[179] For more detail, cf. Dodd 1995, 51–53; see also Bailey 1983, 160–163, who specifically focused on the transitional purpose of διά τοῦτο in 4.17. Fee links the "crisis in authority" which he asserts is at the heart of the next three sections of the letter (5.1–13; 6.1–11; 6.12–20) with the extended argument of the first four chapters (1987, 194–195).

[180] Dodd 1995, 51.

[181] The term φυσιόω, introduced in 4.6, is linked by both Wagner 1998, 283–285, and Dodd 1995, 49, with Paul's citation in 1.31 (which Wagner asserts is a conflation of Jer. 9.23 and 1 Kgdms 2.10). Various forms of φυσιόω are found again in 5.2, 8.1 and 13.4. This attitude is often contrasted with ἀγάπη towards one's fellow Christian, even as Paul referred to those same Corinthians who denigrated him as his "beloved children" (4.14).

[182] The most famous of these family *concilia* was that of Brutus and his family in 44 B.C.E., following the assassination of Julius Cæsar. Cf. Cic., *Att.* 15.11.

[183] See the third-century C.E. account (Marcianus) of the father who killed his son after learning that the latter was having an affair with his step-mother (*Dig.* 48.9.5). Much more will be said about this in Chapter 5 below.

[184] On the choices of marriage partners in the context of the *concilium*, see Pliny, *Ep.* 1.14. Regarding the need to consult with the *concilium* before proceeding with divorce unilaterally, see Val. Max. 2.9.21, about which more will be said below.

[185] On the connection between *concilium familia* and *concilium amicorum* (meeting of friends) see Dixon 1992, 139. On the judicial functions, cf. Pliny, *Ep.* 4.22; 6.22,31; Juv., *Sat.* 4.

[186] Cf. Pickett 1997, 213: Paul viewed the "world's norms and values as a primary cause of the disintegration of the community into elitist splinter-groups."

[187] Carpenter and Kennedy 1988, 3.

[188] Coser 1956, 34ff.

[189] Cf. Barclay 1991, 181, who further notes a tension "between the Pauline ideal of brotherhood and the practical realities of slavery." For more on this, see next chapter.

[190] Cf. Fitzgerald 1988.

[191] See also Eph. 4.28. This corresponds with the use of ἴδιον in Gal. 6.5: "each must carry his (or her) own load."

[192] There, believing wives are urged to "submit to their own husbands" (τοῖς ἰδίοις ἀνδράσιν, Tit. 2.5; cf. 1 Pet. 3.1, 5); slaves are told to obey their own masters and "not to talk back" (δούλους ἰδίοις δεσπόταις ὑποτάσσεσθαι ἐν πᾶσιν, εὐαρέστους εἶναι, μὴ ἀντιλέγοντας, Tit. 2.9; cf. 1 Tim. 6.1); and overseers are instructed to "manage their own households" (1 Tim. 3.4–5). See Winter 1994 for a more detailed analysis of "civic consciousness" which was promoted in the early church.

[193] Only in 1 Cor. 14.35 do we see ἰδίους linked with the subordination principles of the later pseudonymous writings. However, the authorship of 14.34-35 has recently been challenged by several scholars, including Payne (1995 and 1998). Hays notes: "The best way to approach this question is to examine the evidence concerning the roles *actually* played by women in the Pauline communities" (1997, 52).

✧ CHAPTER FIVE
From Courts to Concilium

Following Chapter Three's exploration of the influence of overlapping relational networks on the Corinthian church, Chapter Four focused on the ἔριδες addressed by Paul in 1 Cor. 1–4. There it was argued that Paul did not begin his letter with specific answers to internal conflicts but, instead, confronted underlying systemic issues concerning corporate identity and apostolic leadership. Many Corinthians regarded the ἐκκλησία as simply one more network in their relational world and Paul as one leader among many (and not even the most impressive!). As long as they saw themselves *primarily* as patrons, clients, masters, slaves, Jews, gentiles, males, females, members of this house group or members of that house group, then their roles as fellow believers in Christ were relegated to a secondary status. Paul's response, as we saw, was two-fold: he redefined the boundaries of the ἐκκλησία in light of the cross and he reconfigured its interrelationships in familial terms. At the end of the chapter, it was noted that the apostle's πατήρ imagery not only emphasized the unique position of primacy that he held in the system, but also set the context for bringing up the kind of issues which the *paterfamilias* often addressed in a household *concilium*. Indeed, the question may be put in fundamental terms: *in the kind of relational system Paul had already redefined in 1 Cor.1–4, how were internal problems supposed to be handled?*

With that last question, we turn now to two passages that focus specifically on the question of intra-church discipline or judgment: the case of the incestuous man in 1 Cor. 5 and litigation between fellow members in 1 Cor. 6.1–11. As we shall see, together these two situations can help us explore both the need for, and limitations of, internal conflict management. The conclusion considers these two passages in relation to what follows in the letter.[1] Each section follows the same organizational pattern: an exegetical study of the passage in light of the problem of overlapping relational networks, followed by a systems analysis of Paul's response. Some issues which will be addressed in this chapter include: the need for internal judgment according to standards independent from outside networks and the role of Paul and the Corinthians themselves in such a process. As will be shown below, these systemic issues—far from being artificial constructs imposed on the text from outside—actually arise out of the apostle's own presentation. It is argued here that the standards and demands of the "outside world," i.e. the other relational networks to which many of the Corinthians belonged, were influencing the way that internal problems or disputes were handled in the ἐκκλησία, a situation Paul intended to remedy.

The Need for Judgment

Considering What has Gone Before

In 4.18–19 Paul, the Corinthians' πατήρ, lamented the fact that some of his "beloved children" had become "puffed up" (φυσιόω) in his absence. Only a few verses later, the same word for "arrogance" is mentioned again (5.2), this time in the specific case of the man living with ἡ γυνή τοῦ πατρός. But what was the basis for their arrogance in this situation, and is there a reason for Paul dealing with this problem first, immediately after asserting his role as "father?" After a brief introduction to past interpretations of the passage, this section analyses the problem in 5.1–13 before moving into an analysis of Paul's response, where particular attention is given to scriptural parallels, including Ezek. 16 (LXX) and to Paul's use of familial language (albeit in a unique way).

In considering the history of interpretation of 1 Cor. 5, it might be somewhat surprising to find that, until recently, commentators either ignored the passage altogether or focused solely on one or two verses, out of the larger context. For example, comments on the passage are sought in vain in many of the earliest patristic writings. Irenæus made passing references to two verses (6 and 11).[2] However, 5.7a (ἐκκαθάρατε τὴν παλαιὰν ζύμην, ἵνα ἦτε νέον φύραμα, καθώς ἐστε ἄζυμοι) has been the subject of much discussion from the earliest years. There is a reference in one of Ignatius' letters to "the old corrupt leaven," as well as to the issue of non-association with a fellow member whose behaviour belies his claim to be ἀδελφός (5.11).[3] Outside of these two references, Ignatius had little to say about the passage. In a similar way, Ptolemy, in his Epistle to Flora (a mid-second century gnostic writing), referred solely to 1 Cor. 5.7, speaking explicitly of "leaven" as evil.[4] Chrysostom also focused considerable attention on this verse, arguing that although there was still sin and iniquity within the church, the fact that Paul referred to the Corinthians as "unleavened" implied that "not over very many was the wickedness prevailing."[5] Gregory of Nyssa utilized the metaphor of the leaven in a quite different and more positive sense, speaking about the transformation of the entire body through the receiving of the eucharist, "the visible elements of the immortal body."[6] Centuries later, in his *De Servo Arbitrio,* Luther made two references to Paul's comments on leaven, likening it to "corrupt morals" which needed to be "purged out" of the church,[7] while in his only reference to 1 Cor. 5 in his *Römerbriefvorlesung,* Luther asserted that whenever people grieve over the "old leaven" in their lives and invoke God's grace, then "they are unleavened by God's reckoning."[8] On the other hand, the German reformer's contemporary, Melanchthon, did not wish in any way to lessen the severity of the scandalous sin, but instead asserted that "the sin of a single person is imputed to the whole group and defiles the whole group."[9] What is most interesting in all this is that so much attention was given in earlier years to this one verse,[10] while the remainder of 1 Cor. 5 remained largely untouched.[11] There were exceptions, of course, most notably Chrysostom's homily and, later, Calvin's use of the passage in Geneva (along with Matt. 18 and 1 Tim. 1) to commend the use of excommunication.[12] On the whole, however, 1 Cor. 5 remained largely undiscussed... until recent times.

Examining the Problem

There is an enigmatic quality of 1 Cor. 5 due, in part, to the dearth of hard data concerning the situation in question. Verse 1 speaks of news that reached Paul regarding a member of the Corinthian congregation: ὥστε γυναῖκά τινα τοῦ πατρὸς ἔχειν. Yet neither the source of this information nor the specifics of the situation are made clear by Paul.

Perhaps the news came to him via "Chloe's people,"[13] but no clue is offered from the verb ἀκούεται,the present passive indicative of ἀκούω, which simply means, "It is heard." It was enough to the apostle that "the house of Corinth stank" and the aroma had reached him.[14] Concerning the nature of the scandal itself, there are again only a few hints and even more questions. Most scholars concur that the relationship in question was an ongoing one, and not simply a "one-night stand," as suggested by Paul's use of the present infinitive ἔχειν (from ἔχω), meaning "to go on having."[15] However, whether it was a marriage to which Paul was alluding or simply a long-term relationship is not clear, nor does it appear to be a crucial issue, inasmuch as co-habitation between two citizens with the intention of marriage was regarded as a valid marriage (*iustum conubium*) in the empire.[16] Another point of agreement among most scholars concerns the fact that the woman was probably not a member of the Christian ἐκκλησία, since Paul did not in any way address his remarks to her, which would be in keeping with his statement in 5.12: τί γάρ μοι τοὺς ἔξω κρίνειν.[17]

The most obvious questions arise, however, when we consider the precise nature of the scandal itself. Paul described what was happening as πορνεία (fornication), not μοιχεία (adultery), and added that this was fornication of a kind ἥτις οὐδὲ ἐν τοῖς ἔθνεσιν. Until recently, it was almost universally agreed that the woman in the incident was the man's stepmother.[18] If this was indeed the case, it would account for Paul's vehement declaration. A stepmother-stepson relationship would indeed have been *incestum* and considered abominable by Jews and Romans alike. תורה was clear in its denunciation of anyone who "lay with his father's wife." Lev. 18:8 said: לֹא תְגַלֵּה עֶרְוַת אָבִיךָ הִוא׃ ס עֶרְוַת אֵשֶׁת אָבִיךָ (ἀσχημοσύνην γυναικὸς πατρός σου οὐκ ἀποκαλύψεις ἀσχημοσύνη πατρός σού ἐστιν, LXX). It should be noted that this law was applicable to the resident alien as well as to the Jew (18.26).[19] Likewise, in Deut. 20.27 the same phrase was used— "Cursed be anyone who lies with his father's wife" (γυναικὸς τοῦ πατρὸς αὐτοῦ)[20]—and it was further stated that this would constitute a violation of his father's rights (ἀπεκάλυψεν συγκάλυμμα τοῦ πατρὸς αὐτοῦ).[21] Roman law also stated quite clearly: "I may not marry one who once was my stepmother."[22] For this reason, Paul would have been justified in saying to the Corinthian Christians that their fellow member's lifestyle was ἥτις οὐδὲ ἐν τοῖς ἔθνεσιν.

This raises the thorny issue of why such an illicit relationship, in the eyes of both Jewish and Roman law, would even have been permissible, much less commended, within the Christian ἐκκλησία. Hays lists the more traditional view that the Corinthians' boasting (καύχημα) in this situation was the result of their over-realized sense of freedom in Christ, "celebrating this man's particular act of defying conventional mores."[23] Chow has argued instead along socio-economic lines, suggesting that the man involved in the case was an influential patron in the church and, therefore, deemed "untouchable" by the more numerous clients and poorer members of the ἐκκλησία.[24] "For who would want to dishonour a powerful patron who could provide protection and benefaction to the church?"[25] Clarke adds that those church members who were among the "not many" of 1 Cor. 1.26 would themselves have been reluctant to confront their peer because of the costly nature of *inimicitiae*,[26] a point challenged by De Vos in a recent article.[27]

In that same article, De Vos offers an alternative position that the woman was not the church member's stepmother at all, but rather *his father's concubine*, thus eliminating the charge of incest, at least in terms of Roman law. For while the LXX spoke of concubinage in terms of polygamous situations, "where a concubine (παλλακή) was kept alongside a wife,"[28] Romans understood the relationship as "essentially a monogamous union, characterized by companionship, affection, and mutual respect, with someone who could not be seen as a proper mother of the partner's children *but in other respects performed the offices of a wife.*"[29] De Vos argues that although such an arrangement would have "raised a few eyebrows amongst the Corinthian elite," it was not illegal. However, he contends, such fine distinctions "would have been lost on someone, like Paul, from a Jewish (or more specifically a non-Roman) background."[30] Likewise, Paul's response would have made little sense to many Corinthians who did not share his Jewish paradigm.

Despite the attractiveness of this thesis in explaining the different perceptions of the incident by Paul and his readers, it is not without problems. First, the claim that Paul the Jew simply would not have been aware of the acceptability of the man's actions amongst non-Jewish church members suggests an ignorance on Paul's part out of keeping with the remainder of 1 Corinthians. If De Vos is correct that a relationship between a man and his late father's concubine would have been "fairly normal" in ancient Athens, if not Corinth,[31] then Paul likely would at least have known of this social acceptance, even if he did not approve of it.[32] Although possible, it is not likely that Paul's statement in 5.1 was born out of cultural naiveté.

If Paul was aware of some level of tacit acceptance among many Corinthians, then a more understandable response on his part might have been: "Even if the Gentiles approve of this, yet we in the church do not." Indeed, the irrelevancy of standards in other networks is a common theme in 1 Cor. 5–10, as epitomized in 6.11: ταῦτά τινες ἦτε. Instead, in 5.1, Paul said something quite different: "This does not occur even among the Gentiles!" Whether she was stepmother or *concubina,* the fact remains that the woman who had been "as a wife" *to the father* was now "as a wife" *to the son.* The one who had shared the father's bed was now sharing the son's.[33] Even if such arrangements did occur, it is questionable how these fit into a category of "traditional Græco-Roman mores." It seems far more likely that the man was engaged in some long-term relationship with his deceased father's young second wife,[34] and that other church members hesitated to act because of the status of the offender. Thus, in presenting the Gentiles as "a topic of reproach to the believers,"[35] Paul either revealed his ignorance of Gentile acceptance of such arrangements or he was closer to the reality of the situation than De Vos allows. A scriptural precedent for this kind of language may be found in Ezekiel 16, where Jerusalem's state of immorality and idolatry was said to have *so far exceeded* the abominations of surrounding nations (ὑπέρκεισαι αὐτὰς ἐν πάσαις ταῖς ὁδοῖς σου, 16.47) that Sodom actually appeared righteous (ἐδικαίωσας) in comparison (16.51,52).[36] In fact, even the Philistines were ashamed of the "lewd ways" of God's covenant people (16.57)![37] Indeed, as will be shown below in *5.2.3,* it may be argued that much of 1 Cor. 5 echoes Ezek. 16.[38]

Having said all this, it is important to recall that it was not the actions of the couple upon which Paul focused, but rather the *re*action (or lack thereof) of the Christian network in regards to this situation. "It is striking that although Paul is concerned with the salvation of the man's spirit (v.

5b), his greater concern is with the purity of the community."³⁹ In at least two ways, we can see potential results from this scandal on the life of the ἐκκλησία. First, as seen in verse 1, the church's witness to the "outside" world was affected by the sin. Paul's charge that "it is heard that there is fornication among you" (ὅλως ἀκούεται ἐν ὑμῖν πορνεία) is reminiscent of the last part of Gen. 35.22 (concerning Reuben's sin), where it is said that "Israel heard of it": καὶ ἤκουσεν Ισραηλ. The relationship was not a hidden, private affair. In 1 Thessalonians, Paul spoke with pride of the positive example that particular church was to "other believers": ὥστε γενέσθαι ὑμᾶς τύπον πᾶσιν τοῖς πιστεύουσιν ἐν τῇ Μακεδονίᾳ καὶ ἐν Ἀχαΐᾳ (1.7). In a similar way, the apostle exclaimed to the Roman Christians that their faith was "proclaimed throughout the world" (ἡ πίστις ὑμῶν καταγγέλλεται ἐν ὅλῳ τῷ κόσμῳ, 1.8). The Corinthians' passivity, however, meant that the same scandal which was being "heard" by Paul was most likely being heard by others outside the church, as well.⁴⁰

More than this, there was an underlying issue of definition to be considered. Paul had already delineated the Christian network as a set-apart, sanctified ἐκκλησία, and introduced a new set of dichotomies distinguishing those within from those outside (see *4.3* above). In 5.10, the apostle seems to have taken for granted the fact that in ὁ κόσμος there would be πορνεία and other vices,⁴¹ and he did not address this issue, per se. After all, as he would clearly state in 6.10, these "outsiders" were not even inheritors of God's kingdom. His focus was on the inheritors, the children of God, the ἀδελφοί. Paul's concern in 5.9–11, rather, was that some of the Christian "siblings" were living as those who were not "siblings," the "inheritors" as those who had no inheritance. Thus, the reformer Bullinger noted:

> Outside the boundaries of the church Paul placed those who were not called brothers, that is, those who did not acknowledge the name of Christ or of the Church; inside the society of the church (I mean of the outward Church) he reckoned those who still acknowledged the name of Christian and did not yet withstand ecclesiastical discipline, but who themselves were all the time defiled and spotted with much evil/mischief (Lt. *sceleribus*).⁴²

It remains to be seen whether Paul's response did include recognition of "those who still acknowledged the name of Christian." However, Bullinger was correct in asserting that, for Paul, a boundary differentiated those inside the ἐκκλησία from those outside it. Yet, inasmuch as the same vices could be found inside the church as outside it (5.11), it was as if the boundaries separating ἡ ἐκκλησία from ὁ κόσμος, did not even exist. What was absurd in this scenario was the Christians' willingness to judge those outside the ἐκκλησία in some way, if only through idle talk (5.12), but where they needed to judge—inside their church—they failed to do so.[43]

Paul's solution to this problem will be examined shortly. For now, it is important to notice that, whatever the specifics of the situation, it appears that *"outside" values were influencing those "inside."* Through their passive acceptance of the situation, Paul's "children" revealed their primary allegiances to their "family of origin," that system of relational networks connecting patrons to clients, citizens to citizens, and fellow members of *collegia* to one another.[44] Thus, Chrysostom appears correct in affirming that "the Corinthians' struggle and their danger was for their whole church, not for any one person."[45] Paul's focus on the reactions of the community rather than on the actions of the one member suggests that he saw the KEY problem more in terms of overly permeable boundaries than in terms of purity rules or personal ethics, per se. From the apostle's perspective, the actual incident was a very visible symptom of the larger unresolved problem of the church's identity crisis (see *fig. 4.b*), as the unleavened bread was becoming increasingly infected with yeast (5.8), thereby losing its very identity as *unleavened* bread.

A final note returns us to the beginning of this subsection, where it was said that "it was heard" that πορνεία existed amongst the Christians. As in chs. 1–4, a corollary of the problem of corporate identity was the additional question of Paul's position in the system. In 4.18, Paul recognized that there were some amongst the brethren who were "arrogant" because of the apostle's absence: "Paul is not even here, so why should we listen to him anyway?" Now, in this specific incident, he again noted the arrogance of some in the ἐκκλησία and linked their attitude with his absence (5.2–3). Δύναμις is explicitly mentioned both times (4.19; 5.4).

It may be argued that part of the problem was that the same persons who were threatened by the status of the offending member who was present among them were unruffled by the authority of Paul their spiritual πατήρ, as long as he was an absentee father (see *fig. 5→*).

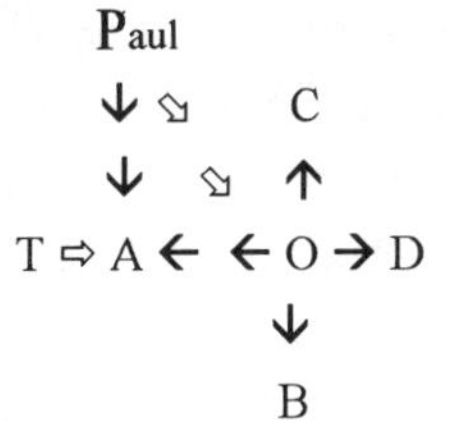

P_{aul}
↓ ↘   C
↓   ↘ ↑
T ⇨ A ← ← O → D
↓
B

T = Timothy, O = Offender

Figure 5–Influences in 1 Cor. 5

Analyzing Paul's Response

If a clear description of the problem in ch. 5 is difficult, then decoding the apostle's response in 5.3–5 is even more troublesome. Fee does a commendable job of laying out the various options for how to read these extended and grammatically complex sentences, which need not be rehearsed in full detail here.[46] What this final subsection on 1 Cor. 5 does consider in some detail are the relational dynamics of Paul's response, both in terms of the context of disciplinary action ("when you are assembled") and his role in the process, as well as the results of the judgment on both the offender and the ἐκκλησία. Attention will be given to possible parallels, such as Ezekiel 16, as well as to Paul's use of familial imagery in the discipline and redefinition of the network.

First, it should be noted that Paul recognized the problem that his absence from Corinth created. In 4.19, he assured his "children" that he would be returning to Corinth, "if the Lord wills." In the meantime, however, he was still far away from them. Returning to *figure 5.a*, we can see that despite his absence, Paul continued to interact with the Corinthians in at least two ways: through representatives like Timothy, his "beloved and faithful son" (4.17), and through an authoritative word on the specific matter before him. Here, the "absentee father" was treading on dangerous ground, by the very fact that the statement was offered *in absentia*. However, Paul acknowledged that his judgment was authoritative precisely because it was given ἐν τῷ ὀνόματι τοῦ κυρίου Ἰησοῦ (5.4).[47] This is important in light of Paul's later nuanced discussion on issues of marriage, where the apostle carefully differentiated between his personal thoughts on a point and the command of the Lord (see 7.10,12,25). There, he would be careful to state that his conclusions regarding remarriage were his judgment alone (7.40), while asserting δοκῶ δὲ κἀγὼ πνεῦμα θεοῦ ἔχειν. However, in the present case, where he was aware of the arrogance of some of the Corinthians in his absence, Paul was clear to say that it was the name and authority of Jesus that underlay his judgment. Far from placing too much weight on his own opinion as the *paterfamilias*, Paul had already admitted in 4.3–5 that his judgment did not count any more than that of the Corinthians. If the Lord had judged the offender's actions to be πορνεία, then in the Lord's name, Paul would voice that judgment. In doing so, he was placing the burden of judgment, albeit in a subtle way, on the Lord rather than solely on himself.

Furthermore, Paul was not willing to carry out this judgment on his own, but instead placed the responsibility in the hands of the entire Corinthian church. We should note that in the oft-cited case of a man who killed his son because the latter had an affair with his stepmother, the emperor Hadrian subsequently sentenced the father to exile *precisely because he had acted in a rash and unilateral fashion.* There were no checks and balances to his decision, no family *concilium* involved.[48] Contrary to those who insist that Paul was despotic in his approach, wielding his patriarchal δύναμις indiscriminately throughout the ἐκκλησία, a closer look at 1 Cor. 5.4–5 quickly reveals a different image. Paul emphasized that the context for a response was in a gathering much like a family *concilium*. "When you (ὑμῶν) are assembled…you are to deliver (παραδοῦναι, aorist active infinitive) this man to Satan." Paul assured the Corinthians that his spirit would be present at this assembly, but he shared the responsibility for sentencing with all his adult "children." Concerning the phrase, *"when you are assembled"* (συναχθέντων ὑμῶν, 5.4), this is the only use of συνάγω in any of its forms in 1 Corinthians or, indeed, anywhere in Paul's letters.[49] When the apostle later referred to the gathering of Christians, i.e. for worship, he used the term συνέχομαι (11.17, 18, 20, 33, 34; 14.26). However, in this one instance (5.4), Paul chose instead to refer to the Corinthian Christians as being συναχθέντων. The term, the aorist passive participial form of συνάγω, suggests a regular gathering, not a one-time event. This raises the question: For what reason would they be assembling? Was it in the context of worship, as with συνέχομαι?[50] There is nothing in the wording or context that suggests this was the case, nor do we see instances of judgment, much less excommunication, in the later chapters on worship (11–14).[51] Was Paul, then, referring here to another kind of assembly?

The word itself was fairly common in other writings, particularly in Plutarch, who in at least one instance made little differentiation in his terms for gathering.[52] While it also occurred fairly frequently in the Septuagint, συνάγω almost never referred to a worship assembly. Instead, it was used largely to describe assemblies of war (Gen. 34.30; 1 Sam. 17.1; 2 Sam. 17.11) or, alternatively, in the context of a pronouncement of divine forgiveness (Jer. 39.37; Is. 56.8). However, in at least one instance, in Ezekiel 16.37, συνάγω was used in the context of judgment. We have already discussed, in the context of 1 Cor. 5.3, the divine accusation in Ezek. 16.47 that Jerusalem's sins surpassed those of the surrounding nations.[53] Now, the prophet said that the Lord was "gathering" the nations as part of the judgment of Jerusalem; the outsiders would see her "nakedness" as her lust and idolatry were laid bare (16.36). Paul used the same word to speak of "gathering" the members of the church to acknowledge the lust (5.1–13; 6.12–20) and, later, idolatry (8–10) of some of its members. What these two situations had in common was an assembly of judgment in which discipline was to be administered. In Ezek 16.39, the prophet went on to say that he would "deliver" (παραδώσω, the future active indicative of παραδίδωμι) guilty Jerusalem into the hands of τὰ ἔθνη. When found in the LXX in this form, παραδώσω, the term almost always has God as its subject. At times God promised to deliver Israel's enemies into their hands (Ex. 23.31; 2 Sam. 5.19; 2 Kin. 3.18).[54] At other times, when Israel (or, more specifically, Jerusalem) became disobedient and courted the favour of other lands and other "gods," God then delivered the "chosen people" into the hands of their enemies (2 Kin. 21.14; Jer. 22.25). The latter case is found far more often in Ezekiel (7.21; 11.9; 16.27, 39; 21.36). In all these instances, the language denotes movement from inside the safety of God's protection to somewhere outside it. Paul, in a similar way, called the Corinthian "assembly" to "deliver" the immoral member out of the safety of the ἐκκλησία into the realm of the Σατανᾶς (5.5).[55] Paul's comment about "removing" (ἐκ+αἴρω) the member from the Christian community also has a precedent in Ezekiel's words concerning Sodom in 16.50: ἐμεγαλαύχουν καὶ ἐποίησαν ἀνομήματα ἐνώπιόν μου καὶ ἐξῆρα (ἐκ+αἴρω) αὐτάς καθὼς εἶδον. It is interesting to note the connection between Sodom's haughtiness and its "removal" by God. In a slightly different way, Paul associated the "arrogance" of some church's members with their refusal to "remove" the offender.

We can see, therefore, that several specific words used by Paul in his response—συνάγω ("gathering," 5.4), παραδίδωμι ("to deliver/hand over," 5.5), and ἐκ+αἴρω ("to remove," 5.3)—are found in Ezekiel 16. More important, perhaps, is the fact that there also is a strong thematic parallel between the two passages. The Ezekiel account is described by Allen as "an extended metaphor," depicting Jerusalem as a young girl saved from early death and loved by her benefactor/husband, whom she then repays with infidelity, thereby revealing her true familial heritage as a child of the ungodly: ἡ μήτηρ ὑμῶν Χετταία καὶ ὁ πατὴρ ὑμῶν Αμορραῖος (16.45).[56] Even so, 1 Cor. 5 is the first of several discussions on intra-church problems and disputes in which Paul challenged the Corinthians to consider whether their behaviour was that of ἀδελφοί ἐν Χριστῷ or that of ἀδελφοί ὀνομαζόμενος (5.11) living "as they used to be" (6.11), as those outside the family and outside the inheritance (6.10).

Most importantly, in the end both Ezekiel 16 and 1 Cor. 5 share an ultimate purpose of reclamation and reinstitution of the offending party, whether it was Jerusalem or the church member. This is evident in Ezek. 16.63, where the Lord said that Jerusalem would be confounded and put to shame *when it ultimately was forgiven by the Lord.*[57] The goal was restoration, which would itself shame the forgiven people. In a similar way, Paul spoke of the salvation of the offending member's spirit, even if it required "delivering the man to Satan for the destruction of his flesh."[58] This is not some kind of dualistic theology on Paul's part, in which the evil flesh is destroyed but the "soul" lives on into immortality. Such thinking would have contradicted his later comments on the "resurrected body" in ch. 15. Rather, if we compare this passage with Paul's very similar words in 11.27–32, it is possible to see that the Lord's judgment is administered *so that* (ἵνα, purpose clause) "we may not be condemned with the rest of the world" (11.32).[59] The apostle did not hesitate to draw correlations between physicial sickness, weakness, death, and the sinfulness of the people (11.30), but these were not the *purpose* of the judgment, simply the results of being in the unprotected world, the domain of Satan. In 11.31, Paul challenged the Corinthians to judge themselves, so that divine judgment would not be needed, but he went on to assure them that the Lord's judgment was intended as discipline, not condemnation. The latter was reserved for ὁ κόσμος, but for the ἀδελφοί the goal was true communion with God and one another (11.33). In light of this, 1 Cor. 5.5 may be read not in terms of the ultimate destruction of the immoral member, but in terms of judgment in the form of exclusion from the sacred assembly in order that one day he might be brought back "inside."[60] The citation from Deuteronomy—ἐξάρατε τὸν πονηρὸν ἐξ ὑμῶν αὐτῶν (17.7; 19.19)—recalls the process of taking the offender outside the gates (17.5) before the sentence of death could be executed. However, the immoral church member in 1 Cor. 5 was to be cast outside the "gates" of the ἐκκλησία into the sphere of "those who are perishing" (1.18), *in the hope* that he might repent and be ashamed and, ultimately, be saved.

Regarding other parallels to 1 Cor. 5, Fee is correct to point out that the curse formulas from the papyri[61] are less important for an understanding of Paul's meaning than other scripture passages, such as 1 Tim. 1.20: ὧν ἐστιν Ὑμέναιος καὶ Ἀλέξανδρος, οὓς παρέδωκα τῷ Σατανᾷ, ἵνα παιδευθῶσιν μὴ βλασφημεῖν.[62] The purpose clause beginning with ἵνα in both 1 Cor. 5.5 and 1 Tim. 1.20 reveals that the ultimate goal is restoration of the guilty one. Similarly, Matt. 11.20ff. shares many characteristics with 1 Cor. 5, including similar echoes of Ezek. 16. In this gospel passage, Jesus reproached the cities which did not acknowledge his deeds of power (δύναμις), and declared that it would be "more tolerable for Sodom on that day of judgment" than for them (11.24).[63] Jesus then praised God for hiding things from the σοφοί and revealing them instead to the νήπιοι, a familiar dichotomy in 1 Corinthians 1–4 (though Paul adds that such νήπιοι needed to grow up). Knowledge of the Father comes only through the Son, Jesus asserted (Matt. 11.27), even as Paul proclaimed that only the Spirit truly comprehends the things of God (1 Cor. 2.11), ἡμεῖς δὲ ὑπ' οὐδενὸς ἀνακρίνεται (2.16). Finally, the call in Matt. 11.28–30 to come into Jesus' rest is not wholly unlike Paul's hope of salvation for the offender.[64]

Paul may or may not have been conscious of one or more of these parallels shown above.[65] What I have tried to show here is that he was not alone in his particular approach to internal judgment, and the danger to which Paul was pointing (much like Ezekiel) was that of neglecting the distinction between "inside" and "outside," thus "surrendering what signified and, by signifying, constituted the unique character" of the ἐκκλησία.[66] What 1 Cor. 5 shares with the Ezekiel passages and even with Matthew, and what is often found lacking in other contemporary sources (e.g. *1QS* 2), is the concern that discipline leads to the restoration of the offender, "as through fire," renewing the temple of which he is but one part (1 Co 3.15–16).

This last point hints at the systemic results of judgment in this case. By *not* judging one of its members, whether it was because of the man's status or other members' acceptance of "unusual" moral situations existing in the πολιτεία, the Corinthian ἐκκλησία was actually damaging itself. The image of the dough in 5.6–8 hearkens back to the temple imagery in 3.16ff., cited above. The church needed to stay true to its identity as something ἅγιος, set apart from the rest of the world, established on the foundation of Jesus Christ (3.11). Inasmuch as there was an overlapping of relational networks through the ongoing involvement of Christians in Corinthian daily life, it was all the more important that the identity of this unique and primary network not be lost. In 1 Cor. 1–4, Paul argued that quarrels about "who belongs to whom" were indicative of the way some members were "behaving according to human inclinations" (3.3) instead of living as true πνευματικοί and ἀδελφοί ἐν Χριστῷ (3.1). Now, when ἀδελφός became synonymous with "immoral and greedy one, idolater, reviler, drunkard, and robber" (4.11), how could the word still mean "fellow Christian"?[67] The actions contradicted the name; but so did the church's lack of response. In using the phrase ἐάν τις ἀδελφός ὀνομαζόμενος, a phrase unique among Paul's letters, indeed, among New Testament writings, the apostle presented the Corinthians with a somewhat disturbing image of a network of ἀδελφοί who may not truly have been ἀδελφοί at all.

Summary and Conclusion

In summarizing what has been discussed in this section, there was a situation in the ἐκκλησία which became known to Paul, which he simply referred to as πορνεία. The specifics of this situation and the reasons why it was not challenged by the other church members are issues which remain debated, although it seems reasonable to assume that the status of the offending member had much to do with the lack of resistance he faced in the church. By not judging the offending member, the ἀδελφοί were actually saying that his and their status "outside" the ἐκκλησία was more important than their common status "inside." In response, Paul focused on the members' corporate responsibility, reminding them once more of their primary place of "belonging"—inside! In this sense, verses 9–13 serve as the lens through which to read the preceding verses, for Paul noted that it was precisely those "inside" that were to be judged by their fellow "insiders." By not dealing with the one "who was called" an ἀδελφός, it could be questioned whether the other members were acting as true ἀδελφοί. For his part, Paul both asserted his unique position as πατήρ by making known his judgment when the rest of the church failed to do so,[68] and at the same time empowered the members to act as adult ἀδελφοί in the context of a "gathering" that resembled a family *concilium*. By offering a new paradigm of Christian interrelationships, where brothers and sisters in Christ saw their mutual responsibilities inside the ἐκκλησία as primary and in which Paul held a unique position without acting unilaterally, Paul upset the equilibrium of the Corinthians who were obviously comfortable with the lack of conflict between themselves and the world around them. He had argued for the need to judge those inside. But how was this to be done so as to honour their "familial" bond?

The Place for Judgment

New Issue, Same Problem

Although Paul's transition statement in 6.1—τολμᾷ τις ὑμῶn—is "as sharp as it was abrupt,"[69] the passage on litigation between church members is really a continuation of his discussion on intra-church conflict.[70] The progession of thought is from consideration of the *need* for judgment in the ἐκκλησία to the question of the *context* in which such judgment should, and should not, occur. As before, this section examines the passage in terms of systemic problem and apostolic response. First, it will be shown how the actions of the Christians in Corinth demonstrated their lack of clarity concerning both their corporate identity as the church and the primary nature of their interrelationships.[71] Here, Carpenter and Kennedy's concept of the "spiral of unmanaged conflict" will be utilized in order to understand the relational implications of litigation. Following this, Paul's response to the situation will be explored, particularly in light of passages from the Hebrew Scriptures (such as Lev. 19 and Deut. 1) as well as Duling's recent research on conflict resolution in a "fictive kin" association. Once again, we will see, Paul seems to have been less concerned with the "what" of the specific issue than with the "how" of Christian interaction (see *figure 2.c* above). The importance of his sibling terminology, more prevalent than in the preceding passage, will again be considered in some detail.

Examining the Problem

Unlike the previous issue, the situation in 6.1–11 is far less ambiguous: quite simply, church members were initiating lawsuits against one another in the "outside" courts. The reasons for their lawsuits are less clear (πρᾶγμα in this forensic sense can simply mean suit), although the apostle's use of ἀποστερεῖσθε in verse 7 ("to be defrauded," the permissive middle of ἀποστερέω), suggests that property rights might have been involved.[72] It is also not certain whether it was a single case to which Paul was referring, or whether several similar litigations were occurring (although it may be argued that the second option is more likely, given Paul's use of the second person plural in verses 7 and 8).[73]

What is indeed clear is that fellow church members were looking outside the ἐκκλησία for resolution of internal disputes and legitimation of their respective rights. Of course, this does not imply that such legal means were available to all the Corinthian Christians.[74] On the contrary, as noted above in chapter 3, the instigators in these lawsuits were most likely among those of higher social status (possibly the "not many" of 1.26), those who operated in the network of the secular ἐκκλησία. As noted, in that system it was either impossible or too costly for household "dependents" or persons of lower rank to initiate persecutions, and when such persons were defendants in a case, they usually found themselves at a disadvantage: "any fruits gained from a prosecution were not worth the price of an undying feud with a man capable of exacting the most harmful revenge."[75] Inasmuch as the stability of the entire hierarchical system depended on the respect and/or submission of inferiors to their superiors,[76] it was unlikely that poor or lower status defendants would receive the kind of hearing that they might have desired in Corinth. Dio Chrysostom alluded to this when he spoke of "lawyers innumerable perverting justice."[77] This favouritism towards the wealthy and influential might have been behind Paul's somewhat enigmatic comment about the ἄδικοι in verse 2.[78] While Moffatt downplayed the pejorative sense of the word "unrighteous," reading it instead in light of the reference to "unbelievers" (ἄπιστοι) in verse 6,[79] Winter has argued that evidence from the period of Roman Corinth suggests that the ἄδικοι were indeed influenced by position, power, influence and even outright bribery.[80] Thus, an important part of the problem regarding litigation between church members was the way it allowed the inequitable standards and relational dichotomies so prevalent in other Corinthian networks to enter the supposedly unique and set-apart network of the Christian ἐκκλησία.

There were other problems inherent in this scenario, including long-term effects on members' interaction as a result of lawsuits. The possiblity of ill will on the part of a losing litigant as a result of a financial settlement or loss of reputation is fairly obvious.[81] What is less obvious, but equally true, was the fact that the enmity that ensued from such a legal battle would move beyond the "combatants" to include those who supported one or the other.[82] Paul had already mentioned conflicting allegiances in the one ἐκκλησία (1–4), different spheres of "belonging." Now, there was the related problem that informal alliances and divisions could arise as a result of the growing enmity between litigating members.[83] It is not suggested that any of this would have been formalized in terms of actual "groups," but rather that persons would "take sides" with one against the other. The cry, "I support...," could easily have caused as much damage to the unity of the church as the boast, "I belong to..." In lamenting the fact that ἀδελφὸς μετὰ ἀδελφοῦ κρίνεται καὶ τοῦτο ἐπὶ ἀπίστων (6.6), Paul was not only pointing to the problem of overly permeable boundaries (going before those "outside"),[84] but also to the fact that these were Christian "siblings" warring against one another. In situations of litigation, "roles change,"[85] and patterns of interaction within the community would be altered to reflect the new roles. This is why victory for either party in a lawsuit between fellow Christians still meant "defeat" (ἥττημα) for the church as a whole.[86] The legal "solutions" to problems between Christian ἀδελφοί could easily create new problems for litigants and supporters who would face each other in "communion" on a regular basis. "Litigation may produce an effective remedy, but it can be worse than the complaint."[87]

In this sense, beyond issues of boundaries and interrelationships, there is also the underlying question of systemic definition to be considered. As A. Mitchell has pointed out, Paul's mention of σοφός in 6.5 suggests that the offenders were not even being true to the contemporary sense of "wisdom" in Corinth. Indeed, the true σοφός would concur with Paul that it was better to be wronged than to initiate prosecution (6.7).[88] "The σοφός would not go to court nor bring indictments..."[89] Yet here, as in the account of the immoral man in 5.1ff., Paul states that these Christian ἀδελφοί were doing precisely what even the Gentile σοφοί did not! Later in the letter, the apostle would speak of the characteristics of true ἀδελφοί: "love is patient; love is kind; love is not envious or boastful or arrogant or rude..." (13.4). However, instead of refraining from ζῆλος (13.4), the childish members of the ἐκκλησία exhibited both ζῆλος καὶ ἔρις (3.3). Instead of refusing to rejoice in ἀδικία (13.6), the Corinthian ἀδελφοί "wronged" one another (ἀδικέω, 6.8) and even took their disputes before the ἄδικοί (6.1). The same Corinthian believers who proclaimed themselves σοφοί and ἀδελφοί denied themselves these claims by their actions. As Pope Gregory later declared: "Those that are at variance...can by no means become spiritual if they neglect becoming united to their neighbours by concord."[90] Earlier, it was asserted that the term "divided church" is an oxymoron; so, too, is the phrase "litigating siblings."[91] When "brother takes brother to court," when "first place is given...to the one who can revile his neighbour most fluently,"[92] then the common bond which makes them siblings is broken. Paul's harsh words in 6.8—"but (ἀλλά, adversative) you (ὑμεῖς, emphatic) wrong and defraud (active voice), and that your siblings" (καὶ τοῦτο ἀδελφούς, same idiom as in 6.6)—point to the "internal contradiction" in the system, *so that at certain points the system seem[ed] to be at war with itself.*[93] The danger of litigation, then even more than now (due to the *inimiticia* involved in any case), was the tendency for all involved—concerned supporters as well as actual litigants—to define themselves not by their common calling or association ἐν Χριστῷ, but rather by their opposition to one another.[94]

Carpenter and Kennedy speak of this systemic phenomenon in terms of a "spiral of unmanaged conflict" which draws all involved into deeper and more intense opposition, so that ultimately "everyone engages in an adversarial battle" that, in turn, leads to the redefining of the entire system.[95] While the specific issues undoubtedly differ from the first-century empire to the modern western world, the principles of progressive movement in their "spiral" resonate with Paul's depiction of life in the Corinthian ἐκκλησία. They argue that "unmanaged conflict seldom stays constant for long." Instead, as time passes, the intensity of the opposition escalates to a crisis point. Carpenter and Kennedy list the major stages in the evolution of a conflict process:

(1) Problem emerges
(2) Sides form
(3) Positions harden
(4) Communication between "opponents" stops
(5) Resources are committed
(6) Conflict goes outside the community
(7) Perceptions of those involved become distorted
(8) Sense of crisis emerges (sanctions and "final options")

In the situation in 1 Cor. 6, whatever the original issue was that led to the initiation of legal proceedings between fellow Christians (a dispute over property rights?), Paul's concern lay in the fact that the situation had already escalated to the point of litigation between ἀδελφοί. Carpenter and Kennedy's reference to the cost of pursuing a course of "destructive conflict," i.e. "damaged reputations, fractured personal relationships, community disruption," certainly was true of first-century legal battles. As we have seen, litigation was a final resort that spelled the end of any possibility of true reconciliation between parties, promising only future enmity. Indeed, in an οἶκος, it was unthinkable that siblings would go outside the family to settle their differences. Thus, while in chs. 1–4 the relational situation seems to have been somewhere between stages (2) and (4), in the case of ch. 6, all communication would have been "suspended"[96] and resources would already have been committed. This was true in terms of finances (for legal fees) as well as human resources (i.e. householders, clients, friends, fellow members of a *collegium).* Finally, whether it was a person of higher status suing a fellow of lower status or one citizen taking another to court, the very fact that the litigants had chosen to deal with their problems by moving out of the church network and into the Corinthian legal system is evidence that perceptions of "the other side" had changed from fellow ἀδελφοί to legal adversaries and/or rivals. In 1 Cor. 1–4, Paul was still able to communicate (or at least attempt to) with those who affiliated themselves in some fashion with either Apollos or himself. His comment μή ᾖ ἐν ὑμῖν σχίσματα (1.10) implied that the ἐκκλησία was still one, despite the ἔριδες. Paul's affirmation of the work of his "rival" (3.5–9), his use of the inclusive "you" plural (e.g. 1.10ff.; 2.1ff.; 3.17), his creative use of irony (4.8–13), and most of all his assertion that he did not want to make his beloved children "ashamed" (οὐκ ἐντρέπων, 4.14) together stand juxtaposed against the apostle's obvious horror at the situation in 6.1 (τολμᾷ τις ὑμῶν), and his bold pronouncement in 6.5 (πρός ἐντροπὴν ὑμῖν λέγω). While earlier in chs. 1–4, Paul was able to address the Corinthian Christians as ἀδελφοί, in 1 Cor. 6 the description itself was suspect when ἀδελφός μετὰ ἀδελφοῦ κρίνεται.[97]

While it would be saying too much to speak of the "spiral" as a kind of template to be placed over the scanty data we have regarding 1 Cor. 6, it does serve as a reminder that any efforts Paul might have made for change and reconciliation in one intra-church situation (the ἔριδες in 1–4) would likely prove ineffective, or perhaps even counterproductive, in a situation "further up the spiral" (the litigation in ch. 6). Paul's response to this problem, while perhaps more subtle than his "sentence" of expulsion for the immoral man, still centered on paradigmatic questions of identity and boundaries rather than on techniques or formulas for resolution.[98] In the following subsection, we will consider Paul's continued focus on an insider-outsider dichotomy, as well as his use of familial imagery to challenge church members to deal with their conflicts in the ἐκκλησία (continuing the theme of the *concilium).* As with 1 Cor. 5, it will be argued here that Paul echoed key Scriptural texts, particularly Lev. 19 and Deut. 1, with his "insider" terminology. In this context, both connections and contrasts between this Pauline passage and Matthew 18 will be considered.

Analyzing Paul's Response

From the start of 1 Cor. 6, it quickly becomes evident that the apostle was more concerned with "separating that which should be separated than protecting the rights" of church members.[99] Building on the contrast in 5.13 between those "inside" and those "outside," in ch. 6 Paul reiterated the fact that membership in the Christian ἐκκλησία meant that a person had now become one of the ἅγιοι—the set-apart, holy ones—in contradistinction to those in the outside world, who once again are depicted in very unflattering fashion. Indeed, here in 6.9–10 Paul would rehearse the same "vice list" as in 5.10–11 to describe those "outside"— πόρνοι, εἰδωλολάτραι, πλεονέκται, μέθυσοι, λοίδοροι, ἅρπαγες—while adding four new terms as well: κλεπτοί (thieves), μοιχοί (adulterers), μαλαχοί (lit. soft-ones, often translated "male prostitutes"), and ἀρσενοκοῖται (trans. in NRSV as "sodomites"). Much has been said of these lists,[100] but the important thing to note for our present purposes is that these were all capital crimes in the Hebrew Scriptures (cf. Deut. 22.21-22; 24.17). In Paul's time, and certainly in Paul's own words, while physical death might no longer have been the penalty for these sins, expulsion from the sanctified community was.[101] The apostle put it in more eschatological terms: "None of these will inherit the kingdom of God."[102] Here, we see a direct connection with Paul's words regarding the man engaged in πορνεία in ch.5; Paul's sentence in that situation, far from being the rash reaction of an oppressive leader, was simply the logical recourse for the "set-apart" ἐκκλησία if they wished to remain holy.[103] Paul himself did not dwell on these trespasses to any great extent, but rather listed them as the collective image of an outside world which formerly defined "some of you." Yet there had been a crossing-over, as it were, a spiritual movement from one system into another. Now, these Christians were ἀπελούσασθε, ἡγιάσθητε, ἐδικαιώθητε ἐν τῷ ὀνόματι τοῦ κυρίου Ἰησοῦ Χριστοῦ καὶ ἐν τῷ πνεύματι τοῦ θεοῦ ἡμῶν (6.11). The *mortis opera* that had been the "marks of their condemnation" were now "erased"; the sinners were destined to judge the angels.[104]

Yet, as we have seen, the same ἅγιοι through whom the world and even angels would one day be judged (6.2-4) were now willingly submitting to the judgments of the ἄδικοι. In placing the ἄδικοι among the disinherited (6.9), Paul set up an ironic, and even pathetic, image. The children were going to those outside the οἶκος to deal with family matters; the heirs were seeking out the disinherited to judge between them; the "sanctified ones" were going to to the "unrighteous" for justice! In speaking of the church members' part in the future eschatological judgment, Paul was actually heightening the sense of division between those inside and those outside the boundaries of the ἐκκλησία. Earlier in the letter, the apostle showed the ἀδελφοί the incongruity of being adult children of the divine Πατήρ, yet defining themselves instead in terms of the household servants (3.1–5). How much more absurd that the ἅγιοι would now choose to be judged by those upon whom they themselves would one day pronounce God's judgment![105]

A large part of Paul's response, therefore, concerned corporate redefinition in relation to the outside world. Though there may not have been *many* within the church who were "competent to comprehend a point [of law],"[106] yet together ἐν Χριστῷ they were the "set-apart ones" who were ἀπελούσασθε καὶ ἡγιάσθητε καὶ ἐδικαιώθητε ἐν τῷ ὀνόματι τοῦ κυρίου Ἰησοῦ Χριστοῦ καὶ ἐν τῷ πνεύματι τοῦ θεοῦ ἡμῶν (6.11). As such, they could not easily keep a foot in both the world of the inheritors and that of the disinherited.[107] An interesting analogy is found in Pliny. When asked by Pompeius Falco whether it was advisable to act as a legal advocate while at the same time serving as Tribune, Pliny responded with a question: How did his friend look upon his office, *inanem umbram et sine honore nomen an potestam sacrosanctam?* The query concerned definition: by what role, in which system, did Pompeius Falco wish to be defined?[108] Even so, Paul pointed to a destiny far greater than that of any tribune, and challenged the Corinthian Christians to choose how they would define themselves, in terms of rights and courts and outside networks, or as ἅγιοι (in relation to the "outside" world) and ἀδελφοί (in relation to their fellow church members). Their paradigm, their choice of how to define themselves, would in turn determine how they would deal with internal disputes.

In following this line of argumentation, Paul carefully avoided a potentially enticing trap. By focusing on the "how" of their interaction rather than on the "what" of the case(s), the apostle was able to look beyond the "symptom" to the underlying chronic problem of identity confusion (see *figure 4.b* above).[109] Instead of getting stuck in a paradigmatic quagmire of "rights" and power struggles, according to the familiar patterns of the secular ἐκκλησία, Paul instead presented them with a wholly different relational image of themselves as siblings and fellow heirs in the network of the Christian ἐκκλησία...an image rooted in the ancient laws of the community of Israel (as we shall see in a moment).

More than this, by dealing with this issue immediately after the case of the incestuous member, Paul presented a contrasting set of images. The apostle had just argued that the sin of the man in ch. 5 was so serious and its effects so far-reaching that it could bring scandal and shame on the entire ἐκκλησία, while the problems in ch. 6 were, at most, "ordinary, trivial cases" between individual members. Did they not have a σοφός amongst themselves who could easily arbitrate in the matter of (to Paul) petty complaints (6.5)? With these words, Paul at the same time *empowered the believers* (to handle their own affairs internally) and *trivialised their grievances* (so that there would be little reason for judgment at all).[110] Ultimately, the choice of the Corinthians in ch. 5 NOT to judge their fellow member and the choice of many of these same church members in ch. 6 to pursue legal action against one another were both born out of the same systemic paradigm that viewed the ways and patterns of the civic ἐκκλησία as more important and relevant than the ways and patterns of the Christian ἐκκλησία. Paul, by taking the opposite course of action— involving himself in the case of one whose immoral actions were "not found even among the Gentiles" (5.1) while also distancing himself from those whose claims to ἐξουσία were no different from those of the Gentiles—actually modelled for the Corinthian church a very different way of viewing the same situation. It was indeed possible to have been wronged by another in the ἐκκλησία, but the one who committed the offence was to be seen as a brother, not simply an adversary. Was Paul thereby allowing for some means of honourable redress?

For the answer to that query, we once again return to the text itself: Τολμᾷ τις ὑμῶν πρᾶγμα ἔχων πρὸς τὸν ἕτερον κρίνεσθαι ἐπὶ τῶν ἀδίκων καὶ οὐχὶ ἐπὶ τῶν ἁγίων...οὕτως οὐκ ἔνι ἐν ὑμῖν οὐδεὶς σοφὸς ὃς δυνήσεται διακρῖναι ἀνὰ μέσον τοῦ ἀδελφοῦ αὐτοῦ; (6.1,5). It is interesting to note that, while there is no clear citation of a Septuagint text in this instance, the apostle's language in these verses is highly reminiscent of Lev. 19.15–18: οὐ ποιήσετε ἄδικον ἐν κρίσει...οὐ μισήσεις τὸν ἀδελφόν σου τῇ διανοίᾳ σου ἐλεγμῷ ἐλέγξεις τὸν πλησίον σου καὶ οὐ λήμψῃ δι᾽αὐτὸν ἁμαρτίαν. Indeed, several points may be made about these two texts:

(1) First, it is not unreasonable to assume that Paul was aware of this section of the Mosaic Law, inasmuch as it was known and adapted by others in the early church. It has been argued, for example, that the Epistle of James comments on all but one verse of Lev. 19.[111] Likewise, in a recent work, Duling has shown evidence that Matt. 18 adapts a "reproof tradition" (ἐλέγξις) introduced in Lev. 19.[112] Duling outlines this process in terms of (1) private, personal reproof (ἐλέγξις, v.15), followed by (2) reproof in the presence of "two or three witnesses" (v.16, a clear allusion to Deut. 19.15),[113] followed by (3) liability before the ἐκκλησία, possibly a subset of leaders or elders in the church network (v.16), followed by (4) expulsion of the offender, who is then to be understood in the same category as ὁ ἐθνικὸς καὶ ὁ τελώνης (v.17).[114] Certainly, among the Qumran texts we can find direct citation of Lev. 19 in the Damascus Rule (CD 9.2–8), and the "reproof tradition" is discussed at length in 1QS 5.24–6.1. It would not be an outrageous suggestion, therefore, that Paul might refer to the ideas or terminology of this important text, even if direct citations are lacking.

(2) On the larger contextual level, several parallels between Lev. 19 and 1 Cor. 5–6 are apparent. Lev. 19 opens with a bold challenge —"You shall be holy (ἅγιοι), for I the LORD your God am holy" (v.2)—and all that follows in that chapter is, in a sense, a commentary on what a holy people look like, i.e. in terms of their actions, and interactions. Similarly, Paul opened his letter by redefining the Christian network as a holy (ἅγιοι) people, a sanctified and set-apart ἐκκλησία ἐν Χριστῷ. All that follows in 1 Corinthians is itself a commentary or elaboration of what that holy network was, and was not, supposed to look like.

(3) Paul's comment in 6.1 about "not going for judgment before the unrighteous" (κρίνεσθαι ἐπὶ τῶν ἀδίκων) is not at all unlike the challenge in Lev. 19.15 "not to render an unjust judgment" (οὐ ποιήσετε ἄδικον ἐν κρίσει). While the apostle certainly was not directly quoting the Mosaic text, it is interesting to see the connection in both passages between "judgment" and "unjust." Lev. 19.16 explicates what ἄδικος might mean in terms of judgment by speaking explicitly about partiality to the poor or to the rich. In his own situation, Paul seems to have assumed that partiality based on status or other outside standards was built into the Corinthian secular court system, so that to go before judges outside the church was to go before the ἄδικοι. In both cases, it was assumed that judgment was to be handled internally.

(4) Both passages utilize familial terminology in describing those involved in the judgment process. In 1 Cor. 6.5, Paul spoke of judging or deciding "between brethren" (ἀδελφοί), even as Lev. 19 continually spoke of ὁ ἀδελφός, who is also defined as a "son of your own people," "neighbour," "kinsman." In both passages, the nature of the relationship regulated the process of judgment: i.e. it was a "sibling," one of your own and not a stranger or outsider, whom you were judging. Likewise, both texts emphasize the internal disposition of all those involved (consider the importance of ἀγάπη in 1 Cor. 13 in light of Lev. 19.18).

(5) What is missing in the Pauline text is a step-by-step "reproof" process, while Lev. 19.17 advocated open reproof (ἔλεγξις) of an erring sibling/neighbour. When the verb ἐλέγχω is found in the LXX, it often refers to confrontation with the ultimate purpose of building up a person, not simply for bringing them to shame or ruin.[115] Only the foolish reject honest reproof, but ἔλεγχε σοφόν καὶ ἀγαπήσει σε (Prov. 9.8; 15.12). This is because, to a person of understanding, reproof can only mean further self-discernment (Prov. 19.25).[116] In this sense, ἔλεγξις is confrontation with a larger purpose in mind, the restoration of a sibling/neighbour. It is not "conflict resolution," but "conflict management," inasmuch as reproof involves not the removal of tension, but actually its increase, though only for a moment. It is not because the words "tickle the ears" that the σοφός receives them well, but rather because true wisdom is able to see the ultimate end of such words, as well as the care and concern behind them. Thus, "the command to confront gently a 'brother' or 'neighbour' is meant to foster an internal disposition designed to avoid with honour destructive interpersonal conflict in a group."[117] In other words, the ἔλεγξις which is commended in Lev. 19 could actually help prevent the escalation of unmanaged conflict by stepping in early in the "spiralling" process. Or, to use Coser's terminology (in *fig. 1.a*), ἔλεγξις is "realistic conflict," a challenging means toward a specific and constructive end. Through it, both the reproved member and the entire group are strengthened. In 1 Corinthians 6, on the other hand, even the term ἔλεγχω/ἔλεγξις is absent. Indeed, "reproof" is found only once in 1 Corinthians: ἐὰν δὲ πάντες προφητεύωσιν, εἰσέλθῃ δέ τις ἄπιστος ἢ ἰδιώτης, ἐλέγχεται ὑπὸ πάντων, ἀνακρίνεται ὑπὸ πάντων (14.24).[118] Here, the context is the Christian worship assembly into which a visiting unbeliever, hearing a prophetic word from all the believers (as opposed to ecstatic tongues), would be both "reproved" (ἐλέγχεται) and "judged" (ἀνακρίνεται) by all (ὑπὸ πάντων).[119] This is particularly interesting in light of what was said earlier about the worship assembly. When Paul used ἐλέγχω in this instance, he was speaking not about formal procedures of discipline for church members (as in Matt. 18), but rather about the distinctive power of orderly Christian worship and teaching to convict outsiders who hear the "word of the Lord." The accent here is on "orderly," for Paul is clear

that an ἄπιστος would be neither "reproved" nor "called to account" if he encountered a scene of religious ecstasy. This would simply be evidence that the Christian network was "one more consumer option in a pluralistic religious market."[120] Order which was rooted in unity, which in turn was rooted in a group-concept of love and interdependence (hence, the emphasis here on σῶμα) was the thing that would be both distinctive and compelling. Put simply, when the church was truly being the church—in its worship—then an outsider looking in would surely be reproved and acknowledge God's presence in their midst (14.25). All this, however, says that the only occurrence of ἔλεγξις in 1 Corinthians is of a different type altogether from what is found in Leviticus 19. Indeed, the very term that later appeared several times in the Pastorals (1 Tim. 5.20; Tit. 1.9,13; 2.15), is almost entirely absent from the undisputed Pauline letters. Not unsurprisingly, the more elaborate processes of later Christian communities, such as *exomologesis*, are missing from 1 Corinthians,[121] but so is the formal procedure of *CD* 9.2–8, with its explicit reference to witnesses (as in Matt. 18.16).

(6) If Paul, then, was echoing Lev. 19, it was not in terms of a specific "reproof" procedure as in Matt. 18 or *CD* 9. However, the *results* of ἔλεγξις, the possible restoration of an offending ἀδελφός and the unity of the community are indeed visible in 1 Cor. 5–6. The apostle contrasted the networks of the outside world, where judgments were made with partiality by the ἄδικοι and slander and enmity were built into the system of prosecutions, with the Christian network, where ἀγάπη οὐ χαίρει ἐπὶ τῇ ἀδικίᾳ, συγχαίρει δὲ τῇ ἀληθείᾳ (13.6) and οὐ λογίζεται τὸ κακόν (13.5). Indeed, more than once (4.6; 8.1; 13.4), Paul contrasted the "arrogance" of those who demanded their rights (ἐξουσία), according to the principles of the secular ἐκκλησία, with the ἀγάπη that sought "the upbuilding of the whole community rather than private advantage."[122] As already mentioned in passing, 1 Cor. 13 could be read as an elaboration of the Mosaic injunction to "love your neighbour as yourself."

(7) The question remains, however, whether Paul had Lev. 19.15–18 in mind when writing 1 Cor. 6. As shown here, although there is no unequivocal answer to this query, there is at least a similarity in both tone and (some) terminology between the two passages. With this in mind, we turn to another possible parallel in the תורה.

Thielman has argued that Paul's question in 6.5, οὕτως οὐκ ἔνι ἐν ὑμῖν οὐδεὶς σοφὸς ὃς δυνήσεται διακρῖναι ἀνὰ μέσον τοῦ ἀδελφοῦ αὐτοῦ, echoes Moses' description of an internal system of adjudication for Israel in Deut. 1.9,12–18:[123]

And I spoke to you at that time, saying "I am unable to bear you all by myself...How can I alone bear you and your burden, as well as your disputes?

So, choose from your own tribes wise men (ἄνδρας σοφούς), discerning and sensible, and I will appoint them as leaders over you." And you answered me, saying, "The thing you have told us to do is good." So I took from among you wise men (ἄνδρας σοφούς), discerning and sensible, and I appointed them as leaders over you, as leaders of thousands, and hundreds, and fifties, and tens, and governors for your judges. I commanded your judges at that time, saying, "Hear the cases of your brothers (τῶν ἀδελφῶν) and judge fairly between a man and his brother or the resident alien amongst you (κρίνατε δικαίως ἀνὰ μέσον ἀνδρὸς καὶ ἀνὰ μέσον ἀδελφοῦ καὶ ἀνὰ μέσον προσηλύτου αὐτοῦ). You shall not be partial in judging, you shall judge the small and the great alike; you shall not show fear before any person, for judgment is God's. And any case that is too difficult for you, bring it then to me and I will hear it. And so I charged you then with all the things that you should do."

Thielman acknowledges that there are differences between the Mosaic Law and Paul's admonitions in the case of the Corinthians, most notably the precise nature of boundary markers with which to set apart the "people of God" from the rest of the world.[124] However, there are several points of contact between these passages, which deserve mention:

(1) The appointed judges in Deuteronomy were described as "wise men" (ἄνδρας σοφούς), the key terminological connection here for Thielman. Paul's use of σοφός certainly tied in with his earlier discussion of the Corinthians' own claim to wisdom, but it is also possible, given the other connections listed below, that the apostle had this text (among others) in mind as he offered his challenge. Could "the household of Stephanas" (16.15–16) be such "wise men" for the church?

(2) It was Moses, the leader and "father figure" for the Israelites, who initiated the search for arbiters/judges between ἀδελφοί. Even so, Paul was clearly the one who challenged the Corinthians on going outside the ἐκκλησία for judgment. After all, it was in the more routine "crises" within familial, or fictive-family, relationships that "family solidarity" could truly show itself.[125]

(3) In Deuteronomy, these judges were to be raised up from within the tribes themselves. Likewise, Paul asked whether there was no one ἐν ὑμῖν to judge.[126]

(4) The judges were to be impartial before different types and ranks of people. Even so, much of what Paul was talking about throughout his letter concerned issues of status, partiality, and possible intimidation (as in the case of the incestuous man, as seen above).[127]

(5) The Deuteronomic judges were not to be intimidated by anyone on account of position or status, since they knew that, ultimately, judgment belongs to God. As we have seen, in 1 Cor. 6.2–4, Paul pointed to the

larger, eschatological reality in which the saints would be co-participants in God's ultimate judgment of the world. Earlier, in 4.1ff., the apostle had warned the Corinthians not to judge prematurely, and certainly not on the basis of "outside" standards of wisdom and eloquence, ὁ δὲ ἀνακρίνων με κύριός ἐστιν.

(6) If these judges did encounter a case too difficult for them to handle on their own, they could then take it to Moses himself. Even so, Paul clearly involved himself in a situation where the church's members failed in their duty of judgment (1 Cor. 5). However, as noted above, situations such as the one in ch. 6 were labelled by the apostle as βιωτικά. The implication in both these passages is that cases which did not need to be brought before Moses or Paul may not have been worthy of all the effort and energy put into them in the first place. After all, the real goal, as Augustine persisted (in commenting on 1 Cor. 6), was to forgive our debtors even as we ask God to forgive us.[128]

Thus, we see that in Paul's words in 1 Cor. 6, there does appear to be an "echo" of Deuteronomy 1. Thielman argues, therefore, that this is evidence that God's people were not to take their disputes outside the community.[129] More than this, however, the link with the LXX passage suggests an alternative system with which to deal with internal grievances, one which involves the leader/father figure (Moses, Paul) working alongside key leaders of the ἐκκλησία to admonish and judge members *on internal matters* as was deemed necessary. Whether we refer to this type of procedure as "reproof" or "private arbitration,"[130] it was still very much a kind of "family meeting." As such, those who said that they were mature and wise children of God were now given the chance to show it. Here again, there is a possible contrast, albeit implicit, with the position of slaves in the οἶκος. Petronius, in his *Satyricon,* presented the fairly common image of a master who intervened in a quarrel between two of his slaves. That was his right.[131] Paul the πατήρ, on the other hand, presented himself and Apollos as examples of ἀδελφοί who chose not to "judge" one another or become "puffed up" one against the other (4.6; on Apollos as ἀδελφός, see 16.12). Would it not have been better for the Corinthians to have no disputes at all? Certainly, Paul's words 1 Cor. 6.7 point to this ideal, but everything else in the letter cries out that the ideal was not yet realized in the ἐκκλησία. The problem, once again, concerned perception and definition.[132] There was never a question that conflicts would occasionally arise between ἀδελφοί, but in the end harmony had to prevail for the sake of the larger family.[133] With 6.5, Paul appears to show one way that such a goal could be achieved, through the intervention of "wise men" who could decide between "brethren" on minor issues and do so without partiality based on the standards of the "outside" networks.

Summary and Conclusion

At first glance, Paul does not appear to have offered any kind of step-by-step procedure for addressing internal conflict, as we might find in the the Dead Sea Scrolls or (if Duling is correct) in Matthew 18. However, when we read 1 Cor. 6.1–11 alongside ch. 5, and in light of the LXX passages listed above, then a "conflict management" pattern begins to emerge.

(1) First, problems inside the ἐκκλησία were to remain inside the ἐκκλησία. As Irenæus later noted, Paul's words in 1 Cor. 6.9–10 were addressed "not to those who are without...but to **us**, lest we should be cast forth from the kingdom of God, by doing any such thing."[134] The apostle's alliterative dichotomy between ἄδικοι and ἅγιοι (6.1) builds on his earlier contrasts in chs. 1–4. The fact that litigation was occurring between fellow members indicated that some church members viewed their private ἐξουσία as more important than the unity of the church and that they likewise viewed each other more in terms of outside roles—clients, slaves, rivals—than in terms of their roles as ἀδελφοί. Paul acknowledged the impossibility of "going out of the world" (5.10), but rather advocated a policy to curb the increasingly permeable boundary between the church and other networks: neither judge those outside the church (5.13), nor allow "those who have no standing in the church" (6.4) to judge the disputes of those inside (6.1).

(2) Internal disputes and problems were to be assessed not according to the standards of the secular ἐκκλησία but, rather, according to the standards of the Christian ἐκκλησία, which sought the upbuilding of other members, not their destruction.

(3) The tools for assessment could be summed up in three questions which Paul himself presented in response to the Corinthian maxim, πάντα μοι ἔξεστιν—(a) Is this "right" for which I am prepared to enter into conflict with a fellow member "beneficial," not only for me but for the whole church? (b) Will this seemingly neutral "right" dominate or consume me? (c) Will it ultimately "build up" the church? (See 1 Cor. 6.12; 10.23.[135]) By its very nature, first-century litigation lawsuits involved seeking one's personal advantage, but Paul's questions challenge the "wronged" Christian to weigh that personal advantage against the needs of the larger church.

(4) All internal judgment or assessment had to be viewed in light of the reality that, ultimately, God is the one true judge (4.4–5).

(5) "Ordinary cases" were to be handled by "wise" leaders in the church, without partiality (6.3–5). Winter adds that these arbiters could be church members who already had some legal training and skills that could be put to good use "in an extra judicial capacity" within the Christian ἐκκλησία.[136]

(6) Larger situations such as disciplinary issues were to be deliberated "when all were assembled" (5.4) in conjunction with Paul or, presumably, a representative (Timothy, Stephanas?).

(7) Expulsion accompanied by ostracism was a viable disciplinary option, but always with the hope "that his spirit may be saved in the day of the Lord" (5.5). Years later, Polycarp followed Paul's lead when speaking to the Philadelphian church about a former presbyter and his wife, who committed some unspecified but grievous sin. Referring to 1 Cor. 5.2, the bishop of Smyrna called for moderation in the church's discipline: "Call them back as suffering and straying members, that you (plural) may save your whole body."[137]

There is much that these steps do not reveal to us. There is no mention here of a gradation of offences and appropriate disciplinary measures (as in *1QS* 7). In fact, there are only two types of situations listed here, one concerning "trivial cases" which may not even deserve the attention of the assembly and the other concerning grossly sinful behaviour which could affect the entire community. Perhaps, however, there is a reason for this silence. As Cousar remarks: "The readers have not been given handy hints about how to resolve their differences, but have been challenged at a very fundamental level to do their theologizing in a different mode."[138] Through his focus on the "how" instead of the "what" of the litigation dispute, Paul made it clear that what was at stake here was the same thing that was at stake in the ἔριδες of chs. 1–4: the clarity of the church's identity and the priority of its claims on its members. Recalling the "spiral of unmanaged conflict" (see *fig. 5.b*), in the initial stages of the spiralling process, sides form and positions harden, leading to the cessation of communication between opposing sides. By calling the Corinthians to see themselves as fellow ἀδελφοί, Paul was attempting to reach them before they reached even this early step in the spiral. This is why there appears to be a tension between his statements in 6.5 and 6.7. By confronting early the underlying issues of definition that actually led to more specific disputes (e.g. "I am a citizen who has rightful demands over this property"), it would be possible to eliminate the need for litigation of any sort, inasmuch as the latter was only needed at a much higher point on the spiral, after communication had stopped and a sense of crisis had emerged. To those who ask whether Paul concurred that there was a need for alternative methods of conflict management or whether he preferred to see no disputes at all between members, the answer might be "yes" to both. It was precisely his desire for unity that led Paul to attempt to manage the conflicts at an early stage—on a paradigmatic level—in order to avoid the necessity of later, more drastic solutions.

In summary, in this section I have attempted to show how the visible issue of litigation pointed to the underlying definitional paradigm in which many Corinthians were obviously still operating: as members of the secular ἐκκλησία in which the litigants (and their supporters) were positioned as adversaries, instead of as members of the Christian ἐκκλησία in which those with disputes were still defined as "siblings." The apostle's "solution," while not as developed in form as may be found in the Dead Sea Scrolls, instead centered on a redefining of the conflictual situation in light of a redefining of the relational system. Together the ἀδελφοί were destined to be instruments of eschatological judgment (6.2–3), even as earlier they had been called co-heirs of the kingdom. It was, therefore, almost inconceivable that these same ἀδελφοί could get tied up in disputes over "rights," much less take such disputes "outside" the family. I have asserted the likelihood of Paul alluding to certain Old Testament passages, not as "proof texts" (which would have meant little, perhaps, to a mainly Gentile congregation), but as precedents for reconfiguring internal relationships independent of the standards and dichotomies of outside networks. Now, we may turn at last to the final section of this chapter, which considers the relationship of the two passages just examined with the rest of the issues in Paul's "family meeting" in 1 Cor. 5–10, as well as with his statement in 4.1ff.

1 Cor. 5–6 as Part of a Larger Unit

What we have seen in both cases above is that judgment and discipline were to be understood in the context of the church's own life and standards. The problem, however, as we saw in ch. 3 above, was that these same church members continued to "belong" to other, overlapping networks. Some members were married to "unbelievers," others were necessarily engaged in business dealings with "outsiders," still others were slaves to "unbelieving" masters. What did internal judgment, discipline, and "conflict management" mean in these instances? In this final section of the chapter, I will argue briefly that these two passages examined above (5.1–13 and 6.1–11), far from being randomly placed at this point of Paul's letter, actually serve to prepare the way for the questions and further problems that follow. While Chrysostom spoke of the collective problems in 1 Cor. 1–6—the ἔριδες, the immoral relationship, and the covetousness resulting in litigation—as "the three heaviest things laid to the [Corinthians'] charge,"[139] there was certainly more to come! The transition verse is 6.12, which Dodd contends "has a formal place within the letter's strategy," forming an *inclusio* with 10.23, even as 4.16 forms a larger *inclusio* with 11.1.[140] As we will see, within this smaller unit we find the *limits* of judgment.

As already noted in chapter 3 above, Winter argues that 6.12–20 depicts "not brothels but banquets," more precisely the private dinners held by and/or for citizens and persons of higher status.[141] Such feasts included programmes called "after-dinners," during which prostitutes would satisfy the sexual appetites of those who had just finished dining. The noteworthy thing here is that such events were both acceptable and familiar within the world of the secular ἐκκλησία. These banquets also served as a visible rite of passage for those young men receiving the *toga virilis*. Seneca the Younger spoke of these culinary and sexual feasts as "symptoms and causes of decadence in the young."[142] Those very persons who only a short time before were not permitted to enjoy such "decadence" found that now, at the "age of reclining" (using Booth's phrase), "all things were permitted" (πάντα ἔξεστιν). Winter makes a strong case for seeing such a situation behind the words in 6.12. This is, of course, quite a different position from that of Fee and others who have argued that the issue in 6.12–20 involved Christian men going to prostitutes because their spirits were now on "a higher plane...where they were unaffected by behaviour that has merely to do with the body."[143] However, in viewing all the various situations that comprise the *inclusio* between 6.12 and 10.23 (not simply the situation in 6.12–20), we see something other than some form of proto-Gnosticism. Instead, each situation appears to concern familiar, acceptable patterns in the outside networks that caused disruption within the very different Christian network. Each of the situations listed in 6.12–11.1 involved a Corinthian "slogan," either quoted verbatim by Paul or, more likely, applied by Paul to the Corinthians (as in "I belong..." in 1.14). These "slogans" suggest behaviour that was acceptable in the Corinthian secular system: πάντα μοι ἔξεστιν (6.12; 10.23), τὰ βρώματα τῇ κοιλίᾳ καὶ ἡ κοιλία τοῖς βρώμασιν (6.13), καλὸν ἀνθρώπῳ γυναικὸς μὴ ἅπτεσθαι (7.1), πάντες γνῶσιν ἔχομεν (8.1), οὐδεὶς θεὸς εἰ μὴ εἷς (8.4). The problem here was not that the Corinthian Christians were doing things that were unlawful (if so, this would certainly have been a helpful point for Paul, see 5.1), but rather that things that were permissible (in the secular networks) did not help the local Christian community.

Returning to 6.12–20, when we view the situation in terms of a coming-of-age ἐξουσία, then we can see that the notion of identity or definition once again played a part in the Corinthian problems. Tacitus described the receiving of the *toga* and the accompanying "right" to attend the banquets as "enticements to Romanization."[144] It was the young men's "right" precisely because they were now able to define themselves as members of the élite. Their actions were based, at least in part, upon their self-definition, which in turn was based on the standards of the network or social system with which they chose to affiliate themselves. Thus, it was recognized by some that "notions concerning what was shameful and not shameful," what was ἔξεστιν and not ἔξεστιν, were relative to the system in which one lived and operated.[145] A recent description of late twentieth-century European culture could very well have been used of the Corinth of Paul's day: "A pluralistic and complex culture tends to produce young people possessing an incomplete and weak identity...[who] appear lost, with few points of reference...*very dependent on the socio-cultural context*, and seek[ing] immediate gratification of the senses."[146]

Likewise, in addressing the issues about which the Corinthians themselves wrote to Paul (7.1), the apostle spoke of the "condition" in which they were at the time of their calling (ἐν ᾧ ἐκλήθη, 7.24), and defined this "condition" in terms of several social dichotomies already discussed: married/unmarried, circumcised/uncircumcised, slave/free. He also linked these defining contrasts as belonging to ὁ κόσμος, the present form of which was "passing away" (παράγω, 7.31). Indeed, in 9.4–6, Paul summarized the ἐξουσίαι which were his (and the Corinthians') in the various networks of the πολιτεία: the right to food and drink, undoubtably a reference to the controversy concerning idol meat; the right to a (believing) wife, continuing the train of thought from 1 Cor. 7; and the right to refrain from working, most likely a reference to the patron-client relationship.[147] In all this, Paul was focusing on "permissible," not illicit, patterns and practices in Roman Corinth. Even more, these "rights" were linked with definitional paradigms, so that what was a "right" for one person in a particular system or network would not necessarily be true for another person not in that system: i.e. masters could boast of "rights" that were not available to slaves, citizens could claim "rights" not open to non-citizens.[148] In what way, then, did Paul's comments in 1 Cor. 5–6 speak to issues that involved persons and systems outside the ἐκκλησία?

Hess and Handel assert that a family system "constitutes its own world, which is not to say that it closes itself off from everything else but that it determines what parts of the external world are admissible and how freely." Quite simply, they summarize, "the family maps its domain of *acceptable and desirable experience.*"[149] Thus, in response to the various "rights" asserted by various church members, Paul reminded them: "you were washed, you were sanctified, you were justified" (6.11). This was their defining "rite of passage" as members of the Christian network, far more important than receiving the *toga* since it involved inheritance not of worldly goods but of God's kingdom.[150] Thus, in dealing with the question of what was permitted, Paul set forth two principles.

First, as he had stated in 5.1–13, Paul continued to argue in subsequent passages that those "inside" were neither to judge nor to be intimidated by those "outside." If something was "acceptable and desirable" in the various networks of Roman Corinth, or in the larger Empire, or in any other lands or groups, what was that to the "kingdom inheritors"? It was precisely because τὸ σχῆμα τοῦ κόσμου τούτου παράγει (7.31) that it made little sense to challenge its norms or "rights." For this reason, he did not say "all things are not necessarily permitted," but rather "not all things are beneficial and build up." Second, as he had said in 6.1–11, Paul continued to assert that the standards and practices of the outside networks had no bearing on life "inside." If something was "acceptable and desirable" in the outside systems, that did not mean it was to be "acceptable and desirable" for the ἀδελφοί. As seen above, the Christian ἀδελφός and ἀδελφή were to follow a different set of standards particular to their familial system.

Taken together, the two complementary principles help explain Paul's otherwise apparent contradictions in the *inclusio* between 6.12–10.23. Divorce was not permitted to fellow believers (7.10–11) and a believer should not initiate divorce even with an unbelieving spouse (7.12–14), *but* if the unbelieving spouse—operating according to the principles of his/her realm, the outside world—initiated separation, then the Christian was "not bound" by the "insider" command.[151] Likewise, there was no fault in a Christian eating whatever was put before him/her (8.8; 10.27), *but* if it was clear that the food had been offered to idols and a "weaker" ἀδελφός was looking on (8.9–13), then it was not beneficial to eat…nor was it ever appropriate to participate in a temple sacrifical meal, which essentially meant accepting the standards of that cultic network (10.14–22). Again, Paul agreed that slaves should make the most of an opportunity of manumission, *but* at the same time he insisted that they should view their present enslaved status "as a matter of indifference."[152] οἱ χρώμενοι τὸν κόσμον ὡς μὴ καταχρώμενοι (7.31). Thus, the apostle's otherwise confusing comments begin to make more sense when we read them in light of the two principles of neither worrying about what happens outside the ἐκκλησία nor letting outside practices influence life inside for the ἀδελφοί.

Returning once more to the chart on ἀδελφός terminology in 1 Corinthians (*fig. 4.a*), we can see in the third column how Paul continued the pattern he began in chs. 5–6 of speaking of the contrast between those inside and those outside in familial terms: ὁ ἀδελφός in contradistinction to ὁ ἄπιστος (7.12ff.). His choice of the nominative case instead of the otherwise more prevalent vocative case clearly is connected with situations where the outside networks were overlapping the Christian network most visibly, i.e. when one married partner was an ἀδελφός and one was not, when a believing slave was under the authority of an unbelieving master, etc. As shown above, Paul utilized the vocative case most especially when he was dealing with purely intra-church issues, such as worship. It is also interesting to see how Paul made unique use of the feminine ἀδελφή (7.15, cf. also 9.5) in order to show how in the Christian network, control in the marriage was not unilateral as in outside networks. One's status as a believer, not one's gender, was the crucial issue for Paul in dealing with delicate issues such as divorce or conjugal rights (7.4). Much has been said, and much more could be said, about Paul's view of women's ἐξουσία in the ἐκκλησία, but here at least, his primary concern was with drawing a contrast between ἀδελφός-ἀδελφή and ἄπιστος. In any case, we can see how Paul continued to utilize familial imagery in redefining members of the Christian network in relation to each other and outsiders.

Thus, in summarizing what has been said in this chapter, I have attempted to show how Paul confronted the Corinthian "double dilemma" by arguing both for the need for conflict where it was lacking, i.e. in the case of the incestuous man, and for the appropriate context for conflict when it did occur, i.e. in the confines of the ἐκκλησία. It has also been suggested here that the placement of these passages in the letter was quite intentional, so that the limits of judgment for the Corinthian Christians— indeed the limits of "insider" standards—were defined quite simply by who and what was their own. Thus, Paul did not offer specific codes of discipline for situations which had already risen to the higher parts of the conflict spiral, but rather he attempted to "manage" them on a paradigmatic level by redefining the "rights" that led to conflict in light of Christian familial bonds.

NOTES

[1] I concur with D. Martin that the issues in 1 Cor. 5–10 are more than simply "separate questions that are addressed seriatim by Paul" (1995, 163).

[2] Iren., *Ag. Her.* 4.27.4

[3] Cf. repectively Ign. *Magn.* 10 and Ign. *Phil.* 3.

[4] Cf. PtF 33.5.15, where the context is a discussion about "fasting according to the visible realm" as contrasted with a "true fast."

[5] Chrys., *Hom. on 1 Cor. 15.3.*

[6] Λόγος κατηχήτικος 37. His fellow Cappadocian, Gregory of Nazianzus, likewise used the leaven image in a positive sense, in his Letter to Cledonius Against Apollinaris (*Ep.* 101).

[7] Luther, *De Serv. Arb.* 5.12, 6.1. Chrysostom defined ἐκκαθάρατε in this way: "to cleanse with accuracy, so that there will not be so much as a remnant nor even a shadow of that sort" (again, see *Hom. on 1 Cor.* 15.3).

[8] See p. 136 in Pauck's edition. On this point, cf. also Paulinus of Nola, *Natalicium* 24.639.

[9] Cf. *Ann. Ep. Pr. ad Cor.* 5.6–7: *Quia unius peccatum imputatur toti multitudini et luit tota multitudnoe.* He further equated the Corinthian situation with the sin of Achan in Josh. 7.1ff. Compare this with Hus' words in *On Simony* 7, where spoke of the church's membership as a whole being leavened, "infected by this same sin, which is communicated to them because of their neglect to eradicate it."

[10] Paulinus of Nola cited 1 Cor. 5.7 directly to affirm that "we are thus loosed from the old laws and no longer dwell in the shadow, for Christ the Son of God has himself enlightened us" *Natalicium* 24.639 (early fifth century C.E.). Cf. also Augustine, in his *Contra Faustum Manichœum* 9.10 and 32.11, who mentioned the leaven in his arguments for keeping the annual festivals. Athanasius made several references to 5.7 in his various Festal Letters (2,3,6,7,10,13,14, 19,42). Contrast Moffatt (1938, 58), who has interpreted these words as the call to celebrate "our festival of faith and fellowship, since thanks to the crucified Christ our whole life is now a festival."

[11] Even so, the chapter has remained absent from most lectionaries, though verses 7b–8a are said regularly at the Breaking of the Bread in the American Book of Common Prayer.

[12] Despite what he saw as papal abuses, Calvin still saw the disciplinary rite as "one of the most profitable and salutary things which the Saviour entrusted to his church." See his *Org. of the Church (1537)*, pp. 50–51 in Reid's edition.

[13] Cf. Horrell 1996, 91; for a more detailed discussion on Paul's sources, see Mitchell 1989.

[14] The illustration comes from Ambrose, in his *Libri duo de pœnitentia* 9.1(against the Novatian heresy, c. 384).

[15] Cf. Fee 1987, 200; Chow 1992, 132; Conzelmann 1975, 96; Barrett 1968, 122.

[16] Dixon 1992, 61, who cites Crook 1967a, 101: "Marriage was a matter of intention; if you lived together as man and wife, man and wife you were". Cf. also De Vos 1998, 105, n. 7. As Dixon has shown, the general understanding of marriage centered on the issue of producing legitimate children. On the question of whether the πατήρ was living or dead at the time of this particular relationship, see De Vos 1998, 105, n. 8.

[17] Certainly, in 1 Cor. 7 he had as much to say to the women in the ἐκκλησία as to the men.

[18] Lattke's suggestion that the woman was actually his biological mother (1994, 39ff.), a situation not uncommon among Persian Magi, lacks the evidence to make it anything more than conjecture. For a counter to Lattke, see De Vos 1998, 105, n. 4.

[19] See also *b. Sanh.* 56A, which lists rabbinic elaborations of the so-called Noahic covenant; their list includes fornication (Gr. πορνεία), as well as idolatry, blasphemy, and the like.

[20] Cf. Jos. *Ant.* 3.274, who said that "union with a stepmother...is viewed with abhorrence as an outrageous crime." See also *Jub.* 33.10; Philo, *De Spec.* 3.14.

[21] This accords with Countryman's suggestion that some sexual actions were considered sin inasmuch as they constituted theft from another male head of the household. Cited in Osiek and Balch 1997, 110. See D. Martin 1995, 174–179.

[22] Gaius *Inst.* 1.63: *Quae mihi quondam socrus aut nurus aut privigna aut noverca fuit.* Cf. also the oft-cited passage from Cicero, *Pro. Cluentio* 5.14–6.15, as well as Ael. Spart., *Life of Ant. Carac.* 10.1–4.

[23] Cf. Hays 1997, 82. Harris speaks of the Corinthians' perception of a "new norm" (1991,7).

[24] Chow 1992, 139–140. In this scenario, Chow further suggests that the man married his stepmother for reasons of financial gain rather than sexual attraction (pp.130–139), a position challenged by Dixon's research (1992, 94). I concur with Witherington that Chow's overall thesis is a plausible one, but that the latter goes too far in his assertion that Paul was encountering basically the same persons—wealthy and influential patrons—throughout 1 Cor. 1–16. See Witherington 1995, 157, n. 20.

[25] Chow 1992, 140. This point was taken up as early as Moffatt 1938, 53. Chrysostom had admitted that the fornicator might very well have been "some wise one," but spoke of the lack of discipline from the church in terms of the fornicator's doctrine, which he said was left "undetermined" by Paul. (15.1)

[26] Clarke 1993, 84–86; cf. Epstein 1987, 92–94.

[27] De Vos 1998, 109. More will be said below about this line of argumentation.

[28] *Ibid.*, 113–114.

[29] Dixon 1992, 94 (emphasis mine), also cited in De Vos 1998, 113. Dixon adds that "there is virtually no evidence" that a married man would simultaneously have a *concubina*.

[30] See p. 113 in De Vos, where he argues that even otherwise Romanised Jews such as Philo and Josephus still failed to comprehend marriage and sexual customs that would have been perfectly normal to non-Jewish members of the πολιτεία.

[31] De Vos 1998, 112, n. 38.

[32] Unlike Josephus or Philo, with whom De Vos links Paul, "the apostle to the gentiles" was deeply involved in a network comprised of both Jews and non-Jews (1.22–24; 12.13).

[33] De Vos is probably correct in his assertion that sexual pleasure, "if not outright lust" was one key factor in irregular relationships such as the one listed in 1 Cor. 5. As early as Augustine, the situation in 1 Cor. 5 was compared to Reuben's "unnatural crime of defiling his father's bed" (Gen. 35.22), a deed which the fourth/fifth-century bishop described as "deliberate incest," although the Genesis passage specifically states that Bilhah, with whom Reuben lay, was his father's concubine, not wife (אביו פִּילֶגֶשׁ; LXX: τῆς παλλακῆς τοῦ πατρὸς αὐτοῦ). See his *Contra Faust. Mani.* 22.64. Cf. also Jerome, *Ep.*147.1.

[34] Osiek and Balch note that such an arrangement was not at all uncommon, given the twin realities of divorce and a father's early death (1997, 109–110).

[35] Chrysostom, *Hom. on 1 Cor.* 15.1; cf. Palladius' brief reference in *Dial. de vita sanct. Joh. Chrys.* 18 (406–408 C.E.). Tertullian used this same approach in regards to the second marriages of Christians, pointing out that "pagans" were more disciplined in this area than many who had "put on Christ": "The false gods, as everybody knows, have widows and monogamists to serve them" (*De Monog.* 17).

[36] There also appear to be echoes of Ezek. 16 in Matt.11.20–24, as Jesus exclaimed: γῆ Σοδόμων ἀνεκτότερον ἔσται ἐν ἡμέρα κρίσεως ἢ σοί.

[37] While the Heb. זמה could refer to "wickedness" in more general terms (as seen in the LXX translation, ἀσέβεια), in both 16.27 and 22.9, the "depravity" in question is clearly sexually oriented. Cf. Allen 1994, 229, n. 27d.

[38] Much more will be said about this in the following section *(5.2.3)*. It is true that Paul did not often appear to cite or allude to Ezekiel, yet Hays has pointed to fairly clear echoes of Ezek. 36 in the apostle's image of the "tablets of fleshy hearts" in 2 Cor. 3–4 (1989, 127).

[39] See Yarbrough 1985, 90; cf. also Harris 1991, 11.

[40] This is the only occurrence of the passive present indicative of ἀκούω in the New Testament (with Eccl. 12.13 being the only one in the Hebrew Scriptures). Nevertheless, whenever a passive form of this verb is found in Scripture, the meaning is that "it is heard/it will be heard" not by a specific person but by people in general. Cf. Ex. 23.13; Is. 58.4; 60.18; 65.19; Jer. 6.7; 27.46; 40.10; Ezek. 19.9; 26.13; Nah. 2.14. Likewise, in the New Testament, the same pattern is found: where a passive form of ἀκούω is found, it invariably means that "it is heard" by an unspecified, unnumbered people. See Lk. 12.3; Rev. 18.22,23. Only Matt. 28.14 breaks the pattern and specifies one person, ὁ ἡγεμών, by whom a sound/message is heard.

[41] In Paul's list, the immoral man is grouped with ὁ πλεονέκτης (an old word for the covetous or greedy, lit. the over-reachers; see Eph. 5.5), ὁ ἅρπαξ (an old word for an extortioner or robber), ἤ εἰδωλολάτρης (lit. a hired hand for the idols). Along with ἤ λοίδορος and ἤ μέθυσος from verse 11, this list is almost entirely comprised of terms found in the New Testament only here and in 6.10. In Deissmann's classic study, this list is shown to correspond with the vices found on counters of virtues and vices used in Roman games (1978, 316).

[42] See Bullinger's treatise, *Of the Holy Catholic Church* (*Dec.* 1; p. 297 in Bromiley's edition).

[43] Cf. Winter 1994, 119.

[44] This should not be surprising, in light of earlier comments concerning homeostatic balance in a social system (see ch. 2 above).

[45] See his *Hom. on 1 Cor.* 15.3.

[46] Fee 1987, 203. Conzelmann 1975, 97, lists six options for reading 5.3–5.

[47] Fee has argued convincingly why, despite the fact "the fact that the phrase is somewhat removed from its verb" (1987, 208), this alone does not make a case against such a reading, especially since it makes far better sense out of the entire passage than either of its two main alternative readings: "when you are assembled in the name of the Lord Jesus" (cf. NIV, JB, Bultmann 1951, 127) or "the one who has done such a thing in the name of the Lord Jesus" (cf. Murphy-O'Connor 1977).

It makes little difference to the argument whether the ἡμῶν in verse 4 in certain ancient MS is genuine or not.

[48] Cf. the *Digest* 48.9.5 in *Corpus Juris Civilis* XI.

[49] It is an often-used term in the gospels, where it is used alternatively for the gathering of grains (Mat. 22.10; 25.26), other inanimate objects (such as branches, Jn. 15.6; Lk.15.13), or people (Mat, 2.4; Mk. 4.1; 6.30). In Acts, συνάγω always refers to the gathering of people (4.5; 11.26; 14.27; 15.30). See also Rev. 16.14; 19.17; 20.8.

[50] Hays thinks this may have been the case, but offers no particular reasons why (1997, 84).

[51] Related to this issue is the fact that 14.23 explicitly states that ἰδιῶται καὶ ἄπιστοι were present in the meeting, while in 5.12–13 it is implied that such outsiders were not present among those "assembled."

[52] Cf. Plutarch, *Tim.* 10.8.3: συναγωνίζεσθαι τοῖς Κορινθίοις καὶ συνελευθεροῦν τὴν Σικελίαν. See also *Comp. Arist. Et Cato.* 4.3.5; *Flam.* 5.5.2. Dio Chrysostom also used συνάγω in one of its various forms (*Or.* 2.77.2; 7.133.7; 48.10.10; 75.8.1). In one particularly interesting example, he spoke of the physician's household assembling, then added οἱ μόνον οἱ ἐλεύθεροι.

[53] Ezekiel's words in 22.9 about the sacrifices and sexual abominations at "the mountain shrines" bring to mind Paul's comments in 6.12ff. about the involvement of some church members in collegial dinners where some form of cultic prostitution was common, as well as his extended argument in 1 Cor. 8–10 regarding the meat used in pagan sacrifices. Though these similarities may be attributed to the common source of the Holiness Code of Leviticus, there are several other points of congruity between 1 Cor. 5 and Ezek. 16.

[54] Contrast God's affirmative reply to David in 2 Sam. 5.19 to the silence that greeted disobedient Saul when asked the same question at an earlier time (1 Sam. 14.37).

[55] Cf. Fee 1987, 209. Hays notes the mystical nature of Paul's language (1997, 84).

[56] Cf. Allen 1994, 223–248, esp. pp. 232–235. Blenkinsopp uses even bolder terms to describe the allegorical character of Ezek. 16 as "the nymphomaniac bride" (1990, 76–79). Allen notes the balance between the focus on the wicked actions of the girl (or her "relatives") and then on God's response in terms of judgment followed by forgiveness.

[57] The word ἐξιλάσκεσθαί (ἱλάσκομαι+ἐκ) referred to atonement made for the sins of another and was often linked with sacrifice. It can be found in Lev. 16.34; 17.11; Num. 8.19; 1Chr. 6.34; Ezek. 45.15,17; Sir. 45.16. Heb. 2.17 speaks of Jesus as one who "had to become like his brothers and sisters in every respect…to make atonement for them."

[58] Augustine noted in his *Contra Faustum Manichæum* 22.79 that Paul was here acting "out of love, not cruelty," and linked this verse with 1 Tim. 1.20.

[59] An early illustration of this principle may be found in the apocryphal *Acts of Thomas* (p. 546ff. in A.C. Coxe's American edition), wherein a young man sees his hands wither upon receiving the eucharist from Thomas, who remarked: "the eucharist of the Lord has convicted you." Following the young man's confession of murder, the apostle instructed him to place his withered hands in water blessed by the apostle,

at which point they were restored. Immediately, both apostle and restored offender went to the victim, who was subsequently restored to life by Thomas. Thus, God's judgment through the eucharist led ultimately to the forgiveness of the sinner and the redress of his wrongs. An interesting side note is the citation of 1 Cor. 6.9 as the basis of living a chaste life.

[60] We see here the chief difference between 1 Cor. 5 and a passage such as *1QS* 2.4b–10, where no pardon was offered for the wicked: "May God not heed when you call on him, nor pardon you by blotting out your sin!" This pardon, however, is precisely the goal Paul had in mind in 1 Cor. 5 and 11. In this sense, Chrysostom was correct to say that the sentence in 1 Cor. 5 was done with "more gentleness" (*Hom. on 1 Cor.* 16.3). Cf. 1QS 2.11–18, which does speak of members of the community who nevertheless held onto the "gods of their hearts." Osiek and Balch note: "Paul is not judging the eternal fate of the son who is committing incest, but insisting that those who *are* 'washed, sanctified, and justified' (6.11) *must act* that way" (1997, 110). Both offender and church were given a chance to repent.

[61] See, for example, the fourth cent. papyrus, *PGM* 4, 1227–64, in which the *demon* is the one who is delivered over to destruction, not the human host.

[62] Cf. Fee 1987, 208, n.62, who asserts that it makes little difference to analysis of the parallelism whether the pastoral epistle is genuinely Pauline or not.

[63] Surprisingly, although this verse seems even more obviously indebted to Ezekiel 16, this connection has usually been ignored in favour of more general comparisons with the "woes of foreign nations" in Ezek. 25–32, Jer. 46–51, and elsewhere.

[64] Cf. also Sirach 4.10–21, which speaks of the children of σοφία, who are described as inheritors (4.12,15), beloved servants (4.13), those who will judge the nations (4.14, not unlike 1 Cor. 6.2), and those whom wisdom disciplines (4.16). Indeed, in Sirach, the "children" are challenged to show no partiality or deference to another person (4.21) and, when they go astray, are "delivered over" (παραδώσω, 4.18) to their own ruin (πτῶσις), so that they may experience the "shame" (αἰσχύνη) that leads to "glory and favor" (4.20).

[65] Wenham argues convincingly for some knowledge on Paul's part of the Jesus tradition underlying Matthew 18 (a point which will be explored further in the following section), but he somehow misses the correlation between Matt. 11 and 1 Cor. 5 (1995, 211–212). I have not even discussed the Passover allusion in Paul's image of the unleavened bread in 1 Cor. 5.6–8, which has been mentioned briefly in *5.2.1* and by many others.

[66] Blenkinsopp 1990, 98; cf. Thielman 1994, 90. Douglas remarks: "Eliminating [dirt] is not a negative movement, but a positive effort to organise the environment" (1966, 2).

[67] Chrysostom pursued this line of argument in *Hom. on 1 Cor.* 16.1.

[68] Cf. Chow 1992, 180: Paul "seems to have expected the church to solve the problem themselves at an earlier stage (1 Cor. 5.2), and gives his decision only when they have not."

[69] Fee 1987, 230. Concerning Paul's words, the 18th-century scholar, J. A. Bengel, noted in his *Gnomen Novi Testamenti: Grandi verbo notatur læsa majestas Christianorum.*

[70] Cf. A. Mitchell 1993, 563. See also Meeks 1983, 128–129; Meeks 1979; Fee 1987, 230.

[71] These twin emphases have been noted by A. Mitchell (1993, 562). As Hays puts it, the Corinthian Christians were "declaring their primary allegiance to the pagan culture of Corinth rather than to the community of faith" (1997, 93).

[72] We see a similar case in Demosthenes' suit against his fraudulent guardian Aphobus in 363 B.C.E. It should be noted that in verse 10, Paul distinguished those who defraud from thieves (κλέπται) and swindlers (ἅρπαγες). A similar distinction is found in Mk. 10.19.

[73] *Contra* Fee 1987, 239.

[74] Cf. Garnsey 1970, 217–218; Chow 1992, 130; Theissen 1982, 97.

[75] Epstein 1987, 94.

[76] Winter notes the concern in the ancient system "for the lack of respect being accorded to one's patron or one's betters" (1991, 561).

[77] Dio Chrys. *Or.* 8.9. His reference was particularly to the time around the Isthmian Games.

[78] The phrase "before the unrighteous" (ἐπί τῶν ἀδίκων) was an idiom, meaning "in the presence of." A similar use of the phrase may be found in 2 Cor. 7.14.

[79] Moffatt 1938, 64: "The derogatory adjective is no more than an equivalent either for unbelievers, much as a strict Jew might speak of Gentile sinners, or for men of no account, judged from the Christian standpoint."

[80] Winter 1991, 563–566. He cites, among others, Cicero, who declared in his own day that *gratia, potentia,* and *pecunia* were all contributors to less-than-impartial justice in the courts (*Pro Cæcina* 73). A particularly intriguing reference to Favorinus (c. 110 C.E.) offers a sharp contrast between Greek Corinth, where citizens were known as φιλοδίκαιοι, and Roman Corinth, where Paul spoke of ἄδικοι (*Or.* 37.16–17; cf. Winter 1991, 564, n. 23).

[81] "No rules of conduct protected a defendant from the most ferocious attacks on all aspects of his public and private life" (Epstein 1987, 91).

[82] Winter 1994, 115. He notes here that the ζῆλος καὶ ἔρις (3.3) that accompanied the leadership/affiliation issues in chs. 1–4 was also "expressed in litigation." Cf. Clarke 1993.

[83] Epstein remarks that "the convicted man's sons and friends were duty-bound to take revenge" against the prosecutor and/or plaintiff (1987, 92).

[84] As early as Tertullian, the connection between 1 Cor. 5.12 and 6.1 was noted (*On Mod.* 2). If the Christian was not to judge those outside, how much more important that s/he was not, in turn, judged by those outside?

[85] A. Mitchell 1993, 575. For this reason, Pliny was reluctant to enter a case against his friend and potential successor (in a post previously held by Pliny) — who now could potentially become an enemy — and did so only because of his even greater loyalty to the late father of the defendant. He "ran the risk of giving offence" (cf. *Ep.* 4.17, "To Gallus").

[86] This word, from the passive verb, ἡττάομαι ("succumb" or "be defeated") is used only here and in Rom. 11.12 in the New Testament. The occurrence in Romans is particularly interesting, since it says there that the ἥττημα of the Jews meant

πλοῦτος for the Gentiles, a way of thinking not wholly unlike that found in Ezek. 16 (seen in the previous section) that stated that Jerusalem's sinfulness actually helped the other nations by making them look righteous.

[87] Derrett 1991, 24.

[88] Cf. Plato *Apol.* 30C–D, 41D; *Gorg.* 468B, 473A. See also A. Mitchell 1993, 573, who remarks: "The philosopher belies his status as wise when he resorts to litigation."

[89] Musonius Rufus, "Will the Philosopher Prosecute Anyone for Personal Injury?", 10.15–23.

[90] See Gregory's *Liber Regula Pastoralis* 22 (Admonition 23), who in the same chapter also draws upon such Scriptures as Matt. 5.23–24; Mk. 9.50; Gal. 5.22; Eph. 4.3–4; Heb. 7.14.

[91] Epstein confirms "the Roman horror of litigation, a certain cause or manifestation of *inimicitiae*...between brothers" (1987, 28–29).

[92] Cf. Greg. Naz., *Or.* 2.79.

[93] Douglas 1966, 122.

[94] See Greg. Naz., *Or.* 2.80: "Men are distinguished not according to personal character but by their disagreement or friendship with us." Cf. Coser 1956, 34, on "reciprocal repulsions."

[95] Carpenter and Kennedy 1988, 11; for what follows on the spiral, see pp. 11–17.

[96] Epstein 1987, 75.

[97] Concerning this, Chrysostom remarked: "For people's offences are not judged by the same rule, when they are committed against any chance person, and towards one's own member" (*Hom.* 16.7).

[98] As Friedman notes: "Efforts to bring about change by dealing only with symptoms (content) rather than process, never will achieve lasting changes in an organic system. Problems will recycle unless the balancing factors in the homeostasis of the system shift" (1985, 202).

[99] Douglas 1966, 53.

[100] The meaning of two of the added terms, μαλαχοί and ἀρσενοκοῖται, has been debated in recent years. Winter 1999 argues that the context of 6.12ff. is not prostitution, per se, but *collegial* banquets where men could indulge in sexual gratification with young boys after the meal. Seneca refers to "luckless boys who must put up with other shameful treatment after the banquet is over" (*Ep.* 95.23–34). Cf. also Suetonius, *Lives* (Nero), 28–29.

[101] On exclusion instead of execution of the offending member, see Horbury 1985.

[102] The list, as Robertson put it in his 1934 study (on 6.9), was "the roll call of the damned."

[103] The chief difference between Paul's reason for not going to court and that of ancient philosophers such as Musonius Rufus (*Will the Philosopher Prosecute Anyone for Personal Injury* 10.15–23) or Epictetus (*Disc.* 3.22.55–56) lies in the apostle's emphasis on the interdependence and corporate identity of those in the community of the saints.

[104] Cf. Tert., *De Pœnitentia* 7. More will be said about this treatise in a moment.

[105] See Chrysostom's comments concerning the absurdity of this situation (*Hom.* 16.4).

[106] *Ibid.*, 16.5.

[107] Irenæus elaborated on this point in *Against Her.* 5.11.1–5.12.1. Tertullian further emphasised that Paul was making the possibility of an eschatological role of "judging the angels" conditional upon present "obedience to the law of God" (*Against Marcion*, 2.9).

[108] Pliny, *Ep.* 1.23. As for himself, Pliny reported that he quit the bar when he became Tribune, since *sapienti viro ita aptanda est, ut perferatur.*

[109] Cf. again Friedman 1985, 202. Carpenter and Kennedy add that, on the positive side, "some conflicts may lead to the sharpening of critical issues and the creation of new systems" (1988, 3).

[110] Augustine argued that Paul granted permission for such "trifling" cases to be decided between Christians as "an indulgence extended to the infirmities of the weak" (*Enc.* 78).

[111] Cf. Johnson 1982, who notes that only Lev. 19.14 is not discussed.

[112] Duling 1998, 281ff. We can also speak of the "reproof tradition" in Ben Sira 19.13–17; *T.Gad* 4.1–3; 6.1–6; and 4 Ezra 14.

[113] *Ibid.*, 279, for more on the importance of two's and three's in the First Gospel.

[114] While only the first stage explicitly adds the possibility of the offending ἀδελφός listening and, thus, being "regained" (v.15), it remains highly significant that all these verses together are bracketed by the parables of the lost sheep on the one hand (vs.10–14) and the unforgiving debtor on the other hand (vs.21–35), stories that "dramatise the conviction that God's desire is that the sinner be saved, not condemned" (cf. Hare 1993, 213). It is not surprising, then, that the closing statement of Lev. 19.15–18, "You shall love your neighbour as yourself," is found not once, but twice in the First Gospel (19.19; 22.39).

[115] Thus, the Psalmist declared, "Let the righteous smite me with kindness and reprove (ἐλέγχει) me" (141.5). In the Book of Job, ἐλέγχω is found several times and particularly concentrated in ch. 13, where the Divine reproof is said to be aimed at those who show partiality (13.10). Isaiah pointed out the righteousness and positive end of God's reproof (2.4; 11.3–4) and Jeremiah asserted that the people's own "apostasies," when revealed to them, would reprove them (2.19).

[116] Indeed, as still another Proverb states: "Well meant are the wounds of a friend" (ἀξιοπιστότερά ἐστιν τραύματα φίλου, 27.5–6).

[117] Duling 1998, 269. In n. 36, the author points out the interchangeable nature of the Greek terms used in the LXX to translate both עֵד and אַף.

[118] Instead, what we find throughout 1 Corinthians is the term ἀνακρίνω, a word unique in the New Testament to Luke (see Lk. 23.14; Acts 4.9; 12.19; 17.11; 24.8; 25.26; 28.18) and to Paul, who used it only in 1 Corinthians (2.14,15; 4.3,4; 9.3; 10.25,27; 14.24). The word signifies a sifting process, an examination "from top to bottom" (ἀνα+κρίνω).

[119] On the relationship between prophecy and "inspired speech," see Forbes 1995.

[120] Hays 1997, 239.

[121] This ecclesiastical discipline, consisting of exclusion from the congregation and subsequent public acts of penitence, followed by readmission to the community, appears in Clement of Alexandria's *Stromata* (2.13.56ff.), but receives special attention from Tertullian in his *De Pœnit.* 9–10: "There still remains for you, in

exomologesis, a second reserve of aid against hell; why do you then abandon your own salvation?" (ch. 12).

[122] Hays 1997, 35.

[123] Thielman 1994, 90–91.

[124] *Ibid.* "The Mosaic Law is important to Paul, and its call for sanctity among God's people authoritative, but the boundary markers for the sanctity of God's people are not identical to those within the Mosaic Law."

[125] Dixon 1992, 28.

[126] The οὐκ-οὐδείς double negative in 6.5 expects an affirmative answer.

[127] In a fascinating legal case against a group consisting of both influential ssociates and inferior officers, Pliny spoke of the readiness on the part of those of higher status to make scapegoats of their co-defendants, *cum sub aliqua specie severitatis delitescere potest* (*Ep.* 3.9).

[128] Augustine, *Enchiridion* 78.

[129] Thielman 1994, 91. Certainly, the familial language in this passage suggests that by going outside the Christian network, these litigating "brothers" were "bringing the whole family into disrepute" (cf. Hays 1997, 95).

[130] Cf. A. Mitchell 1993, 567–569, 585. See also Meeks 1983, 104.

[131] Cf. Petron. *Satyr.* 70. Of course, in the story the slaves do not heed their master, Trimalchio's words, the latter being portrayed as a drunken and vulgar member of the *nouveau-riche*. See Gardner and Wiedemann's comments on the passage (1991, 20).

[132] Segal remarks: "Given their future role [as judges of the world and heirs of the kingdom], Paul despairs of their present moral naïveté" (1990, 158).

[133] Cf. Dixon 1988, 29. See also Albini 1997, 67, who commenting on Plutarch's *De fraterno amore*, summarises: "Brothers should stick by one another, defend and help one another."

[134] Irenæus, *Ad. Haer.* 4.27.4.

[135] B. Dodd's argument that 6.12 as a whole was "a Pauline literary invention" will be discussed briefly in the final section of this chapter (see Dodd 1995, 53).

[136] Winter 1991, 568–569, where he adds that this does not mean that Paul was setting up "a quasi-permanent court parallel to the Jewish ones." Rather, Winter stands in the line of Augustine in his assertion that Paul's preference was for no intra-church disputes at all. On this last point, see also Héring 1962, 41; Conzelmann 1975, 105; Talbert 1987, 21ff. Derrett's alternative case (1991, 26) for "an ascetic's non-judgmental advice to antagonists," which he likens to the role of the Buddhist monk who serves as a reconciler and challenger (p.36, n.44), remains unconvincing.

[137] Polycarp, *Phil.* 11.

[138] Cousar 1993, 98.

[139] Chrysostom, *Hom. on 1 Cor.* 19.1.

[140] Dodd 1995, 53.

[141] Winter 1997b, 77.

[142] Seneca, *Ep.* 95.24, as cited in Winter 1997b, 87. See also Booth 1991, 106ff.

[143] Fee 1987, 251. See also Osiek and Balch 1997, 113..

[144] Tacitus, *Ag.* 21, as cited in Winter 1997b, 86.

[145] Cf. Sextus Empiricus, *Outlines of Pyrrhonism* 3.199–200, circa 200 C.E.

[146] *In Verbo tuo* 1997, 11.c (p.16), my emphasis. Commenting on 1 Cor. 6.12, Jerome warned the widow Furia to beware of a temptation common to the young "to misuse their own discretion and to suppose that things are lawful because they are pleasing" (*Ep.* 54).

[147] Cf. Winter 1997a.

[148] In this sense, Aageson appears correct in asserting that many of the definitional contrasts in the Empire were associated with "the exercise of control and power" (1996, 87).

[149] Hess and Handel 1959, 14. Broderick notes that one way of doing this— mapping the domain—is by "channeling" the members' associations with potentially dangerous persons or situations (1993, 136–137).

[150] Polycarp thus cited 1 Cor. 6.9–11 in his admonition to youth to be "cut off from the lusts that are in the world" and to "abstain from all things inconsistent and unbecoming" for those who were to inherit the Kingdom (*Phil.* 5).

[151] While Luther would later suggest that the believing partner was now free to remarry, this is not at all clear from the text itself.

[152] Concerning the enigmatic 7.21 and Paul's use of diatribe to make his point, see Deming 1995, 137. Also cf. Aageson 1996 (concerning "arrangements of control"); Bradley 1994 and 1984; Dodd 1996. On the related issues of circumcision and epispasm, see Winter 1994, 147ff. On the possibility of a servile origin for Paul himself, see van Minnen 1994.

✧ CONCLUSION

In the preceding pages, I have explored the notion of conflict in the Corinthian church from a systems perspective. From the beginning, I sought to engage with Coser's challenging premise that conflict is not always a negative process and can be instrumental in challenging old paradigms of community and replacing them with new orders and new understandings. Previous attempts to discuss the nature of the intra-church conflict in Corinth were examined in terms of the inadequacies of their conclusions. More was needed to interact with what has here been termed the conflictual "double dilemma" facing Paul.

Thus, in chapter 2, I turned to the methodological approach utilized here: systems thinking. I focused on the key concepts or principles of homeostatic balance, the danger of triangles, and the importance of differentiation and interdependence in a system. It was noted here that family-like networks lend themselves more easily to systems analysis, and it was tentatively suggested that the Pauline Christian community had the characteristics of a fictive family or family-like system.

In chapter 3, intra-church conflict was described as a multi-faceted problem, largely the result of multiple overlapping relational networks. After exploring the kinds of networks that existed in Roman Corinth, evidence for these networks in 1 Corinthians was considered.

Chapters 4 and 5 dealt specifically with a few key problems and Paul's responses. The situations in 1 Cor. 1-6 were chosen as foci of analysis primarily because Paul himself put these issues first, before the items addressed to him by the Corinthians. Chapter 4 considered the ἔριδες in 1 Cor. 1-4 in terms of an overall identity crisis in the church, as evident in confusion regarding the importance of baptism as a boundary marker for the church. Paul's two-level response, in terms of a redefining of the church as the set-apart ἐκκλησία and a reconfiguring of the members' interrelationships in familial terms, was then examined. Chapter 5 carried forward the focus on system redefinition through its exploration into the cases of the incestuous man (1 Cor. 5) and the litigious members (1 Cor. 6). Here, the model of the 'conflict spiral' was utilized in order to consider how Paul dealt with issues at different points of intensity. It was also suggested that his ongoing use of familial imagery helped redefine the situations by redefining the group.

Two questions, therefore, remain. First, is it possible to speak of a 'Pauline conflict management approach'? It has been argued here that *a major part of the apostle's response to conflicts in the church was the redefinition of the overall system as the* ἐκκλησία *and the reconfiguration of interrelationships from collegial to familial terms.* Within this paradigm, special consideration has been given to the role of the *concilium* or 'family meeting' as the context for dealing with internal conflict and providing a measure of independence from the surrounding Corinthian society with its overlapping networks. It is important, therefore, to conclude this thesis with the reiteration that when Paul was confronted with the 'double dilemma' of lessening conflicts within the church while shoring up the boundaries around the church, he responded with the redefining of the system itself. Inasmuch as the critical task of a mediator was to bring two antagonists together "to reduce their mutual suspicions,"[1] Paul used the language of ἀδελφοί to call for a new way of approaching one's fellow Christians. By placing himself in the role of father of the family, Paul did not so much reinforce existing social norms as challenge those norms by transforming congregational authority.

Second, was Paul's attempt in 1 Corinthians, then, a failure in its immediate context, as M. Mitchell (1991) has suggested? Certainly, things seemed to get worse before they got better, if the harsh rhetoric in 2 Corinthians is any indication. Yet this is not altogether uncommon when conflict management involves system redefinition, and not simply a "quick fix." In drawing out some of the underlying paradigms of community, of interdependence, of leadership, it was inevitable that the apostle would meet with considerable resistance. Unlike the more common "first-order attempts at dealing with environmental demands" which generally prove ineffective, "problem resolution from the systems perspective involves...second-order change, or change of the system itself."[2] Such change was, and continues to be, uncomfortable for all involved, since redefining the system or network means realigning the familiar roles and positions of those linked together into new configurations. Masters, patrons, citizens, men—those who were somehow in power positions as a result of their participation in outside networks—undoubtedly would have found a new arrangement based solely on being ἐν Χριστῷ quite difficult to accept. However, the fact that communication had not ceased altogether between the church members and their apostle was one positive sign. Furthermore, Johnson notes two signs that eventual reconciliation did occur: "when writing to the Romans, Paul later reports: 'For Macedonia and Achaia have been pleased to make some contribution for the poor among the saints in Jerusalem' (Rom. 15.26). And [the Corinthians] saved his letters."[3]

In the end, it has never been suggested that this approach to conflict in 1 Corinthians is anything more than an added voice in the conversation. To say otherwise would be to contradict the very essence of systems thinking, which is intentionally complementary with other methodologies. However, it is hoped that by seeing the problems less in terms of linear, single-cause thinking (higher status versus lower status), we may recognize and respect the more dynamic complexities of the Corinthian situation, in which various networks of people interacted, overlapped, and often challenged one another. I also hope that Paul's use of familial terminology, a point which has in the past often been overlooked in favor of more obvious imagery used by the apostle, may receive more careful attention in future studies. Indeed, Paul's attempts to deal with intra-church conflict by looking at individual manifestations in light of underlying definitional paradigms, may have much to say to today's churches, who continue to wrestle with internal disputes and often look no different than "those outside."

NOTES

[1] Epstein 1987, 5-6. Consider Cicero's explanation of the need for a third party in his attempted reconciliation with Caesar (following the Conference of Luca): "Cur igitur exspectem hominem aliquem qui me cum illo in gratiam reducat? Reduxit ordo amplissimus, et ordo is qui est et publici consili et meorum omnium consiliorum auctor et princeps." (*Prov. Cons.* 25, as cited in Epstein 1987, 131, n. 21.)

[2] Morgan, et al. 1981, 137-138.

[3] Johnson 1986, 299.

✧ APPENDIX

Because of space limitations, it was impossible in this book to examine in detail all the conflictual issues addressed by Paul. Therefore, in order to present a broader view of Paul's letter, as well as to encourage further research into the Corinthian conflicts from a systemic or network approach, the following overview is provided.

1 Corinthians 1.10–4.21

→   persons affiliating themselves with Paul
persons affiliating themselves with Apollos
persons affiliating themselves with Cephas
"those of Chloe" (indirectly, informants to Paul)

Summary: The focus here appears to be not on theological issues as much as on issues of "belonging," as affiliations to key leaders/figures in the church (even if these leaders are not personally involved) have resulted in different allegiances. There is no indication that formal "groups" or associations are suggested by the slogans listed. The key issue appears to be "who belongs to whom."

Timing: It may be presumed from Paul's response to the situation that these "allegiances" began to take shape only after he had left Corinth. The vacuum left by the apostle's departure seems to have been filled to some extent by Apollos, a learned and effective speaker who (probably unknowingly) raised questions in Christians' minds concerning the impressiveness of their founder.

Networks involved: There appears to be an interplay here between household loyalties, political systems (as seen in the form of the slogans), and even rhetorical schools (as suggested by the σοφία motif). Socio-economic differences in the congregation clearly contribute to the conflictual mixture (1.26), but seemingly in an indirect fashion, as issues of personal "belonging" (1.12) and spiritual maturity (2.6) take the forefront. Jews and Greeks are differentiated not as much from one another here as (respectively) from "the called" (οἱ κλητοί, 1.24).

Paul's position: Here, the apostle is at the heart of the disputes, albeit against his desires. As much as he is being compared to other leaders, notably Apollos, Paul is not simply an outside spectator in this drama.

Paul's response: There is a focus on wisdom, but even more on relational roles of belonging, i.e. Paul as "father" and founder in relation to the Corinthians and as servant/steward in relation to God. For more, see chapter 4 above.

1 Corinthians 5.1–13; 6.12–20
Individual immorality and
corporate responsibility→   the incestuous church member
the rest of the congregation
those for whom "all things are lawful"

Summary: The issues here appear again to center not on theological issues, but on issues of influence and rights (ἐξουσία). The key themes in both instances involve the "position" in the network of those acting in immoral ways without consequences as well as the role the church as a whole should play in judging such matters.

Timing: These issues reflect a still-young social system that is not yet clear about its own internal organization and discipline.

Networks involved: In the first situation, the suggestion that a patron-client relationship exists between the incestuous member and the others seems plausible, and explains the hesitation on the part of church members to act with decisiveness. Beyond personal patronage, public benefaction and citizenship might also explain the "untouchable" nature of the offender, especially since ἐξουσία is a key theme. In the second case, it has been argued that the most likely candidates to express such a phrase as "all things are lawful" would be those who could not say this at a prior time and now can, namely, those young men who have received the *toga virilis* and the rights and privileges that accompany it. In this case, there would also be an overlap with collegial or cultic networks, as this is where opportunities would take the newly "legal" young men.

Paul's position: Here, the apostle is not in the middle, but more on the side and seemingly unaware of all the specific details concerning the situations. Inasmuch as his information probably came from "Chloe's people," his position might best be described as that of the unwelcome and uninvited critic.

Paul's response: Paul's language in this section focuses on "insider" and "outsider" distinctions, as well as on judgment. For more, see chapter 5 above.

1 Corinthians 6.1–11

Litigation →   plaintiffs (who are church members)
                   defendants (who are church members)

Summary: The issue here is certainly not the *what* of the litigation, for we are told nothing about why certain Christians are taking fellow church members to court. Rather, the problem is in *how* fellow members were handling their internal disputes.

Timing: We still see here a neophyte system.

Networks involved: The question to ask is what kind of people in first-century Corinth would have had the ability to initiate civil prosecution, and who would likely be on the receiving end. The answers, at least tentatively, involve persons of influence, probably fellow citizens/ benefactors and members of the secular ἐκκλησία.

Paul's position: The apostle is again the outsider looking in, or the parent who has heard the news about his "children" through outside means.

Paul's response: Again, we see Paul use "insider/outsider" distinctions as well as a focus on judgment in and by the congregation. Again, see chapter 5 above.

1 Corinthians 7

Uneven relationships→   believing spouse   *also:*   free and slave
                            unbelieving spouse   circumcised
                            fiancé   uncircumcised

Summary: On the surface, the issue is marital relations, but on a deeper level, Paul makes it clear (through his analogy of circumcision and manumission) that what is happening here involves issues of control and change, as well as the question of the relevance of societal standards for those who are now among "the called."

Timing: The general issue of marital relations has clearly been raised by the Corinthians themselves in a letter to Paul (7.1). This might well reflect the lack of clear direction in the (new) church in areas of day-to-day interpersonal relationships.

Networks involved: While the household network is certainly involved, there is also evidence of even more specific networks such as "widows" (who could also have been wealthy benefactors in the church) and "virgins," as well as the "unmarried" (who are apparently male, and might be young men such as those indicated in 6.12–20). The inclusion of freedmen, slaves, circumcised and uncircumcised (7.17–24) is certainly not for theoretical illustration only, for Paul's language suggests that such were church members.

Paul's position: Here, Paul's opinion has been sought out by at least some in the church, but the care with which he answers throughout suggests that not all in the congregation are awaiting his "words of wisdom." He is also in the position of being asked to speak on areas on which Jesus did not directly comment.

Paul's response: Paul's language in this section focuses on control, i.e. self-control in terms of sexual desires, control over one's body, control over the other person, control over one's time and how to use it, God's control over all.

1 Corinthians 8–10

The case of "idol meat" → those with no problem eating "idol meat"

those who refuse to eat meat offered to idols

Summary: The focus here seems, at first glance, to concern Jewish food laws in what is becoming a predominantly Gentile congregation. However, underlying issues include participation and belonging in social contexts where such meat would be offered. Questions arise concerning the occasions for eating such meat, the relation of meals in the names of gods and professional meetings or *collegia*.

Timing: Apparently, this was not an issue when Paul founded the Corinthian community. One possible scenario is that something had happened to change the rights of Jewish Christians to purchase food before it is taken to market.

Networks involved: Clearly, both Jewish and collegial networks are involved, clashing together over the question of food laws and fellowship. As seen above, other networks enter the mix, including those of patrons and clients, pagan cults, and even young men able to go to collegial banquets for the first time (10.23ff.).

Paul's position: It is, at best, ambiguous. While he appears to have received this news directly from some in the congregation, there is certainly some anti-Paul sentiment showing through in his apostolic *apologia* of 1 Cor. 9. There are also issues here concerning Paul's relation to the Jerusalem apostles, to those claiming to have some form of γνῶσις, and to those in the patron-client network who were suspicious of his refusal to enter that network.

Paul's response: Paul's language of "building up" challenges fellow members to re-prioritize their place of belonging (to the table of the Lord or to the table of collegial/cultic banquets). The "building up" imagery suggests a reconfiguration of interrelationships between fellow members.

1 Corinthians 11.17–34

Communion or segregation
in the Lord's Supper → those who eat before all have arrived
                                  those who arrive late and have nothing to eat

Summary: Socio-economic differences among church members appear to be at the heart of this tension-laden situation, as patterns familiar to those of higher status and means take precedence over the common brother/sisterhood ἐν Χριστῷ.

Timing: This represents maintenance of familiar patterns of household etiquette by members following the departure of the founder.

Networks involved: Some members are clearly part of a network of those of higher status, and appear to be householders, while others seem to be either slaves or clients who neither have the leisure to be at the meal early nor have their own food resources to bring with them.

Paul's position: It seems that he is at least recognized by some as an interpreter of early Jesus tradition, as well as one whose commendation was sought (by some).

Paul's response: Paul's language focuses on "houses" and judgment. Connections between this passage and 1 Cor. 5 were considered briefly in chapter 5 above.

1 Corinthians 11:1–16; 12–14

Tensions in worship→ women who do not cover their heads

those who have no need for "less honorable"

"less honorable members"

those who speak in tongues

those who do not speak in tongues

those who do not sit down for others to speak

prophets and spectators

Summary: The issues here do not seem to concern socio-economic status as much as Greek versus Roman propriety (i.e. women's presence and conduct in a meeting), the influence of pagan mystery cults, and questions about leadership. Order in worship is a key theme.

Timing: The problems that have arisen seem to have much to do with the growing number of "liberated" women and with the introduction into the church of sophisticated oratory, wisdom and signs. Is it completely unrealistic to think that there is a connection here with the coming of Apollos following Paul's departure?

Networks involved: Certainly, we can point to networks of "liberated" women on the one hand and possibly θίασοι on the other.

Paul's position: The apostle here appears to be the sensitive consultant, with little of the polemic found in other sections, with the notable exception at the end of ch. 14.

Paul's response: Paul's language in this section focuses on order, onlookers (whether angels or unbelieving or untrained human spectators), and the body. Regrettably, space limitations do not allow for more than a brief word to be offered on this much-discussed section of 1 Corinthians.

1 Corinthians 15

The resurrection of the dead→ those who accept bodily resurrection

those who do not

Summary: The issue here appears to involve theological issues, not unrelated to the Lukan controversy in Acts between the Pharisees and Sadducees. There may be links with concerns for the proper handling of the dead in the *collegia* and specifically in burial clubs.

Timing: Some have clearly challenged the Corinthians' faith since Paul's departure.

Networks involved: As already suggested, *collegia* or burial guilds might have been involved (15.31-32), as these were obvious places for such questions to be raised.

Paul's position: He himself is not the issue, *per se*, and yet there are certainly questions (implied) concerning his standing in relation to the other apostles.

Paul's response: Paul's language in this section echoes what has been used in previous sections, especially in terms of the dichotomies of chs. 1-4 and the issue of order and subjection.

Summary

When all these conflicts are seen together in this way, it becomes clear that although socio-economic differentials may indeed have been contributing factors in the problems, they were not always so. When the question is raised regarding the identity of the players in different situations, then the answers—persons with different personal allegiances, fellow citizens vying for power in the court system, conservative Jewish Christians and their Gentile counterparts in the *collegia*—reveal a complexity to the church's membership and common life that is not always recognized. We cannot, therefore, throw out the importance of socio-economic factors, any more than we can dispense with religious, ethnic, theological, or gender elements. This is, of course, the main point: a multiplicity of factors underlay the intra-church conflict in Corinth precisely because multiple relational networks overlapped.

✦ BIBLIOGRAPHY

Aageson, J. W. (1996). 'Control' in Pauline Language and Culture: A Study of Rom. 6. *NTS* 42, 75–89.

Achtemeier, P. J. (1987). *The Quest for Unity in the New Testament Church.* Philadelphia: Fortress.

Albini, F. (1997). Family and the Formation of Character in Plutarch. In J. Mossman (Ed.), *Plutarch and His Intellectual World* (pp. 59–72). London: Duckworth.

Allen, L. C. (1994). *Ezekiel 1–19* (Word 28). Dallas: Word.

Alvarez-Pereyre, F. and F. Heymann. (1996). The Desire for Transcendence: the Hebrew Family Model and Jewish Family Practices. In A. Burguière, C. Klapisch-Zuber, M. Segalen, and F. Zonabend (Eds.), *A History of the Family:Distant Worlds, Ancient Worlds* (Vol. 1, pp. 270–312). Cambridge, MA: Belknap.

Applebaum, S. (1989). *Judaea in Hellenistic and Roman Times.* Leiden: E. J. Brill.

Baird, W. (1990). "One Against the Other": Intra-Church Conflict in 1 Corinthians. In R. T. Fortna and B. R. Gaventa (Ed.), *The Conversation Continues: Studies in Paul and John* (pp. 116–136). Nashville: Abingdon.

Balch, D. L. (1981). *Let Wives Be Submissive: The Domestic Code in 1 Peter.* Chico, CA: Scholars Press.

Balch, D. L. (1988). Household Codes. In D. E. Aune (Ed.), *Greco-Roman Literature and the New Testament* (pp. 25–50). Atlanta: Scholars Press.

Banks, R. (1994). *Paul's Idea of Community.* (Revised). Peabody, MA: Hendrickson.

Barclay, J. M. G. (1992). Thessalonica and Corinth: Social Contrasts in Pauline Christianity. *JSNT 47* (September), 49–74.

Barclay, J. M. G. (1991). Paul, Philemon, and Christian-Slave Ownership. *NTS 37,* 162–187.

Barrett, C. K. (1989). *The New Testament Background: Selected Documents.* (Revised Ed.). San Francisco: HarperCollins.

Barrett, C. K. (1984). *Paul: An Introduction to His Thought.* Louisville: Westminster/John Knox Press.

Barrett, C. K. (1982). *Essays on Paul.* London: SPCK.

Barrett, C. K. (1968). *A Commentary on the First Epistle to the Corinthians.* New York: HNTC.

Barrett, M. and McIntosh, M. (1982). *The Anti-Social Family.* London: Verso.

Barton, S. C. (1997). Christian Community in the Light of 1 Corinthians. *Studies in Christian Ethics, 10*(1), 1–15.

Barton, S. C. (1996). "All Things to All People": Paul and the Law in the Light of 1 Corinthians 9:19–23. In J. D. G. Dunn (Ed.), *Paul and the Mosaic Law* (pp. 271–285). Tübingen: Mohr/Siebeck.

Barton, S. C. (1986). Paul's Sense of Place: An Anthropological Approach to Community Formation in Corinth. *NTS 32*, 225–246.

Bassler, J. M. (Ed.). (1991). *Pauline Theology: Thessalonians, Philippians, Galatians, Philemon.* (Vol. 1). Minneapolis: Fortress.

Beavers, W. R. (1977). *Psychotherapy and Growth: A Family Systems Perspective.* New York: Brunner/Mazel.

Beker, J. C. (1984). *Paul the Apostle: The Triumph of God in Life and Thought.* Philadelphia: Fortress.

Bertalanffy, L. von (1972). History and Status of General Systems Theory. In G. J. Klir (Ed.), *Trends in General Systems Theory* (pp. 21–41). New York: Interscience.

Best, E. (1986). *Paul and His Converts.* Edinburgh: T. & T. Clark.

Best, E. (1980). The Power and the Wisdom of God. In L. DeLorenzi (Ed.), *Paul a una Chiesa Divisa.* Rome: Abbazia d. S. Paulo fuori le mura.

Bettini, M. (1991). *Anthropology and Roman Culture: Kinship, Time, Images of the Soul* (Van Sickle, John, Trans.). Baltimore and London: Johns Hopkins Univ. Press.

Betz, H. D. (1985). *2 Corinthians 8 and 9: A Commentary on Two Administrative Letters of the Apostle Paul.* Philadelphia: Fortress.

Blenkinsopp, J. (1990). *Ezekiel* (Interpr.). Louisville: John Knox Press.

Blue, B. (1994). Acts and the House Church. In D.W.J. Gill and C. Gempf (Ed.), *The Book of Acts in Its Graeco-Roman Setting* (pp. 119–122). Grand Rapids: Eerdmans.

Booth, A. (1991). The Age for Reclining and its Attendant Perils. In W. J. Slater (Ed.), *Dining in a Classical Context* (pp. 101–115). Ann Arbor: University of Michigan.

Boring, M. E., K. Berger and C. Colpe (Eds.). (1995). *Hellenistic Commentary to the New Testament.* Nashville: Abingdon.

Bornkamm, G. (1969). *Paul* (Stalker, D. M. G., Trans.). New York: Harper & Row.

Bott, E. (1971). *Family and Social Network.* (Second Ed.). London: Tavistock.

Bowersock, G.W. (1965). *Augustus and the Greek World.* Oxford: Clarendon Press.

Bradley, K. R. (1994). *Slavery and Society at Rome.* Cambridge; London; New York: Cambridge University Press.

Bradley, K. R. (1984). *Slaves and Masters in the Roman Empire: A Study in Social Control.* (Vol. 185). Bruxelles: Latomus.

Brawley, R. L. (1987). *Luke-Acts and the Jews.* Atlanta: Scholars Press.

Broderick, C. B. (1993). *Understanding Family Process.* Newbury Park; London; New Delhi: Sage.

Brooten, B. (1982). *Women Leaders in the Ancient Synagogue.* Chico: Scholars Press.

Brown, R. E. (1997). *An Introduction to the New Testament.* New York: Doubleday.

Bruce, F. F. (1985). *The Pauline Circle.* Carlisle: Paternoster Press.

Bruce, F. F. (1971). *1 and 2 Corinthians* (New Century Bible). London: Oliphants.

Bultmann, R. (1951). *Theology of the New Testament, vol. 1.* New York: Scribners.

Burr, W. R., R. Hill, F. I. Nye and I. L. Reiss (Eds.). (1979). *Contemporary Theories About the Family*. New York: Free Press.

Callan, T. (1990). *Psychological Perspectives on the Life of Paul*. Lewiston, Queenston, Lampeter: Edwin Mellen Press.

Campbell, R. A. (1991). Does Paul Aquiesce in Divisions at the Lord's Supper? *NovT 33*(1), 61–70.

Carlson, R. P. (1993). The Role of Baptism in Paul's Thought. *Int 47*.

Carpenter, S. L., & Kennedy, W. J. D. (1988). *Managing Public Disputes: A Practical Guide to Handling Conflict and Reaching Agreements*. San Francisco and London: Jossey-Bass.

Castagnoli, F. (1971). *Orthogonal Town Planning in Antiquity*. Cambridge: Cambridge University Press.

Castelli, E. A. (1991). *Imitating Paul: A Discourse of Power*. Louisville, KY: Westminster/John Knox Press.

Chance, J. K. (1994). The Anthropology of Honor and Shame: Culture, Values and Practice. *Sem.* 68, 139–151.

Chow, J. K. (1992). *Patronage and Power: A Study of Social Networks in Corinth* (JSNTS 75). Sheffield: Sheffield Academic Press.

Clarke, A. D. (1993). *Secular and Christian Leadership in Corinth: A Socio-Historical and Exegetical Study of 1 Corinthians 1–6*. Leiden, New York and Köln: Brill.

Cohen, S. J. D. (Ed.). (1993). *The Jewish Family in Antiquity*. Atlanta: Scholars Press.

Conzelmann, H. (1975). *1 Corinthians* (Hermeneia). Philadelphia: Fortress.

Coser, L. A. (1967). *Continuities in the Study of Social Conflict*. New York: Free Press.

Coser, L. A. (Ed.). (1965). *Georg Simmel*. Englewood Cliffs, NJ: Prentice-Hall.

Coser, L. A. (1956). *The Functions of Social Conflict*. New York: Free Press.

Cotter, W. (1996). The Collegia and Roman Law: State Restrictions on Voluntary Associations, 64 BCE – 200 CE. In J. S. Kloppenborg and S. G. Wilson (Eds.), *Voluntary Associations in the Graeco-Roman World* (pp. 74–89). London and New York: Routledge.

Cotter, W. (1994). Women's Authority Roles in Paul's Churches: Countercultural or Conventional? *NovT* 36/4, 350–372.

Cousar, C. B. (1993). The Theological Task of 1 Corinthians. In D. M. Hay (Ed.), *Pauline Theology II: 1 and 2 Corinthians* (pp. 90–102). Minneapolis: Fortress.

Covey, S. (1989). *The 7 Habits of Highly Effective People: Powerful Lessons in Personal Change*. New York: Simon & Schuster.

Crafton, J. A. (1990). *The Agency of the Apostle: A Dramatistic Analysis of Paul's Response to Conflict in 1 Corinthians*. Sheffield: JSOT Press.

Crook, J. (1967a). *Law and Life of Rome*. London: Thames and Hudson.

Crook, J. (1967b). Patria Potestas. *Church Quarterly, 17*, 113–122.

Davis, J. A. (1984). *Wisdom and Spirit: An Investigation of 1 Corinthians 1.18–3.20 Against the Background of Jewish Sapiential Traditions in the Greco-Roman Period*. New York and London: University Press of America.

De Boer, M. C. (1994). The Composition of 1 Corinthians. *NTS 40*, 229–245.

DeMaris, R. E. (1995). Corinthian Religion and Baptisms for the Dead (1 Corinthians 15.29): Insights from Archaeology and Anthropology. *JBL* 114/4, 661–682.

de Ste. Croix, G. E. M. (1981). *The Class Struggle in the Ancient Greek World: From the Archaic Age to the Arab Conquests.* London: Duckworth.

De Vos, C. S. (1998). Stepmothers, Concubines and the Case of Πορνεία in 1 Corinthians 5. *NTS 44(1),* 104–114.

Deissmann, A. (1978). *Light from the Ancient East* (rep.). Grand Rapids: Baker.

Delcor, M. (1968). The Courts of Corinth and the Courts of Qumran. In J. Murphy-O'Connor (Ed.), *Paul and Qumran: Studies in New Testament Exegesis* (pp. 68–79). London: Geoffrey Chapman.

Deming, W. (1995a). A Diatribe Pattern in 1 Cor.7.21–22: A New Perspective on Paul's Directions to Slaves. *NovT 37,* 130–138.

Deming, W. (1995b). *Paul on Marriage and Celibacy: The Hellenistic Background of 1 Corinthians 7.* Cambridge: Cambridge University Press.

Derrett, J. D. M. (1991). Judgement and 1 Corinthians 6. *NTS 37,* 22–36.

Dixon, S. (1988). *The Roman Mother.* Norman, OK and London: University of Oklahoma Press.

Dixon, S. (1992). *The Roman Family.* Baltimore and London: Johns Hopkins Press.

Dodd, B. J. (1996a). Christ's Slave, People Pleasers and Gal. 1.10. *NTS 42,* 90–104.

Dodd, B. J. (1996b). *The Problem with Paul.* Downers Grove, IL: InterVarsity Press.

Dodd, B. J. (1995). Paul's Paradigmatic 'I' and 1 Corinthians 6.12. *JSNT 59,* 39–58.

Donaldson, T. L. (1997). Israelite, Convert and Apostle to the Gentiles: The Origins of Paul's Gentile Mission. In R. N. Longenecker (Ed.) *The Road from Damascus* (pp. 62–84). Grand Rapids and Cambridge: Eerdmans.

Donaldson, T. L. (1993). Thomas Kuhn, Convictional Worlds, and Paul. In B.H. McLean (Ed.), *Origins and Method: Towards a New Understanding of Judaism and Christianity: Essays in Honour of John C. Hurd* (pp. 190–198). Sheffield: JSOT.

Donfried, K. P. (1981). *The Dynamic Word: New Testament Insights for Contemporary Christians.* San Francisco: Harper & Row.

Douglas, M. and A. Wildavsky (1982). *Risk and Culture.* Berkeley, Los Angeles and London: University of California Press.

Douglas, M. (1973a). *Natural Symbols.* New York: Penguin.

Douglas, M. (1973b). *Rules and Meanings.* Harmondsworth: Penguin Education Press.

Douglas, M. (1966). *Purity and Danger.* London: Routledge and Kegan Paul.

Dubisch, J. (1993). "Foreign Chickens" and Other Outsiders: Gender and Community in Greece. *Amer. Ethn.* 20, 272–287.

Duling, D. C. (1998). Matthew 18:15–17: Conflict, Confrontation, and Conflict Resolution in a 'Fictive Kin' Association. In *SBL 1998 Seminar Papers* (pp. 253–295). Atlanta: Scholars Press.

Dunn, J. D. G. (1999). Who Did Paul Think He Was? A Study of Jewish Christian Identity. *NTS* 45, 174–193.

Dunn, J. D. G. (1998). *The Theology of Paul the Apostle.* Grand Rapids and Cambridge: Eerdmans.

Dunn, J. D. G. (1995). *1 Corinthians.* Sheffield: Sheffield Academic Press.

Dunn, J. D. G. (1994). Prolegomena to a Theology of Paul. *NTS* 40, 407–432.

Dunn, J. D. G. (1991). *The Partings of the Ways*. London, Philadelphia: SPCK and Trinity Press Intl.

Dunn, J. D. G. (1990). *Jesus, Paul and the Law: Studies in Mark and Galatians*. London: SPCK.

Dunn, J. D. G. (1985). Works of the Law and the Curse of the Law (Galatians 3.10–14). *NTS* 31, 523–542.

Dunn, J. D. G. (1975). *Jesus and the Spirit*. London: SPCK.

Eisenstadt, S. N. (1984). *Patrons, Clients and Friends: Interpersonal Relations and the Structure of Trust in Society*. Cambridge: Cambridge University Press.

Elliger, W. (1987). *Paulus in Griechenland*. Stuttgart: Verlag Katholisches Bibelwerk.

Ellingworth, E. and H. Hatton (1985). *A Translator's Handbook on Paul's First Letter to the Corinthians*. London, New York and Stuttgart: United Bible Society.

Elliott, J. (1995). *Social Scientific Criticism of the New Testament*. London: SPCK.

Engberg-Pedersen, T. (1993). Proclaiming the Lord's Death. In D. M. Hay (Ed.), *Pauline Theology: 1 and 2 Corinthians* (Vol. 2, pp. 103–132). Minneapolis: Fortress.

Engels, D. (1990). *Roman Corinth: An Alternative Model for the Classical City*. Chicago and London: University of Chicago.

Epstein, D. F. (1987). *Personal Enmity in Roman Politics, 218 –43 B.C.* London, New York, Sydney: Croom Helm.

Eyeben, E. (1991). Fathers and Sons. In B. Rawson, Ed. *Marriage, Divorce, and Children in Ancient Rome* (pp. 114–143). Oxford: Clarendon Press.

Fee, G. D. (1993). Toward a Theology of 1 Corinthians. In D. M. Hay (Ed.), *Pauline Theology, Volume II: 1 & 2 Corinthians*. Minneapolis: Fortress.

Fee, G. D. (1987). *The First Epistle to the Corinthians*. Grand Rapids: Eerdmans.

Feldman, L. H. (1996a). *Studies in Hellenistic Judaism*. Leiden, New York, Köln: Brill.

Feldman, L. H. and M. Reinhold. (1996b). *Jewish Life and Thought among Greeks and Romans*. Edinburgh: T. & T. Clark.

Feldman, L. H. (1993). Palestinian and Diaspora Judaism in the First Century. In H. Shanks (Ed.), *Christianity and Rabbinic Judaism: A Parallel History of their Origins and Early Development* (pp. 1–39). London: SPCK.

Fiorenza, E. S. (1987). Rhetorical Situation and Historical Reconstruction in 1 Corinthians. *NTS 33*, 386–403.

Fitzgerald, J.T., Ed. (1996). *Friendship, Flattery and Frankness of Speech: Studies on Friendship in the New Testament World*. Leiden, New York, Köln: Brill.

Fitzgerald, J.T. (1988). *Cracks in an Earthen Vessel* (SPLDS 99). Atlanta: Scholars Press.

Forbes, C. (1995). *Prophecy and Inspired Speech in Early Christianity and its Hellenistic Environment*. Tübingen: Mohr.

Friedman, E. H. (1985). *Generation to Generation: Family Process in Church and Synagogue*. New York and London: Guilford Press.

Frör, H. (1995). *You Wretched Corinthians!* (trans. J. Bowden). London: SCM Press.

Furnish, V. P. (1993). Theology in 1 Corinthians. In D. M. Hay (Ed.), *Pauline Theology: 1 and 2 Corinthians* (Vol. 2, pp. 59–89). Minneapolis: Fortress.

Furnish, V. P. (1984). *II Corinthians* (AB 32A). New York and London: Doubleday.

Gardner, J. F. and Wiedemann, T. (1991). *The Roman Household: A Sourcebook*. London and New York: Routledge.

Garnsey, P. (1970). *Social Status and Legal Privilege in the Roman Empire*. Oxford: Clarendon Press.

Garrison, R. (1997). *The Graeco-Roman Context of Early Christian Literature* (JSNTS 137). Sheffield: Sheffield Academic Press.

Gathercole, S. and G. W. Hansen. (forthcoming). *Support the Progress of the Gospel: Christians as Partners and Stewards*. Carlisle: Paternoster.

Gaventa, B. R. (1993). Apostle and Church in 2 Corinthians. In D. M. Hay, Ed. *Pauline Theology: 1 and 2 Corinthians* (Vol. 2, pp. 182–199). Minneapolis: Fortress.

Geertz, C. (1973). *The Interpretation of Cultures: Selected Essays*. New York: Basic.

Giddens, A. (1976). *New Rules of Sociological Method: A Positive Critique of Interpretative Sociologies*. London: Hutchinson.

Giddens, A. (1990). Structuration Theory and Sociological Analysis. In J. Clark, C. Mogdil, S. Mogdil (Eds.), *Anthony Giddens: Consensus and Controversy* (pp. 297–315). London: Falmer.

Gill, D. W. J. (1994). Acts and the Urban Élites. In D. Gill and C. Gempf, Ed. *The Book of Acts in Its Graeco-Roman Setting* (pp. 105–118). Grand Rapids: Eerdmans.

Glancy, J. A. (1998). Obstacles to Slaves' Participation in the Corinthian Church. *JBL* 117 (3), 481–501.

Gooch, P. W. (1987). *Partial Knowledge: Philosophical Studies in Paul*. Notre Dame: University of Notre Dame Press.

Gordon, J. D. (1997). *Sister or Wife? (JSNTS* 149) Sheffield: Sheffield University Press.

Goulder, M. (1994). *St. Paul versus St. Peter: A Tale of Two Missions*. London: SCM.

Grosheide, F. W. (1953). *Commentary on the First Epistle to the Corinthians* (NICNT, repr. 1980). Grand Rapids: Eerdmans.

Hallett, J. P. (1984). *Fathers and Daughters in Roman Society*. Princeton: Princeton University Press.

Hanges, J. C. (1998). 1 Corinthians 4:6 and the Possibility of Written Bylaws in the Corinthian Church. *JBL* 117(2), 275–298.

Hanson, P. D. (1985). Conflict in Ancient Israel and Its Resolution. In J. T. Butler, et al. (Eds.), *Understanding the Word* (pp. 185–206). Sheffield: JSOT Press.

Hardy, E. G. (1906). Christianity and the *Collegia*. In *Studies in Roman History*, I (pp. 129–150).

Hare, D. A. (1993). *Matthew* (Interpretation). Louisville: John Knox Press.

Harris, G. (1991). The Beginnings of Church Discipline: 1 Corinthians 5. *NTS* 37, 1–21.

Hartman, L. (1996). Baptism. *ABD* I, 583–594.

Hay, D. M., Ed. (1993). *Pauline Theology: 1 & 2 Corinthians*. Minneapolis: Fortress.

Hays, R. B. (1999). Conversion of the Imagination. *NTS* 45, 388–408.

Hays, R. B. (1997). *First Corinthians* (Interpretation). Louisville: John Knox Press.

Hays, R. B. (1996). *The Moral Vision of the New Testament: Community, Cross, and New Creation.* San Francisco: HarperSanFrancisco.

Hays, R. B. (1989). *Echoes of Scripture in the Letters of Paul.* New Haven and London: Yale University Press.

Héring, J. (1962). *The First Epistle of Saint Paul to the Corinthians.* London: Epworth.

Herman, G. (1987). *Ritualised Friendship and the Greek City.* Cambridge: Cambridge University Press.

Hess, R. S. and Handel, G. (1959). *Family Worlds: A Psychosocial Approach to Family Life.* Chicago: University of Chicago Press.

Himmelweit, H. (1964). Deviant Behaviour. In J. Goulder & W. L. Kolb (Eds.), *A Dictionary of the Social Sciences* (pp. 196–197). New York: The Free Press.

Hock, R. F. (1980). *The Social Context of Paul's Ministry: Tentmaking and Apostleship.* Philadelphia: Fortress.

Holmberg, B. (1990). *Sociology and the New Testament.* Philadelphia: Fortress.

Horbury, W. (1985). Extirpation or Excommunication. *VT* 35, 13–38.

Horrell, D. G. (2001). From ἀδελφοί to οἶκος θεοῦ: Social Transformation in Pauline Christianity. *JBL* 120, 293-311.

Horrell, D. G. (1997). Theological Principle or Christological Praxis? Pauline Ethics in 1 Corinthians 8.1–11.1. *JSNT* 67, 83–114.

Horrell, D. G. (1996). *The Social Ethos of the Corinthian Correspondence: Interests and Ideology from 1 Corinthians to 1 Clement.* Edinburgh: T. & T. Clark.

Hurd, J. C. (1983). *The Origin of I Corinthians* (repr. in 1983). London: SPCK.

In Verbo tuo: Final Document of the Congress on Vocations to the Priesthood and to Consecrated Life in Europe (1997). Vatican City: Libreria Editrice Vaticana.

Jewett, R. (1979). *Dating Paul's Life.* London: SCM Press.

Johnson, L. T. (1986). *The Writings of the New Testament.* Philadelphia: Fortress.

Johnson, L. T. (1982). The Use of Lev. 19 in the Letter of James. *JBL* 101, 391–401.

Jones, C. P. (1978). *The Roman World of Dio Chrysostom.* Cambridge, MS and London: Harvard University Press.

Judge, E. (1960). *The Social Pattern of Christian Groups in the First Century.* London: SPCK.

Kee, H. C. (1995). Defining the First-Century CE Synagogue: Problems and Progress. *NTS* 41/4, 481–500.

Kee, H. C. (1993). After the Crucifixion – Christianity Through Paul. In H. Shanks, Ed. *Christianity and Rabbinic Judaism: A Parallel History of their Origins and Early Development* (pp. 85–124). London: SPCK.

Kelly, J. F. (1997). *The World of the Early Christians.* Collegeville, MN: Liturgical.

Kennedy, G. (1975). *New Testament Interpretation through Rhetorical Criticism.* Chapel Hill: University of North Carolina Press.

Kent, J. H. (1966). *Corinth VIII/3. The Inscriptions 1926-1950.* Princeton.

Kidd, R. M. (1990). *Wealth and Beneficence in the Pastoral Epistles: A "Bourgeois" Form of Early Christianity?* Atlanta: Scholars Press.

Klein, D. M. and J. White. (1996). *Family Theories: An Introduction*. Thousand Oak, CA; London; New Delhi: Sage.

Kloppenborg, J. S. and S. G. Wilson, Eds. (1996). *Voluntary Associations in the Graeco-Roman World*. London and New York: Routledge.

Kraabel, A. T. (1979). The Diaspora Synagogue: Archaeological and Epigraphic Evidence since Sukenik. *ANRW* 2(19), 477–510.

Kraybill, J. N. (1992). *Cult and Commerce in Revelation 18*. A Dissertation for Union Theological Seminary, Richmond, VA.

Kuck, D. W. (1992). *Judgment and Community Conflict: Paul's Use of Apocalyptic Judgment Language in 1 Cor. 3.5–4.5*. Leiden: Brill.

Lampe, P. (1989). *Die stadtrömischen Christen*. Tübingen: J.C.B. Mohr-Siebeck.

Lattke, M. (1994). Verfluchter Inzest: war der 'Pornos' von 1 Kor. 5 ein persicher 'Magos'? In A. Kessler, T. Ricklin and G. Wurst, Eds. *Peregrina Curiositas:Eine Reise durch den Orbis Antiquus*. Freiburg: Universität Verlag.

Lightfoot, J. B. (1957). *Notes on the Epistles of St. Paul: from unpublished commentaries*. (Reprinted Ed.). Grand Rapids: Eerdmans.

Litfin, D. (1994). *St. Paul's Theology of Proclamation: 1 Corinthians 1–4 and Graeco-Roman Rhetoric*. Cambridge: Cambridge University Press.

Longenecker, R. N. (1997). *The Road from Damascus*. Grand Rapids: Eerdmans.

MacRory, J. (1915). *The Epistles of St. Paul to the Corinthians*. Dublin: M.H. Gill & Son.

Malherbe, A. J. (1994). Determinism and Free Will: The Argument of 1 Corinthians 8 and 9. In T. Engberg-Pedersen, Ed. *Paul in His Hellenistic Context* (pp. 231–255). Edinburgh: T. & T. Clark.

Malherbe, A. J. (1987). *Paul and the Thessalonians*. Philadelphia: Fortress.

Malherbe, A. J. (1983). *Social Aspects of Early Christianity*. Philadelphia: Fortress.

Malina, B. J. and Neyrey, Jerome H. (1996). *Portraits of Paul: An Archaeology of Ancient Personality*. Louisville, KY: Westminster/John Knox Press.

Malina, B. J. (1993). *The New Testament World* (rev.). Atlanta: John Knox Press.

Marshall, P. (1987). *Enmity in Corinth: Social Conventions in Paul's Relations with the Corinthians*. Tübingen: J.C.B. Mohr (Siebeck).

Martin, D. B. (1996). The Construction of the Ancient Family: Methodological Considerations. *JRS 86*, 40–60.

Martin, D. B. (1995). *The Corinthian Body*. New Haven and London: Yale Univ. Press.

Martin, D. B. (1990). *Slavery as Salvation: The Metaphor of Slavery in Pauline Christianity*. New Haven, CT: Yale University Press.

Martin, F. M. (1988). *Narrative Parallels to the New Testament*. Atlanta: Scholars Press.

Martin, R. P. (1981). *Reconciliation: A Study of Paul's Theology*. London: Marshall, Morgan & Scott.

Mattila, S. E. (1996). Where Women Sat in Ancient Synagogues: The Archaeological Evidence in Context. In J. S. Kloppenborg and S. G. Wilson (Eds.) *Voluntary*

Associations in the Graeco-Roman World (pp. 266–286). London and New York: Routledge.

McCready, W. O. (1996). *Ekklêsia* and Voluntary Associations. In J. S. Kloppenborg and S. G. Wilson (Eds.) *Voluntary Associations in the Graeco-Roman World* (pp. 59–73). London and New York: Routledge.

Meeks, W. A. (1986). *The Moral World of the First Christians.* Philadelphia: Westminster.

Meeks, W. A. (1983). *The First Urban Christians: The Social World of the Apostle Paul.* New Haven and London: Yale University Press.

Meeks, W. A. (1979). 'Since Then You Would Need to Go Out of the World': Group Boundaries in Pauline Christianity, in T. J. Ryan, Ed. *Critical History and Biblical Faith: New Testament Perspectives* (pp. 4–29). Villanova, PA: College Theological Society.

Mercadante, L. (1978). *From Hierarchy to Equality, A Comparison of Past and Present Interpretations of 1 Cor. 11.2–16 in Relation to the Changing Status of Women in Society.* Vancouver: University of Vancouver Press.

Merton, R. K. (1968). *Social Theory and Social Structure.* (1968 enlarged edition). New York: Free Press.

Metzger, B. M. (1992). *The Text of the New Testament.* New York and Oxford: Oxford University Press.

Millar, F. (1995). Popular Politics at Rome in the Late Republic. In Malkin & Rubinsohn, Eds. *Leaders and Masses in the Roman World* (pp. 91–113). Leiden: E. J. Brill.

Mitchell, A. C. (1993). Rich and Poor in the Courts of Corinth: Litigiousness and Status in 1 Corinthians 6.1–11. *NTS* 39(4), 562–586.

Mitchell, M. M. (1991). *Paul and the Rhetoric of Reconciliation: An Exegetical Investigation of the Language and Composition of 1 Corinthians.* Tübingen: J. C. B. Mohr (Siebeck).

Mitchell, M. M. (1989). Concerning Peri. De. in 1 Corinthians. *NovT* 31(3), 229–256.

Moffatt, J. (1938). *First Corinthians.* London: Hodder and Stoughton.

Morgan, D. D., D. H. Levandowski, & M. L. Rogers. (1981). The Apostle Paul: Problem Formation and Problem Resolution from a Systems Perspective. *JPT* 9(2), 136–143.

Moxnes, H. (1994). The Quest for Honor and the Unity of the Community in Romans 12 and in the Orations of Dio Chrysostom. In T. Engberg-Pedersen, Ed. *Paul in His Hellenistic Context* (pp. 203–230). Edinburgh: T. & T. Clark.

Müller, P. (1970). *Die soziale Gruppe im Prozess der Massenkommunikation.* Stuttgart.

Munck, J. (1959). *Paul and the Salvation of Mankind.* London: SCM Press.

Murphy-O'Connor, J. (1997). *An Introduction to the New Testament.*

Murphy-O'Connor, J. (1996). *Paul: A Critical Life.* Oxford: Clarendon Press.

Murphy-O'Connor, J. (1992). Corinth. In D. N. Freedman, Ed. *ABD* (1), 1134–1139. New York; London; Toronto; Sydney; Auckland: Doubleday.

Murphy-O'Connor, J. (1984). The Corinth That Saint Paul Saw. *BA 47*, 147–159.

Murphy-O'Connor, J. (1983a). *St. Paul's Corinth.* (Vol. 6). Wilmington, DE: Michael Glazier, Inc.

Murphy-O'Connor, J. (1983b). Corinthian Bronze. *RB 90*, 23–36.

Murphy-O'Connor, J. (1981). "Baptised for the Dead" [I Cor. XV, 29] A Corinthian Slogan? *RB* 88, 532–543.

Murphy-O'Connor, J. (1979). *1 Corinthians* (New Testament Message). Dublin: Veritas Publications.

Murphy-O'Connor, J. (1977). 1 Corinthians, V, 3–5. *RB* 84, 239–245.

Orr, W. F. and J. A. Walther (1976). *1 Corinthians*. New York: Doubleday.

Osiek, C. and D. L. Balch (1997). *Families in the New Testament World*. Louisville, KY: Westminster/John Knox Press.

Osiek, C. (1996). Family in Early Christianity: "Family Values" Revisited. *CBQ 58*, 1–24.

Osiek, C. (1992). *What are They Saying about the Social Setting of the New Testament?* New York and Mahwah: Paulist Press.

Packer, J. E. (1974). Housing and Population in Imperial Ostia and Rome. In R. McMullen (Ed.) *Roman Social Relations: 50 B.C. to A.D. 284*. New Haven: Yale University Press.

Parsons, T., & Bales, R. (1955). *Family, Socialization, and Interaction Processes*. New York: Free Press.

Parsons, T. (1952). *The Social System*. London: Tavistock.

Patterson, J. R. (1992). Patronage, *Collegia* and Burial in Imperial Rome. In S. Bassett, Ed. *Death in Towns: Urban Responses to Dying and the Dead, 100–1600*. Leicester: Leicester University Press.

Payne, P. B. (1998). MS. 88 as Evidence for a Text without 1 Cor. 14.24–35. *NTS 44(1)*, 152–158.

Payne, P. B. (1995). Fuldensis, Sigla for Variants in Vaticanus, and 1 Cor. 14:34–35. *NTS* 41(2), 240–262.

Petersen, N. (1985). *Rediscovering Paul: Philemon and the Sociology of Paul's Narrative World*. Philadelphia: Fortress.

Pickett, R. (1997). *The Cross in Corinth* (JSNTS 143). Sheffield: Sheffield Academic Press.

Pitt-Rivers, J. (1977). *The Fate of Shechem, or the Politics of Sex*. Cambridge: Cambriege University Press.

Pogoloff, S. M. (1992). *Logos and Sophia: The Rhetorical Situation of 1 Corinthians*. Atlanta: Scholars Press.

Pomeroy, S. (1996). Families in Ptolemaic Egypt: Continuity, Change, and Coercion. In R. W. Wallace and E. M. Harris, (Ed. *Transitions to Empire: Essays in Graeco-Roman History, 360–146 B.C., in honor of E. Badian* (pp. 241–253). Norman, OK and London: University of Oklahoma Press.

Raaflaub, K. A. (1996). Born to be Wolves? Origins of Roman Imperialism. In R. W. Wallace and E. M. Harris (Ed.) *Transitions to Empire: Essays in Graeco-Roman History, 360–146 B.C., in honor of E. Badian* (pp. 273–314). Norman, OK and London: University of Oklahoma Press.

Redfield, R. (1953). *The Primitive World and Its Transformation.* Ithaca, NY: Lee.

Remus, H. (1996). Voluntary Association and Networks: Aelius Aristides at the Asclepieion in Pergamum. In J. S. Kloppenborg and Stephen G. Wilson (Eds.) *Voluntary Associations in the Graeco-Roman World* (pp. 146–175). London and New York: Routledge.

Rex, J. (1981). *Social Conflict.* London and New York: Longman.

Richardson, P. (1996). Early Synagogues as Collegia in the Diaspora and Palestine. In J. S. Kloppenborg and Stephen G. Wilson, Eds. *Voluntary Associations in the Graeco-Roman World* (pp. 90–109). London and New York: Routledge.

Robertson, A. T. (1934). *Word Pictures in the Greek New Testament.* New York: Broadman Press.

Romano, D. G. (1994). Post–146 B.C. Land Use in Corinth, and Planning of the Roman Colony of 44 B.C. In T. E. Gregory, Ed. *The Corinthia in the Roman Period* (pp. 9–30). Ann Arbor, MI: JRASup 8.

Rossouw, G. J. (1993). Theology in a Postmodern Culture: Ten Challenges. *HervTS 49* (4), 894–907.

Rouselle, A. (1996). The Family under the Roman Empire: Signs and Gestures. In A. Burguière, Klapisch-Zuber, C., Segalen, M., and Zonabend, F., Eds. *A History of the Family: Distant Worlds, Ancient Worlds* (Vol. 1, pp. 270–312). Cambridge, MA: Belknap Press.

Ruef, J. (1971). *Paul's First Letter to the Corinthians.* Philadelphia: Westminster.

Rutgers, L. V. (1995). *The Jews in Late Ancient Rome: Evidence of Cultural Interaction in the Roman Diaspora.* Leiden; New York; Köln: E. J. Brill.

Saller, R. P. (1994). *Patriarchy, Property and Death in the Roman Family.* Cambridge: Cambridge University Press.

Saller, R. (1991). Corporal Punishment, Authority, and Obedience in the Roman Household. In B. Rawson, Ed. *Marriage, Divorce, and Children in Ancient Rome* (pp. 144–165). Oxford: Clarendon Press.

Saller, R. P. (1988). *Pietas,* obligation and authority in the Roman family, *Alte Geschichte und Wissenschaftsgeschichte: Festschrift für Karl Christ* (pp. 393–410). Darmstadt.

Saller, R. P. (1986). *Patria potestas* and the stereotype of the Roman family. *ContCh 1,* 7–22.

Saller, R. P. (1984). *Familia, domus,* and the Roman conception of the family. *Phoenix 38,* 336–355.

Saller, R. P. (1982). *Personal Patronage Under the Early Empire.* Cambridge: Cambridge University Press.

Schreiber, A. (1977). *Die Gemeinde in Korinth.* Münster: Aschendorff.

Schürer, E. (1973). *The History of the Jewish People in the Age of Jesus Christ* (2 vols., rev. and Ed. by G. Vermes and F. Millar). Edinburgh: T. & T. Clark.

Schütz, J. H. (1975). *Paul and the Anatomy of Apostolic Authority.* Cambridge: Cambridge University Press.

Schweitzer, A. (1912). *Paul and His Interpreters: A Critical History* (W. Montgomery, Trans.). London: Adam and Charles Black.

Segal, A. F. (1990). *Paul the Convert: The Apostolate and Apostasy of Saul the Pharisee.* New Haven: Yale University Press.

Seitz, C. R. (1994). Pluralism and the Lost Art of Christian Apology. *First Things* (June/July), 15–18.

Seland, T. (1996). Philo and the Clubs and Associations of Alexandria. In J. S. Kloppenborg and S. G. Wilson, Eds. *Voluntary Associations in the Graeco-Roman World* (pp. 110–127). London and New York: Routledge.

Sellin, G. (1991). 1 Korinther 5–6 und der 'Vorbrief' nach Korinth. *NTS* 37, 535–558.

Skidmore, C. (1996). *Practical Ethics for Roman Gentlemen.* Exeter: University of Exeter Press.

Smit, J. (1991). The Genre of 1 Corinthians 13 in the Light of Classical Rhetoric. *NovT* 33(3), 193–216.

Spawforth, A. J. S. (1994). Corinth, Argos and the Imperial Cult: Pseudo-Julian, Letters 198. *Hesp.* 63 (2), 211–232.

Stambaugh, J. E. and D. L. Balch. (1986). *The New Testament in Its Social Environment.* Philadelphia: Westminster.

Stanley, C. D. (1996). 'Neither Jew nor Greek': Ethnic Conflict in Graeco-Roman Society. *JSNT* 64, 101–124.

Strauss, B. S. (1993). *Fathers and Sons in Athens: Ideology and Society in the Era of the Peloponnesian War.* London: Routledge.

Swain, S. (1996). *Hellenism and Empire.* Oxford: Clarendon.

Talbert, C. H. (1987). *Reading Corinthians: A Literary and Theological Commentary on 1 and 2 Corinthians.* New York: Crossroad.

Taylor, N. (1992). *Paul, Antioch and Jerusalem: A Study in Relationships and Authority in Earliest Christianity.* Sheffield: JSOT.

Theissen, G. (1982). *The Social Setting of Pauline Christianity* (J. H. Schütz, Trans.). Philadelphia: Fortress.

Theissen, G. (1978). *Sociology of Early Palestinian Christianity* (J. Bowden, Trans.). Philadelphia: Fortress.

Thielman, F. (1994). *Paul and the Law.* Downers Grove, IL: InterVarsity Press.

Thrall, M. E. (1965). *The First and Second Letters of Paul to the Corinthians.* Cambridge: Cambridge University Press.

Troeltsch, E. (1931). *The Social Teaching of Christian Churches.* New York: Macmillan.

Turcan, R. (1996). *The Cults of the Roman Empire.* Oxford: Blackwell.

Van Minnen, P. (1994). Paul the Roman Citizen. *JSNT* 56, 43–52.

Van Stempvoort, P. A. (1950). *Eeheid en Schisma.* Uitgeuer, Nijkerk: Callenbach.

Veyne, P. (Ed.). (1978). *A History of Private Life, vol. 1: From Pagan Rome to Byzantium.* (Vol. 1). Cambridge, MS, and London: Harvard University Press.

Wagner, G. (1967). *Pauline Baptism and the Pagan Mysteries.* Edinburgh & London: Oliver & Boyd.

Wagner, J. R. (1998). "Not Beyond the Things which are Written": A Call to Boast Only in the Lord (1 Cor. 4.6). *NTS 44, 2*, 279–287.

Walbank, F. W. (1995). Polybius' Perception of the One and the Many. In I. Malkin and Z. W. Rubinsohn (Eds.), *Leaders and Masses in the Roman World* (pp. 201–222). Leiden: E. J. Brill.

Walker-Ramisch, S. (1996). Graeco-Roman Voluntary Associations and the Damascus Document: A Sociological Analysis. In Kloppenborg and Wilson (Eds.) *Voluntary Associations in the Graeco-Roman World* (pp. 128–145). London: Routledge.

Wallace-Hadrill, A. (1991). Houses and Households: Sampling Pompeii and Herculaneum. In B. Rawson (Ed.) *Marriage, Divorce, and Children in Ancient Rome* (pp. 191–227). Oxford: Clarendon Press.

Waltzing, J. P. (1895). *Étude Historique sur Les Corporations Professionelles chez Les Romains, Vols. 1–4*. Brussells: F. Hayez.

Ward, R.B. (1990). Musonius and Paul on Marriage. *NTS* 36, 281–289.

Watson, A. (1987). *Roman Slave Law*. Baltimore: Johns Hopkins University Press.

Watzlawick, P., J. H. Weakland, and R. Fisch (1974). *Change: Principles of Problem Formation and Problem Resolution*. New York: Norton.

Webb, B. G. (1994). Judges. In G. J. Wenham, J. A. Motyer, D. A. Carlson, R. T. France (Eds.) *New Bible Commentary*, pp. 261–286. Leicester: Inter-Varsity.

Wedderburn, A. J. M. (1987). *Baptism and Resurrection: Studies in Pauline Theology Against its Graeco-Roman Background* (WUNT 44). Tübingen: Mohr.

Weiss, J. (1936). *The History of Primitive Christianity*. New York: Wilson-Erickson.

Weinfeld, M. (1986). *The Organisation Pattern and the Penal Code of the Qumran Sect* (NTOA 2). Göttingen: Vandenhoeck and Ruprecht.

Welborn, L. L. (1987). On the Discord in Corinth. *JBL* 106, 83–111.

Wendland, H. (1962). *Die Brief an die Korinther*. Göttingen: Vandenhoeck & Ruprecht.

Wenham, D. (1995). *Paul: Follower of Jesus or Founder of Christianity?* Grand Rapids Cambridge: Eerdmans.

Westermann, W. L. (1955). *Slave Systems of Greek and Roman Antiquity: Memoirs of the American Philosophical Society 40*. Philadelphia: APS.

Whitehead, A. (1929). *Process and Reality*. New York: Macmillan.

Wiles, M. F. (1978). The Domesticated Apostle. In W. A. Meeks (Ed.), *The Writings of St. Paul* (pp. 207–213). New York and London: W. W. Norton & Co.

Williams, C. K., II. (1994). Roman Corinth as a Commercial Center. In T. E. Gregory, Ed. *The Corinthia in the Roman Period* (pp. 31–46). Ann Arbor, MI: JRASup 8.

Willis, W. L. (1985). *Idol Meat in Corinth: The Pauline Argument in 1 Corinthians 8 and 10*. Chico, CA: Scholars Press.

Wilson, A. N. (1997). *Paul: The Mind of the Apostle*. New York and London: Norton.

Wilson, R. M. (1982). Gnosis at Corinth. In M. D. Hooker and S. G. Wilson (Eds.), *Paul and Paulinism: Essays in Honour of C. K. Barrett* (pp. 102–114). London: SPCK.

Winter, B. W. (1999). *After Paul left Corinth: The Influence of Secular Ethics and Social Change*. Pre-publication proof.

Winter, B. W. (1997a). *Philo and Paul Among the Sophists* (*SNTS* Monograph Series 96). Cambridge: Cambridge University Press.

Winter, B. W. (1997b). Gluttony and Immorality at Élitist Banquets: The Background to 1 Corinthians 6:12–20. *Jian Dao* 7, 77–90.

Winter, B. W. (1994). *Seek the Welfare of the City: Christians as Benefactors and Citizens*. Grand Rapids: Eerdmans.

Winter, B. W. (1991). Civil Litigation in Secular Corinth and the Church: The Forensic Background to 1 Corinthians 6.1–8. *NTS 37*, 559–572.

Wire, A. C. (1990). *The Corinthian Women Prophets*. Minneapolis: Fortress.

Wiseman, J. (1979). Corinth and Rome I: 228 B.C. – A.D. 267. In H. Temporini (Ed.), *Austieg und Niedergang der römischen Welt* (Vol. 7, pp. 428–548). Berlin.

Witherington, B., III. (1995). *Conflict and Community in Corinth: A Socio–Rhetorical Commentary on 1 and 2 Corinthians*. Grands Rapids: Eerdmans.

Witherington, B., III. (1994). *Paul's Narrative Thought World: The Tapestry of Tragedy and Triumph*. Louisville, KY: Westminster/John Knox Press.

Witherington, B., III. (1988). *Women in the Earliest Churches*. Cambridge: Cambridge University Press.

Wright, N. T. (1997). *What Saint Paul Really Said*. Grand Rapids: Eerdmans.

Wright, N. T. (1992). *The New Testament and the People of God*. London: SPCK.

Yarbrough, O. L. (1985). *Not Like the Gentiles: Marriage Rules in the Letters of Paul*. (SBL Dissertation Series 80). Atlanta: Scholars Press.

Yorke, G. L. (1991). *The Church as the Body of Christ in the Pauline Corpus: A Re-examination*. Lanham, MD and London: University Press of America.

Ziesler, J. (1990). *Pauline Christianity* (rev.). Oxford: Oxford University Press.

Zonabend, F. (1996). An Anthropological Perspective on Kinship and the Family. In Burguière, Klapisch-Zuber, Segalen and Zonabend, Eds. *A History of the Family: Distant Worlds, Ancient Worlds* (pp. 8–70). Cambridge, MS: Belknap.

✧ INDEX

A

Acts of Paul and Thecla, 14
Acts of Thomas, 219
Ἀδελφοι, 57, 85, 141–151, 164, 172–173, 194, 197, 201–209
Aelius Aristides, 63, 101, 170
Allen, L. C., 217–218
Alvarez-Pereyre, F. and Heymann, F., 57, 99, 103, 105
Ambrose, 215
American Sociological Association, 5
Appelbaum, S., 101, 103
Aristides, 135
Aristotle, 101, 176
Asconius, 102
Augustine, 160, 178, 216, 225
Aulus Gellius, 101, 104

B

Baird, W., 10
Balch, D., 96
Banks, R., 172, 174
Baptism, 119–123, 135, 151-154
Barclay, W., 97, 100, 113, 166, 174, 179
Barrett, C. K., 110, 165, 168, 170–173
Barton, S. C., 51, 167–168, 174
Baur, F. C., 9–10, 90
Beker, J. C., 178
"Belonging," 55–57, 73–74, 117–125, 152–159, 193–197, 212
Ben Sira, 105, 224
Bernard, J., 5
Best, E., 51, 167

Blenkinsopp, J., 218–219
Blue, B., 81–82, 107–108
Booth, A., 112
Boring, W., 105, 109
Bott, E., 51
"Boundaries with gates," 16, 26
Boundary markers, 116–121, 130–139
Bowersock, G. W., 102
Bradley, K. R., 100, 176
Broderick, C. B., 50–51, 168
Brown, R. E., 98
Bruce, F. F., 101, 107, 165
Bullinger, G., 187-18, 8, 219
Burial clubs, 55
Burr, W. R., 51

C

Callan, T., 178
Calvin, J., 183, 217
Carpenter, S. L. and Kennedy, W. J. D., 52, 179, 195, 223
Castelli, E. A., 178
Chance, J. K., 104, 176
Chloe, "those of," 83–84, 108, 118
Chow, J., 23–26, 33, 53–54, 91, 104, 110, 166, 185, 216, 220
Chrysostom, 173, 178, 183, 188, 212, 217, 219, 221, 224, 226
Cicero, 58, 99–100, 107–108, 218, 222
Clarke, A., 25, 54, 104, 166, 175, 185, 218
Clement of Alexandria, 177, 225
Clement of Rome, 160
Collegia, 55, 65–76, 87–89, 97–98
Conflict, realistic and non-realistic, 6
Conflict management, 1–4, 53

Studies in Biblical Literature

This series invites manuscripts from scholars in any area of biblical literature. Both established and innovative methodologies, covering general and particular areas in biblical study, are welcome. The series seeks to make available studies that will make a significant contribution to the ongoing biblical discourse. Scholars who have interests in gender and sociocultural hermeneutics are particularly encouraged to consider this series.

For further information about the series and for the submission of manuscripts, contact:

Hemchand Gossai
Department of Religion
Muhlenberg College
2400 Chew Street
Allentown, PA 18104-5586

To order other books in this series, please contact our Customer Service Department:

(800) 770-LANG (within the U.S.)
(212) 647-7706 (outside the U.S.)
(212) 647-7707 FAX

or browse online by series at:

WWW.PETERLANGUSA.COM